# ROUTLEDGE LIBRARY EDITIONS: ROMANTICISM

Volume 23

# ROMANTICISM

# ROMANTICISM
Comparative Discourses

Edited by
LARRY H. PEER AND DIANE LONG HOEVELER

LONDON AND NEW YORK

First published in 2006 by Ashgate Publishing Limited

This edition first published in 2016
by Routledge
2 Park Square, Milton Park, Abingdon, Oxon OX14 4RN

and by Routledge
711 Third Avenue, New York, NY 10017

*Routledge is an imprint of the Taylor & Francis Group, an informa business*

© 2006 Larry H. Peer and Diane Long Hoeveler

All rights reserved. No part of this book may be reprinted or reproduced or utilised in any form or by any electronic, mechanical, or other means, now known or hereafter invented, including photocopying and recording, or in any information storage or retrieval system, without permission in writing from the publishers.

*Trademark notice*: Product or corporate names may be trademarks or registered trademarks, and are used only for identification and explanation without intent to infringe.

*British Library Cataloguing in Publication Data*
A catalogue record for this book is available from the British Library

ISBN: 978-1-138-64537-0 (Set)
ISBN: 978-1-315-62815-8 (Set) (ebk)
ISBN: 978-1-138-64369-7 (Volume 23) (hbk)
ISBN: 978-1-138-64370-3 (Volume 23) (pbk)
ISBN: 978-1-315-62926-1 (Volume 23) (ebk)

**Publisher's Note**
The publisher has gone to great lengths to ensure the quality of this reprint but points out that some imperfections in the original copies may be apparent.

**Disclaimer**
The publisher has made every effort to trace copyright holders and would welcome correspondence from those they have been unable to trace.

# Romanticism
Comparative Discourses

*Edited by*

LARRY H. PEER

DIANE LONG HOEVELER

© Larry H. Peer and Diane Long Hoeveler 2006

All rights reserved. No part of this publication may be reproduced, stored in a retrieval system, or transmitted in any form or by any means, electronic, mechanical, photocopying, recording, or otherwise without the prior permission of the publisher.

Larry H. Peer and Diane Long Hoeveler have asserted their moral right under the Copyright, Designs and Patents Act, 1988, to be identified as the editors of this work.

Published by
Ashgate Publishing Limited
Gower House
Croft Road
Aldershot
Hants GU11 3HR
England

Ashgate Publishing Company
Suite 420
101 Cherry Street
Burlington, VT 05401-4405
USA

Ashgate website: http://www.ashgate.com

**British Library Cataloguing in Publication Data**
Romanticism : comparative discourses.—(The nineteenth century series)
   1.European literature—18th century—History and criticism 2.European literature—19th century—History and criticism 3.Romanticism—Europe
   I.Peer, Larry H.  II.Hoeveler, Diane Long
   809.9'145'09033

**Library of Congress Cataloging-in-Publication Data**
Romanticism : comparative discourses / edited by Larry H. Peer and Diane Long Hoeveler.
    p. cm.—(Nineteenth century series)
  Includes bibliographical references and index.
  ISBN 0-7546-5374-9 (alk. paper)
   1. European literature—18th century—History and criticism—Congresses. 2. European literature—19th century—History and criticism—Congresses. 3. Romanticism—Europe. I. Peer, Larry H. II. Hoeveler, Diane Long. III. Nineteenth century (Aldershot, England)
  PN751.R75 2005
  809'.9145'09033—dc22

2005019319

ISBN-10: 0 7546 5374 9

Printed and bound in Great Britain by MPG Books Ltd. Bodmin, Cornwall.

# Contents

Acknowledgements ix

1 Prologomenon to the Study of
  Romanticism's Comparative Discourses 1
  *Larry H. Peer and Diane Long Hoeveler*

**Part 1 Language and Romantic Discourse Systems**

2 Gothic Opera as Romantic Discourse in Britain
  and France: A Cross-Cultural Dialogue 11
  *Diane Long Hoeveler and Sarah Davies Cordova*

3 Pursuing the Plerotic Sublime:
  Romantic Poetry and the Failure of Language 35
  *Richard A. Nanian*

4 Half-Asleep on Thresholds: Fragile Boundaries
  in Coleridge's "Fears in Solitude" 55
  *Onita Vaz*

5 Romantic Drama and the Discourse of Criminality 73
  *Marjean D. Purinton*

**Part 2 Women Writers and Romantic Constructions of Power**

6 Towards Constructing a "Poetics of Space" for the
  Sentimental Novel: A Topo-analysis of
  Charlotte Smith's *The Old Manor House* 87
  *Nancy Metzger*

7 The Second Soul-less Sex? Mary Wollstonecraft
  and the "Mahometan" 99
  *Carolyn A. Weber*

| 8 | Ithuriel's Spear and Detecting the Counterfeit: Edgeworth's Miltonic Allusions in *Belinda*<br>*Jeffrey Cass* | 117 |
|---|---|---|
| 9 | Parting Songs: Hemans, Landon, and Barret Browning Rewrite Friederike Brun<br>*Kari Lokke* | 131 |
| 10 | The Discourse of Religious *Bildung* in Anne Brontë's *Agnes Grey*<br>*Larry H. Peer* | 143 |

**Part 3  Varieties of Revisionist Discourse in Romanticism**

| 11 | Readerly Agency and the Discourse of History in *The Antiquary*<br>*Bonnie J. Gunzenhauser* | 155 |
|---|---|---|
| 12 | Reading Beyond Body, Cane, and Crosier: Talleyrand as Romantic Discourse<br>*Rodney Farnsworth* | 165 |
| 13 | Byron and *Manfred*: Epistolary Journal into Dramatic Poem<br>*D.L. Macdonald* | 181 |
| 14 | The Romantic Artist on the Couch: A Freudian Approach to Wackenroder's Musician, Berlinger<br>*Sonja E. Klocke* | 191 |

*Index*     203

# Acknowledgements

The authors would like to thank the editorial and marketing teams at Ashgate Press for their professionalism, expertise, and patience with the occasional fugitive flaw. Larry H. Peer thanks Ashleigh Self for unstinting service in setting up the copy and Janet for everything. Diane Long Hoeveler acknowledges Michael McKinney, Dean of the Helen Way Klingler College of Arts and Sciences and Tim Machan, Chair of the Department of English, Marquette University, for their financial support of the 2003 International Conference on Romanticism meetings held at Marquette University.

Chapter One

# Prologomenon to the Study of Romanticism's Comparative Discourses

Larry H. Peer and Diane Long Hoeveler

Literary historians of the cultural phenomenon we call "Romanticism" have been circling this elegant but ungainly manifestation for a good two hundred years, with their attempts at definition meeting with greater or lesser success. If minds like Schlegel and Heine, or de Staël and Manzoni, or Wordsworth and Coleridge could not agree on the meaning or shape of the cultural constructions that were swirling around them, then there is little hope that any literary critic writing in the early years of the twenty-first century can capture more than a glimpse of "Romanticism's" intentions and "truth." The essays collected for this volume—all original—are not animated by the attempt to pay "homage" to these authors and works or by the need to catalogue or neatly codify the movement we know as "Romanticism." Instead, each essay seeks to capture one aspect of the discursive field that we label "Romantic studies" today. And, as it is fair to assume not only that there is no agreed-upon canon of literary texts in the field today, but also that there is no methodology that literary critics can all subscribe to, "Romanticism" has become, in Foucault's terms, a "discourse system," and it is the multiplicity and polyvalent quality of that discourse system that we intend to explore in the various essays collected in this volume.

Michel Foucault has given a number of definitions for the term *discourse*, all of which are, perhaps, vague, but nonetheless suggestive for the sort of critical work currently being currently practiced in the field of Romanticism. For Foucault, the term "discourse" can first be understood as all or any utterances and texts that produce or construct how we conceptualize the world around us. Second, discourses can be understood as common linguistic structures or rhetorical tropes and conventions shared by a number of written productions (hence "Romantic discourse" or "gothic discourse" or "sentimental discourse"). Finally, Foucault talks about discourse as a system of rules and structures that combine to produce a wide variety of utterances and texts. This last meaning of the term suggests that discourse is less the actual text under consideration than the rules governing the text produced (80).[1] Although these definitions might suggest that Foucault's notion of *discourse* is little more than genre theory and hence a slightly dressed-up version of formalism, the crucial difference for contemporary literary critics lies in recognizing the importance of the issue of power.

Discourse criticism, as currently practiced, acknowledges the deeply ideological nature of literary productions, recognizing in them a way that culture speaks and silences at the same time. Louis Althusser has defined the power that emanates from literary works as a form of ideology, while ideology itself operates through a series of gaps, omissions, or fissures that conceal more than they reveal. Ideologies, in fact, operate by papering over their contradictions, masquerading as coherent systems of values so as to dupe or lull the unwary or naïve. The "Romantic ideology," as Jerome McGann has defined it, was a successful poetic construction that attempted to dazzle its consumers with a belief in the divinity of the imaginative potential with all of us. Granted, such an ideology was seductive for a secularizing age, and it explains more than a little why we are still in thrall to its siren song. Foucault, however, would argue that all literary works are ideologically bifurcated, split along progressive and conservative lines that most often their authors cannot recognize, let alone acknowledge themselves. But because of their complicity in, as well as their assault on, their cultures' power structures and values, literary works accomplish potent cultural work on many different levels. The essays in this volume interrogate exactly this ideological bifurcation in Romanticism through examining a number of literary texts that can be approached through several of the contemporary paradigms of discourse criticism as it is practiced today.

Any new volume of essays on Romanticism needs to justify itself fairly strenuously, and this collection is no exception. Without rehearsing all of the contentious battles that have been critically fought over the body of what has become a ravaged textual terrain, suffice it to say that literary critics of Romanticism are *beyond* anxiety. No longer able to assume the stability of any subject, let alone their own, they have increasingly tightened their lenses, intent on exploring a variety of overlooked or "non-canonical" texts that have not yet been overcultivated. Certainly, the critical battles between Meyer Abrams and J. Hillis Miller for the soul of Anglo-American nineteenth-century studies assumed epic, if not comic, proportions, while it was repeated less than a decade later in the dispute between McGann and critics like Harold Bloom. More recently, Jerome Christensen, in fact, has referred to "the contemporary moment of [critical] discursivity," positing it against the tendency to make supersaturated sets of statements from an expired past. Historically constructed, Romanticism "remains under construction in the history that we are making" (3). Christensen, though, does attempt to define the field, claiming that "Romanticism is an ethics of imaginative, collaborative work" (8). Very few literary critics today, however, would be bold enough to even attempt to define the field, nor would they claim that there is any one "Romantic aesthetic," let alone any monolithic approach to understanding so vast a cultural entity as "Romanticism." Instead, contemporary critics tend to situate themselves along one of the various fault-lines that run through such a large discursive field. This volume is organized, then, along those fault-lines, all the while recognizing that any number of other organizations or other fault-lines would allow us to approach the field with a variety of new critical lenses.

One of our chief concerns here is to use and mix, for purposes of grinding new critical lenses, two chronological levels of discourse—namely, discourses *of* Romanticism and discourses *on* Romanticism. Thus this book suggests a critical formulation that seeks not to construct a theory of Romanticism but to find a *concept*, in the sense of Hegel's dialectical *Begriff*, that can account for intersecting fault-lines in both Romanticism's texts and subsequent critical texts about Romanticism. This will not result in the construction of a typology of Romanticism, as Löwy's and Sayre's book does, but will form a new and concentric hermeneutic horizon implicitly examining how both these evolving discourse levels affect a text's interpretation. It seems right that Romanticism would disseminate an infinite number of possible meanings with each new interpretation, that its force in modern critical discourse should be dynamic and ideologically saturated, and that each critical response to each Romantic text produces a discursive vantage point like an ocular flexor reshaping the eye's lens.

This volume begins with four essays that focus on discourse as a species of ideological construction, implicated with the power structures that were operating in Britain and France during the height of the Romantic period. The first essay in Part 1 is by Diane Long Hoeveler and Sarah Davies Cordova, "Gothic Opera as Romantic Discourse in Britain and France: A Cross-Cultural Dialogue," and it explores the power of one particularly popular discourse system, opera, to translate and stage potent ideological materials in a revolutionary age. As gothic novels quickly made their way onto the popular stage, they also were adapted in a series of gothic operas that we now designate as "rescue" operas. Centering on motifs of escape from unjust imprisonment, rescue operas, in complex social and psychological ways, became vehicles of secularization, modernization, and nationalism, implicating the gothic discourse in a political agenda that ambivalently constructed revolution, citizenship, and nationality in new ways.

The second essay in this section, Richard A. Nanian's "Pursuing the Plerotic Sublime: Romantic Poetry and the Failure of Language," examines some of the philosophical problematics in any discussion of the way language works. Specifically focusing on the poetic values of nothingness and everythingness by representing the achievement of perfect order and perfect disorder through language, Nanian asserts that as language approaches either order or disorder, it fails, even though language is most powerful at these points of failure. The discourse of Romantic poetry is plerotic, a climb into the eventual failure of inarticulate venting, the most moving kind of cognitive disorder, multiple and expanded signifiers, and loss of articulation rather than a fall into silence.

Complementing Nanian's exploration of how Romantic language operates as an ideological construction, Onita Vaz's "Half-asleep on Thresholds: Fragile Boundaries in Coleridge's 'Fears in Solitude'" focuses on one of the central assumptions of Romantic discourse, the epistemological instability of generic categories. For Vaz, this instability is joined in Coleridge's "Fears in Solitude" to another Romantic construction, the recreative power of the "secondary imagination," in a pattern that links Coleridge's poem with the Romantic discourse of his time. "Fears in Solitude" functions as a key text in understanding and observing Romanticism's mode of imaginative utterance.

The final essay in Part 1, Marjean D. Purinton's "Romantic Drama and the Discourse of Criminality," examines the public humiliation and punishment of criminals in the European eighteenth and nineteenth centuries as a highly theatricalized spectacle, intended as social education. By focusing on a series of dramas that were popular during the heyday of the period, Purinton is able to examine such theater as implicated in the evolving discourse of criminality, crime, punishment, and retribution. The stage drama of British Romanticism reflects not only a fascination with criminal punishment, but also a strong support of new penal codes in England that sought reformation rather than retribution.

Part 2 consists of five essays, each of which focuses on a particular female writer and her attempt to wrestle with control of property, spiritual power, or literary traditions. The first essay in this section, Nancy Metzger's "Towards Constructing a 'Poetics of Space' for the Sentimental Novel: A Topo-Analysis of Charlotte Smith's *The Old Manor House*" examines the metaphorical use of the manor house to reflect socio-political relationships in England by using Gaston Bachelard's theory of the "poetics of space." With Bachelard as her theoretical framework, Metzger is able to reveal the intimate domestic relationships at the heart of Smith's discourse and, indeed, at the core of the entire sentimental novel tradition in English.

The next essay, Carolyn A. Weber's "The Second Soul-less Sex? Mary Wollstonecraft and the 'Mahometan,'" very usefully examines what she claims is one of Wollstonecraft's primary concerns in her *Vindication*: the "ensouling" of women. Weber chooses, however, to focus on Wollstonecraft's association of Islam ("Mahometan") with British Protestantism, and she reveals that both religions were implicated in the explicit and implicit denial of women's souls. Weber shows how Wollstonecraft's use of the term "Mahometan" reveals a complex appeal to both sympathy and shock in her call for women's equality.

The third essay in this section, Jeffrey Cass's "Ithuriel's Spear and Detecting the Counterfeit: Edgeworth's Miltonic Allusions in *Belinda*," focuses on the issue of literary tradition as a discourse system operating in a particularly uneasy manner. Unfortunately, Edgeworth criticism has generally followed the Bloomian psychoanalytic reading of Gilbert and Gubar (*Madwoman in the Attic*), especially in its insistence upon female modesty and reticence as tools of patriarchal compliance and complicity. Cass argues that this line of criticism is fundamentally incorrect and, in the case of Edgeworth's *Belinda*, reflects back to a fundamental misreading of Milton and the implicit theology of the Fall that he presents in *Paradise Lost*. Milton's poetic universe does not blame Eve for the postlapsarian punishment of the human race, and does not completely absolve Adam for his sin, in spite of a popular line taken in Anglo-American criticism. Instead, an alternative reading of his *Paradise Lost* offers a new reading of Edgeworth's *Belinda*, since the Miltonic allusions in her novel are key to understanding its meaning..

In another examination of literary anxiety, Kari Lokke, in "Parting Songs: Hemans, Landon, and Barrett Browning Rewrite Friedericke Brun," explores the ways in which the refrain of Brun's poem "Ich denke Dein" was reworked throughout the nineteenth century by several British women poets. We observe here the resonance of a lively international construction of Romantic women poets' constituting themselves as audiences for each other's work.

The final essay in this section of the volume, Larry H. Peer's "The Discourse of Religious *Bildung* in Anne Brontë's *Agnes Grey*," focuses on one of the most ignored texts in the discussion of Romantic discourse, Anne Brontë's *Agnes Grey*. The profound view into the notion of Romantic *Bildung* and religiosity offered by Brontë's governess novel links it to the great continental *Bildungsromane* of the early nineteenth century. Centering on the inner development of piety through suffering as the route to individuality, Brontë's novel participates in the particular discourse of "development" at the root of continental Romanticism.

Finally, Part 3 presents four essays, all of which examine some aspect of what was considered, during the period, as "revisionist" discourse. By focusing on some of the most prominent Scottish, British, and German male Romantics, this section seeks to interrogate how "revision" was constructed as a potent display of power, celebrity, and agency. The first essay in this section, Bonnie J. Gunzenhauser's "Readerly Agency and the Discourse of History in *The Antiquary*," examines Walter Scott's novel *The Antiquary* as participating in a discourse rooted in his efforts to establish an Edinburgh antiquarian society known as the Bannatyne Club that would publish documents from the Scottish past. Just as history plays the most important role in shaping the course of human progress, as Scott maintained, so does the collection and study of historical documents play a significant role in shaping the discourse of his historical novel writing.

The second essay in this section is Rodney Farnsworth's "Reading Beyond Body, Cane, and Crosier: Talleyrand as Romantic Discourse." Contemporaneous writers typically read Talleyrand's actions through the Romantic metaphors of the body, with his crosier and cane becoming the signifiers that motivate the revisionism of negative discourse. Both Napoleonists and Monarchists participated in and further constructed this discourse, and only in the later Romantic period did the pattern moderate. The legacy of the change in the body metaphor is that we now conduct discourse according to this later, more moderate paradigm, speaking typically of Talleyrand as a negotiator between extremes.

The next essay, David Lorne Macdonald's "Byron and *Manfred*: Epistolary Journal into Dramatic Poem," is a response to the frequently-made suggestion that Byron imitated Goethe's *Faust* in creating his drama *Manfred*. Byron insisted that his play's actual inspiration was the scenery he had seen on his 1816 tour of the Swiss Alps. Macdonald shows how the discourse of Byron's travel journal is transferred into numerous passages throughout the first half of *Manfred*, particularly in Manfred's famous soliloquy, producing a unique expression of Romantic irony hitherto unappreciated in scholarship on Byron.

The final essay in the volume, Sonja E. Klocke's "The Romantic Artist on the Couch: A Freudian Approach to Wackenroder's Musician Berglinger," focuses on the German Romantic tradition. By examining the so-called overly sensitive Romantic artist, Klocke notes that prior explanations for this trope are misguided. Furthermore, such explanations as have been put forward and repeated tend to be about the Romantic artist rather than about the artist's creations. Arguing that Romantic artists were increasingly interested in the unconscious and its power to more or less control the products of the creative mind, Klocke takes Wackenroder's *Herzensergiessungen eines kunstliebenden Klosterbruders* and its character Berglinger as a kind of case study for Freudian analysis of the Romantic artist as literary character. Her conclusion, that Berglinger suffers from a classic case of unsolved oedipal conflict, suggests a new approach to this *topos* in Romanticism.

In conclusion, we acknowledge that, in assembling yet another collection of essays on the Romantic period, we are attempting to carve yet more letters on the large tree of literary productivity and we are reminded of Heine's observation:

> Der Baum der Menschheit vergißt des stillen Gärtners, der ihn gepflegt in der Kälte, getränkt in der Dürre und vor schädlichen Thieren geschüzt hat; aber er bewahrt treulich die Namen, die man ihm in seine Rinde umbarmherzig eingeschnitten mit scharfem Stahl, und er überleifert sie in immer wachsender Größe den spätesten Geschlechtern. (8/1, 208)

(Mankind is a tree that forgets the quiet gardener who cared for it in the cold season, watered it during the drought, and protected it from harmful animals; but it faithfully preserves the names ruthlessly carved in its bark with sharp steel and passes them on in ever increasing size to the latest generations.)

The act of continuing to carve is what is important to us.

**Notes**

1   Foucault's definition of discourse can be compared to a number of the "theses on the Philosophy of Criticism" which Jerome McGann has appended to his *The Beauty of Inflections*. For instance, consider thesis one: "Poetry is, from the individual's point of view, a particular type of human experience; from a social point of view, however, it is an event. Criticism studies these experiences and events in their successive and interrelated apparitions. A work of poetry is not a thing or an object, nor should criticism conceive it as such; it is the result of an interactive network of productive people and forces" (343). See all the theses (343–44) for an interesting historical comparison of how far (or how little) new historicism has traveled in the past twenty years.

**Works Cited**

Althusser, Louis. "Ideology and Ideological State Apparatuses." In *Critical Theory Since 1965*. Ed. Hazard Adams and Leroy Searle. Tallahassee: UP of Florida, 1986. 239–50.
Christensen, Jerome. *Romanticism at the End of History*. Baltimore: Johns Hopkins UP, 2000.
Foucault, Michel. *The Archeology of Knowledge*. trans. A.M. Sheridan Smith. New York: Pantheon, 1972.
Heine, Heinrich. *Sämtliche Werke: Düsseldorfer Ausgabe*. Ed. Manfred Windfuhr. Hamburg: Hoffman und Campe Verlag, 1979.
Löwy, Michael and Sayre, Robert. *Romanticism Against the Tide of Modernity*. trans. Catherine Porter. Durham: Duke UP, 2001.
McGann, Jerome. *The Beauty of Inflections*. Oxford: Oxford UP, 1985.

# Part 1
# Language and Romantic Discourse Systems

Chapter Two

# Gothic Opera as Romantic Discourse in Britain and France: A Cross-Cultural Dialogue

Diane Long Hoeveler and Sarah Davies Cordova

... Mais ce n'est pas aux orateurs révolutionnaires que les romantiques vont demander des leçons de style, c'est à la Révolution en personne, à ce langage fait Histoire, lequel se signifie par des évènements qui sont des déclarations: La Terreur, on le sait bien, ne fut pas seulement terrible à cause des exécutions, elle le fut parce qu'elle se revendiqua elle-même sous cette forme majuscule, en faisant de la terreur la mesure de l'histoire et le logos des temps modernes. [1]

**Introduction**

The term "British opera" has often been thought an oxymoron. In fact, as the Italian opera made its way into eighteenth-century London it was greeted by outright hostility and contempt by such intellectuals as Jonathan Swift, Samuel Johnson, and numerous others.[2] As a wholly imported art form, arriving fully developed and with its own conventions set largely in place already, opera somehow had to find a way to adapt to British culture before it could be accepted by the public as a legitimate and viable art and form of entertainment. That opera did survive—and thrive—in late eighteenth- and early nineteenth-century Britain is due, we think, not to the quality of the music, most of which is forgettable, but to the power of the genre's ability to translate and stage potent ideological materials in a revolutionary age. And that ideological material—fear of violent revolution and its effects on what had been a stable class system—is largely the same content that was developed in the gothic novels of Horace Walpole, Ann Radcliffe, Matthew Lewis, and Charlotte Dacre, and then in the gothic dramas of such adapters as James Boaden, Henry Siddons, and Lewis. These gothic novels and dramas most frequently took as their subjects the unlawful imprisonments of innocent victims of tyranny, released after heroic efforts by disinherited men who regain their rightful lands and titles only after proving their worth. Most of these works read now like wish fulfillment, fairy tales or worse, but they were extremely popular and, as such, deserve our critical attention as important ideological markers for their culture.

Paula Backsheider has suggested that gothic dramas are "the earliest example[s] of what we call mass culture ... an artistic configuration that becomes formulaic and has mass appeal, that engages the attention of a very large, very diverse audience, and that stands up to repetition, not only of new examples of the type but production of individual plays" (150). But why, we might ask, were gothic dramas quickly transformed into gothic operas or what are known now as "rescue operas"? This essay examines the social and political ideologies that are explicit in the major gothic operatic adaptations of the most popular gothic novels of Britain, while at the same time examining British opera's very close connections with French models as well as French adaptations of British cultural works.

What is most curious about all of these works is their use of the theme of escape from unjust imprisonment. In fact, the endlessly repeated motif of imprisonment and escape (from a tunnel, a tower, a labyrinth, a camp of pirates, a boat of kidnappers, etc.) is so pervasive that the modem critic knows that it bears the weight of the opera's ideological meaning. But that is precisely where the confusion begins. Is the capture and escape meant to embody a politically and socially conservative message and a direct warning to the protagonists of the drama, and, by extension, to the audience? Or is the message one of revolution and liberation from tyranny and injustice? When one examines these rescue operas in and of themselves and not simply as inferior productions intended for a mass audience, one can see that each of the operas—in both Britain and France—participates in the ongoing national debate about the proper role of the monarchy, the threat of violent revolution, the shock of sudden class transformation, the anxiety of changing gender roles within the family structure, and, finally, the construction of newly nationalistic countries that seek to justify the means they have each taken to modernize and secularize.

Jeffrey Cox has observed, in relation to romantic drama and the French Revolution, that when history itself becomes theatrical, theater responds by "translating the representation of revolt from history to myth" (241). With this in mind, we might ask, what ideology undergirds gothic drama and opera? Are they, as Peter Brooks has observed about melodrama, essentially conservative, a means of reinstating social and political order (15), or can they be understood as a species of what Hayden White has called "anarchistic," in that it calls for a dissolution of current institutions in order to reclaim a more humane community that existed sometime in the past? (24–5) "Rescue operas" are not simply a politically conservative discourse system as has generally been argued, but rather they intend to present something like an anarchistic warning by constructing a distant past that the opera reshapes as redeemable through the elimination of corrupt aristocrats. Each opera presents a political and social warning to the monarchy: reform or be overthrown by violence, which certainly would seem to constitute something of an anarchist message. The specter of the French Revolution hangs over each of these works, and all of them introduce middle-class characters who embody the best of what Britain and France must become if they are to avoid violent and chaotic fates. The operas are clearly attempting to mediate between classes, races, and genders that saw themselves as being at odds over the shape and power structure of the newly evolving bourgeois society. In fact, the operas, like dramas, actually function as cathartic forms, public rituals in which the middle class haunted itself with its own act of imagined, fantasized revolution, usually depicted as some form of matricide or fratricide in a series of what we might see as social and political morality plays. The middle-class audience flocked to these plays that presented its own mythology of origins, its own "Hyperion"-like creation of a new order built on the shorn backs of an aristocracy that quite simply did not deserve to survive.

As Robert Miles has noted, those involved in the invention of the gothic embraced the hieratic function of keeping alive the sacred mementoes of the race. But ideological conservatism intersected with the democratic nature of artistic production for the masses, creating what Foucault has called a site of "power/knowledge" at odds with itself. As a site of opposing strategies, rescue operas became a "hazardous play of dominations" seeking to compose for themselves a coherent position amid rapid social, historical, and cultural transformations. It is, according to Miles, in the moments of slippage and discontinuity that the ideological business of the gothic aesthetic is most apparent (32). For him, the gothic aesthetic incorporates an idealized national identity together with a myth of origins (50). This position is similar to that most recently put forward by James Watt in his *Contesting the Gothic* (1999). For Watt, the 1790s through the early 1800s were dominated by what he calls the creation of "Loyalist Gothic" romances. He sees these works as reactions to Britain's defeat in America in that they consistently portray a proud heritage of military victory played out within an unambiguous moral and political agenda. Setting their action around besieged castles, these operas present a stratified yet harmonious society, use real historical figures from the British military pantheon (Richard the Lion Heart was a particular favorite), and consistently depict the defeat of effeminate or foreign villains. Loyalist gothics are structurally bound to depict an act of usurpation that is always corrected, often through the supernatural agency of a ghost (7). We might legitimately ask, however, why loyalty gothics would be so popular in a country like France, on the verge of overthrowing its king and establishing a republic. Was the viewing of opera and melodrama in which the rightful heir is rescued from those infinitely lower in rank and honors a form of nostalgic denial—a denial of parricide?

When Handel died in 1759 the *Universal Chronicle* printed an epitaph that saluted him as a musician "whose compositions were a sentimental language rather than mere sounds; and surpassed the power of words in expressing the various passions of the human heart."[3] Delight and the expression of strong emotions was seen in this era as a part of the human condition, and Handel's oratorios fit into the three main compositional styles that had been defined by Charles Avison in his *Essay on Musical Expression* (1752): the grand or sublime, the beautiful or serene, and the pathetic or devout, plaintive, or sorrowful. In a similar vein, James Beattie observed that "mere descriptions, however beautiful, and moral reflections, however just, become tiresome, where our passions are not occasionally awakened by some event that concerns our fellow-men" (cited in Schmidgall, 37). The operas and oratorios of this period can be "read" as a "series of passionate or affective vignettes" which appear to portray the actions and emotions of their characters in a piecemeal fashion. Schmidgall sees Handel as working in the "passion-based aesthetic" of his time. His airs particularly attempt to express idealized versions of one of the passions of the human heart and therefore they reveal the eighteenth-century bias toward generalizing, and one thinks of Joanna Baillie's *Plays on the Passions* in this context. The Cartesian assumption that passions or emotions are definite in character, concrete in form, and separable in the mind led Shaftesbury to claim that human passions, rather than reason, were the "springs of action." Shaftesbury attempted then to categorize the passions as "natural or social" affections directed toward the general welfare; "the self or private" affections directed toward the individual's own good; and the "unnatural" affections directed toward neither. In Germany this tendency to systematize led to the theory of *Affktenlehre*, the doctrine that explained how the passions could be portrayed in music, leading to the belief that dramatic music must deal in various specific human emotions in order to evoke a pathetic response from its audience (Schmidgall, 38–9). But this brings us to the Germanic attempt to define "rescue opera," that musical experiment to translate the British gothic sensibility, complete with all its paranoia, claustrophobia, persecution mania, and ambivalence toward authority, onto the opera stage and which probably had its first incarnation in Friedrich von Schiller's 1781 robber rescue drama, *Die Raüber*.

**Definitions**

Defining "rescue opera" musicologically and developing a clear and concise history for this genre has been fraught with difficulty. David Charlton has claimed that the term itself is unhistorical and of limited usefulness because it "plays false on three levels [of] the musical theatre that it purports to represent" ("On Redefinitions", 169). First of all, the term does not distinguish between works of different moral purposes or dramatic styles. Secondly, the term relies on a blanket notion of "rescue," but does not take into consideration all of the other moral actions involved. Thirdly, the term ignores eighteenth-century definitions of its own theatrical era. In summarizing all of the meanings for the term that have been proposed by musicologists as eminent as Winton Dean et al., Charlton claims that all of these attempts at definition "fail to account for certain operas and tendencies" ("On Redefinitions", 169). For him, rescue operas are not part of what he calls "an authentic genre like 'opera buffa.'" Instead, the term was coined only in the late nineteenth and early twentieth centuries as a legacy of that movement that sought to label music by the use of one word (e.g., *Humanitätsmelodie*). Dyneley Hussey used the term "rescue opera" to describe Beethoven's *Fidelio* in 1927, while Karl M. Kolb labeled these works "das sogenannte Rettungsoder Befreiungsstück," (our translation: "the genre of the so-called rescue or deliverance operas"), suggesting that the term had become useful as a means of connecting the German *Fidelio* to the French tradition. As Charlton observes, the term "rescue" is problematic in that it suggests a happy resolution, the use of a *deus ex machina* to resolve complications much in the manner of *opera seria*.[4] Yet the sudden reversals of fortune which many of the rescue operas stage resemble less the *coup de théâtre* of classical theater which corresponded to the shifting alliances among royals and more to the "tableau" in which everyone is (re)united because of their desire to be happy. For our purposes it might be useful to draw the following analogy: the genre of "opera semiseria" is the musical equivalent of the literary genre of melodrama, while rescue opera is the staged correlative of the *roman frénétique/noir* or gothic novel.

Most musicologists agree that Michel-Jean Sedaine (1719–97) was the founder of the rescue opera melodrama. They cite his very successful *Richard coeur-de-lion* (1784) as the originator of the genre. Indeed, it was, in its genre, as successful as Beaumarchais's *Mariage de Figaro* for the 1780s decade.[5] Claiming that he wrote light *opéras comiques larmoyants* in the Italian style, Sedaine particularly influenced René-Charles Guilbert de Pixérécourt (1773–1844), who in turn recognized his artistic paternity when he stated that melodrama was a "musical drama in which the music is played by the orchestra instead of being sung" (cited in Rahill, 18) and was to be known as "l'école de Sedaine perfectionnée" (trans: "the school of Sedaine perfected" [Ledbury, 248]).

Sedaine's originality stemmed from his belief that drama should deal with political and moral issues and, in the rescue operas, he explores the theme of "unjust detention." In each case the reasons for detention are different, and even though the plot emphasizes the excitement of the danger and tension found in the actual rescue, the underlying ideology portrayed avoided the simplistic moral categories of the popular melodramas dominating the French stage. The dungeon, which did not originate as a metaphor because of the Bastille but because of its role in medieval literature, had by then become popular in England with the successes of such gothic novels as *The Monk* and *The Italian*. By the mid-eighteenth century, the prison was the trope most frequently referenced in these works, in addition to the imprisonment of the *Philosophes* for their publications and work on the *Encyclopédie*, as well as the arbitrary and infamous uses of the *lettres de cachet*.

Whereas *Richard coeur-de-lion* and *Le Comte D'Albert* (1786) concern the rescue of an aristocrat after violent assaults on prisons and the dramatic collapse of much pasteboard scenery on stage, *Le Roi et le fermier* (1762), one of many operas Sedaine wrote celebrating "freedom," has the heroine Jenny happily escaping from her abductor. Therein the motif of endangered female innocence and sexual victimization is played out in a spectacularizing manner with the peasant girl, Jenny, cast as the victim of the lust of the aristocrat Lurewel. Although Richard says in Act I, scene iv that she has been "enlevée, séduite, trompée" (trans: "kidnapped, seduced, betrayed"), Lurewellater tells a courtier that 'elle fait la sotte,' (trans: "she is acting foolishly") which represents his view (a literary–aristocratic cliché) of her defense of her honor. By having her embody some of the characteristics which patriarchal society desired of the ideal woman at this period ("Ma Jenny est si douce, si timide," [Act I, v: trans. "My Jenny is so sweet, so timid"]), the libretto sets her up both to validate the patriarchal mode of female subjugation and to put it into question since she escapes by using her wits (Dunkley, 55).[6]

By the 1790s rescue operas were extremely popular, both in Britain and France, and adaptations of popular gothic novels about victimization and persecution reached all classes in a variety of theatrical and operatic venues. There were dozens of gothic novels written in England between 1764 and 1799, a large number of which attempted to defend the increasingly serious threats posed against the monarchy and the aristocracy more generally in England. The gothic began as an ideologically conservative genre committed to shoring up the claims of primogeniture and inheritance by entail. Novels such as Walpole's *Castle of Otranto* (1765) and Clara Reeve's *Old English Baron* (1778) were concerned with unjust tyrants, imprisonments, escapes, disinheritances, wrongful claims on an estate, threatened assaults on virginal females, and the eventual triumph of the "true" aristocrat as rightful heir. The staged form of these plots stressed the dramatic effects, and, as the Terror's impact spread, melodramatic villains appeared in increasingly horrific manifestations.

The popularity of the gothic as a genre was conveyed almost immediately to France, where translations and stage adaptations of the British novels were in vogue. The first example of a British rescue opera was an adaptation of Sedaine's libretto and André-E.-M.Grétry's musical score for *Richard coeur-de-lion*, which was staged in London in two different versions in 1786. The most accomplished British musical composer of rescue operas was Stephen Storace, whose popularity was based on such escape operas as *The Haunted Tower* (1789), *The Siege of Belgrade* (1791), *The Pirates* (1792), and *Lodoiska* (1794). The last work, set in Poland during the Tartar invasion, was adapted as a text by John Philip Kemble for Storace from Kreutzer's French version (1791). Like the others in this genre, it concerns a beautiful countess imprisoned by an evil baron and rescued by her beloved count and his servant, with the unwitting aid of the Tartars (Taylor, 94–5). The other dominant example of British rescue/gothic drama was *Blue Beard* (1798) by the well-known playwright George Colman and the successful singer-composer Michael Kelly. Their collaboration, again adapted from the French *Barbe bleue* by Gréty (1789), placed Blue Beard in the Orient and relied on references to Napoleon's campaign in Egypt (Taylor, 113). And if its political insinuations were not potent enough, this time the heroine has to escape from the harem of an accomplished wife-killer (Taylor, 113).

It was a short step from the gothic novel to the "rescue opera," with several versions of the same novel often appearing on stage within the same year even. For instance, in 1798, François B. Hoffman and Nicolas Dalayrac adapted Radcliffe's novel *The Mysteries of Udolpho* (1794) as the "tyrant" rescue opera *Léon, ou Le Château de Montenero*. And Pixérécourt, dubbed the "Corneille of the Boulevards" because most of his works were played on the boulevards that had replaced the old walls of Paris, turned the same British gothic story into *Le Château des Appenins ou le fantôme vivant* (1798), transforming, as he went, the ghostly apparitions of his source into hoaxes perpetuated on the gullible. Other less prominent French melodramatists utilized all the gothic devices at their disposal; hence there were bleeding nuns, *doppelgängers*, evil dukes, and eventually vampires all over the French stage. M.-C. Cammaille-Saint-Aubin and César Ribié adapted Lewis's *Monk* in 1797, causing a sensation and fostering a continuing obsession with the gothic on the Boulevard stage (Rahill, 27). *Le Moine* was so popular that it was performed 116 times at a variety of Parisian theaters, including eighty performances at the Théâtre de la Gaîté.

But notice how rescue/exile/outlaw opera is transformed and anglicized in a typical example of a later native British "comic-opera," Balfe's *The Maid of Artois* (1836), with a libretto by Bunn. The heroine Isolde has been kidnapped by the villainous marquis, while the hero Jules attempts to rescue her, but instead is captured by the marquis's henchmen and sent to a penal colony in Guiana. During the second act, however, Isolde manages to escape her jailors and travel across the ocean disguised as a sailor. Once safely landed, she then disguises herself as a Sister of Charity and rescues Jules herself. During their daring and dangerous escape, the lovers are rescued yet one more time, now by the reformed and repentant marquis, who begs them for forgiveness so that they can all live happily ever after. The dialogue was spoken and interspersed between the arias, but clearly the genre was infused with melodramatic as well as gothic tropes (and reminds us more than a little of Beethoven's *Fidelio*). To conclude, the British rescue opera focused on material that was almost uniformly adapted from earlier French operas, but it tended to emphasize gothic elements that its populace would easily recognize from both their readings of the novels and their attendance at the gothic dramas that were so quickly staged and based on those novels.

**French Sources**

It is necessary, therefore, to turn now to the situation in France, as there was as much artistic collaboration between the two countries as there was political angst and economic rivalry. While it is common to claim that the British imported melodrama from France (cf. Brooks) as they had earlier adopted opera from Italy, it is also possible to see a more convoluted pattern of influences by shifting our gaze back to the mid-eighteenth-century or thereabouts. All sorts of diversions moved across the English Channel in both directions, and in Paris there was a full-blown "cult of all things English" during the mid-eighteenth century (Rahill, 109), including entertainment enterprises modeled on the Vauxhall and the Ranelagh, which had established themselves in the British capital in 1774. The availability of a growing number of translations of fictional and philosophical British and French texts encouraged the exchange of fashionable ideas and an examination of different sources of inspiration. Pixérécourt's favorite reading in 1793, for instance, was Revd. James Hervey's *Meditations and Contemplations Among the Tombs* (1746–47) and Revd. Edward Young's *The Complaint, or Night Thoughts* (1742–45), both works typifying what the French referred to as *le spleen anglais*. As Rahill has noted, the two authors were popular in France because of their "resolute moral didacticism, a morbid preoccupation with grief and misfortune, a noxious and all-pervading sentimentality, and an almost total absence of a sense of humor. All of these were to be in the inheritance of melodrama" (7).

In Paris, during the 1792 theater season, *Le Château du diable*, a four-act drama by Joseph Loaisel-Tréogate, was a huge success at the Théâtre de la Rue Martin. For many reasons, 1792 marks a turning point in the French Revolution and in the use of political representations and symbols. The First Republic was proclaimed on September 21; the *Marseillaise* was composed and reached Paris on July 30; the name "Marianne"[7] designated the Republic for the first time; the female figure of Liberty with her phrygian bonnet emblematized the nation; and Louis XVI was imprisoned in August, tried in December and executed on January 20, 1793. Thus the events of 1792 point to gender as a founding category of modern politics, culture and ideology, even though the revolutionary era's gender politics repressed women as subjects—they were excluded from citizenship in June 1793—and attempted to reconfigure them into subjects of masculine desire. On the theatrical stage, the years leading up to and encompassing the 1789 Revolution realized a transformative shift in the dramatic arts with such works as Jean-Jacques Rousseau's 1775 *Pygmalion*, Pierre Augustin Caron de Beaumarchais's 1784 *Mariage de Figaro*, Sedaine's 1784 *Richard coeur-de-lion* and Pixérécourt's 1800 *Coelina ou l'enfant du mystère*, which emerged, according to Charles Nodier, as the first representative piece of the "modern" melodramatic genre.[8]

Three legal events transformed the French theatrical world during the Revolution. First, actors were granted the status of "citizen" in December 1789; second, in 1790 the Catholic Church, which no longer bestowed legitimacy upon the king, had to swear allegiance to the Republic's constitution; and, third, the advent of the 1791 legislation of the National Convention broke up the Comédie Française's near-monopoly of the repertoire which had limited smaller theaters to productions which differed little from the pantomimic, acrobatic and trained animal entertainment offered at the fairgrounds on the outskirts of Paris. The abolition of state control of theater venues brought about a proliferation of new theaters, creating rivalries in the productions they presented to their newly formed audiences. Spectators were drawn in by the promise that the action would go beyond the excitement and fears of the events witnessed during the Revolution. With the multiple daily beheadings serving as a backdrop to street "performances," the excitement on stage had to surpass real disembodiments in order to compete. The Boulevard du Temple, in particular, became popularly and humorously known as the "Boulevard du crime" because of all the staged abductions, murders, rapes and other heinous crimes committed on the theaters' stages (see Brooks, *passimond* and Roots-Bernstein). However, the theatrical world's freedom proved to be short-lived. The Reign of Terror gradually reinstated modes of censure as certain dramaturges denounced the government's power struggles and, early in the nineteenth century, Napoleon reinstituted the hierarchy of theaters and designated what sorts of spectacles could be performed on the various stages.

The new dramas—most of which changed their categorization (*comédie, tragicomédie, opéra comique, drame, mélodrame* etc.) depending often on the venue of the particular performance—alluded frequently, yet indirectly, to current events but in terms of individual stories which were displaced to other locales and times. The plots were borrowed from British successes as well as French literary and feudal histories even as the plays were enrolled by the state to promulgate didactically civic messages of virtue and republicanism. Rereadings of history which conformed (evidently or not) to the principles of the society the Republic was forging underpinned many of the most popular spectacles, while anti-clericalism guaranteed the popularity of a particular entertainment with its portrayal of the abuses perpetrated by convents and cloisters. Thus the ontology of melodrama situates itself within the framework of popular agitation surrounding the abolition of religious orders as well as of slavery and divorce legislation (Didier, 120). After 1789, operas increasingly took on the characteristics of popular melodrama, with a simple moral structure (the Manichean good versus evil) and a conclusion that emphasized social and communal freedom rather than personal or individual redemption. The example already mentioned above of *Le Château du diable* follows this pattern. Consisting of equal parts melodrama and fairy tale, it charts the struggles of a young knight forced to penetrate a perilous castle filled with ghosts, ghouls, and all manner of sensual temptations. After many harrowing adventures endured while surviving his ordeal, the knightly hero learns that his fiancée's father has staged all of these horrors, in order to test his loyalty and courage.[9]

Other works attempted to explore regicide and the instability associated with the founding of the French Republic. In particular, the recurrent thematics of the imprisonment of women dramatized in different ways the successful and not so effective efforts of the male population to restrain and contain women, especially those of lower social rank who had shown their energy and strength during the period of 1789–1792 by expressing their discontent at the misogynist, racist, and violent injustices of patriarchal society. According to David Charlton, the phases of the French Revolution produced melodrama's thematics in accord with the moment: the early years, 1789–1792, gave rise to works

> espousing hope in the equality of citizens, hope for constitutional monarchy, and for the self-determining unity of the French nation. The Terror years, 1793–94, produced intense didactic works about sacrifice and patriotism and works celebrating military victories. Then the fall of Robespierre (9 Thermidor II/27 July 1794) saw a resurgence of counter-revolutionary movements of all kinds; some contained old fashioned royalists, others, constitutionalists; but they were all united against the memory of Robespierre and his 'drinkers of blood.' (French Opera IX, 57)

Encouraged by the success of *Le Château du diable*, Loaisel-Tréogate went on to write a number of other popular pieces including, for the 1797 theater season, *La forêt périlleuse des brigands de la Calabre*, one of the most popular melodramas to play nightly to a packed house on the Boulevard du Temple. Over-populated with banditti, the melodrama featured a beautiful heroine, Camille, and her devoted lover, Colisan, struggling against the evil machinations of an outlaw who kidnaps Camille and imprisons her in a cave where he threatens to starve her unless she becomes his mistress.[10] In his attempt to rescue Camille, Colisan stumbles into a secret passageway to the cave and is eventually forced to fight against his own rescuing party because his bandit captors have coerced him to join them. Such melodramatic effects suffuse French popular theater and connect these plays with such British gothic novels as Radcliffe's *A Sicilian Romance* (1790), or to the French *roman noir* and *roman frénétique* with their utilization of medieval, chivalric, pantomimic, melodramatic, and gothic conventions.[11]

The popularity of Loaisel-Tréogate's melodramatic pieces rested upon new conceptions of theatrical spectacle largely elaborated by Rousseau, Denis Diderot, Jean-Georges Noverre, Beaumarchais, and Sedaine, which brought together the distinct genres of seventeenth-century classical theater to enact the blurring of their differences. With the politicization of literary and aesthetic criticism in the 1770s, opposition to the Académie's rigidity in differentiating between the genres situated parodic and satirical discourse against a revival of "a formal and civic vocabulary of virtuous emulation" (Ledbury *Genre*, 224) and led to the exploitation of sentiment and emotional anguish, crime and horror on stage. Moving performance style toward pre-Romantic topics and conventions, these transfigurations opened the door to melodramatic staging.

Melodrama, therefore, embodied the desires and expectations of audiences changed by the events of the period into representations of what Nodier called "the morality of the Revolution," including messages about the pathos and appeal of virtue in distress, a scenario which enticed its audience, even if it did so with increasingly convoluted plots. Democratic in their appeal to a variety of spectators, these works advocated standing up to tyrants, traitors, or villains in order to find happiness and respect. Further, in their democratic emphasis, they placed on an equal footing all the arts associated with the theater, including the musical (song and instrumental accompaniment), the corporeal (dance and mime), costuming, stage effects and the decor. Clearly breaking with the non-native classical theater elaborated in the seventeenth century, music and pantomime became constitutive staples of French melodrama in large part because of the expressive possibilities of the body. The language of gesture, which Noverre (the "Shakespeare of dance," as David Garrick nicknamed him) observed at fair theaters, as well as during his tours at the Garrick theater in London, and which he advocated in his development of the *ballet d'action*, was presumed universally understandable to a variety of audiences, and thus transferable to other stages. As the performers communicated feelings derived from their moral response to various human conditions, they embodied either concepts of *sensibilité*, which encompassed domestic loyalty, and the work ethic with docile bodies, or absolutist values with satirical moves from heavy conformity to grotesque excesses (Foster, 42). Noverre's insistence upon the readability of facial expression extended the melodramatic exploitation of the verbal language's inability to convey the necessary emotion with its alternating use of emphatic music and spoken word.

These physical, visual, and aural complements to the declarative mode of classical theater underscored the emotional intensity of crisis, added legibility to the characters' turmoil and allowed for the body politic, disengaged from the symbolic of the state by the Revolution, to be represented on the stage as actual embodiments of domestic life. The action of the melodramatic plot worked through confrontations having largely to do with questions of identity, misidentification of lineage and social position, together with such conflations as that of social rank and the *droit du seigneur* mentality; economic class and male (virtual) blindness; or naïveté (often portrayed by mute male characters) and virtue. Thus, although many, including the critics of the time, have emphasized how conservative and simplistic the messages of these melodramas and rescue operas appear, the episodes in the characters' lives and their desires reflect often indirectly and ironically on both the domestic sphere and the political, public arena.

**Cross-Cultural Dialogue**

But why did "rescue operas" and their progenitors, gothic melodramas, become so popular before, during, and after the Revolution, and what does such a cultural phenomenon reveal about the vexed and ambivalent cultural relationship between France and England during this period? In our attempt to answer those two questions, we have briefly examined the cultural fluidity of the gothic as a genre and pointed to the increasing interaction between librettists, composers and artists of the two countries who "borrowed" ideas, ideologies, acting styles, and even scripts and libretti from each other. Another important constituent of the genre's success was how audience dynamics impacted and reflected upon the popularity of the genre together with the changing French public which started to resemble the more established British tradition of a diversified audience. With working citizens increasingly attending the theater and with Shakespeare's growing popularity in France, spectators' tastes were altered, and this called for a theatrical experience full of emotional appeal and involvement. This new audience was interested in action-packed scenarios (the three-unities rule of classical theater forbidding actions on stage clearly did not apply to the melodramatic plots) and rapidly developing intrigues, rather than the slow-building *tableaux* that had been popular earlier. Even though some theater critics considered the new theater to be blatantly pandering to the lowest elements, with its heavy reliance on grotesque prison scenes, dramatic escapes, wild crowd scenes, and the simplistic triumph of the just over the unjust, the public that sought entertainment rather than edification nevertheless expected to witness recognizable personal experiences which could serve as a means to self-knowledge (Kennedy, 19–21).

Rescue operas, therefore, developed along two somewhat different lines: "tyrant" operas and "humanitarian" operas within the general category of opera semiseria, or opéra comique. The first type corresponds to the conservative British "loyalty gothic," with its focus on the trials and tribulations of the aristocracy, while the second type draws upon the sentimental "virtue in distress" or "woman in jeopardy" genre, with its focus on middle-class characters or women as the captured or besieged. The first category emphasized political injustice or abstract questions of law and embodied the threat of tyranny in an evil man who imprisons unjustly a noble character. Etienne Méhul's *Euphrosine* and H.-M. Berton's *Les rigueurs du cloître* (both 1790) are typical examples of the genre. "Humanitarian" operas, on the other hand, do not depict a tyrant, but instead portray an individual—usually a woman or a worthy bourgeois—who sacrifices everything in order to correct an injustice or to obtain some person's freedom. Dalayrac's *Raoul, Sire de Créqui* (1789) or Bouilly's and Cherubini's *Les deux journées* (1800) are examples, along with Sedaine's pre-1789 works. This tendency to depict, in a grandiose manner, an act of humanity ties in with the general mood of the times and figures prominently in all the arts including painting, where such works have been labeled, according to R. Rosenblum, as *exemplum virtutis*. The parallels, which Ledbury has examined between the works of Sedaine and the painter Jean-Baptiste Greuze (1725-1805), illustrate this correspondence, while Sedaine's father-like mentoring of David bears witness to the close collaboration that existed between the arts in the staging and representation of ideology.

Opera semiseria, combining comic and horrible events with both aristocratic and lower-class characters, was well suited to the sentimentality of the period. Ironically, in a manner reminiscent of Sade, these operas specialized in juxtaposing the pathetic with the appalling without having to carry through the action to a tragic conclusion. Ferdinando Paër (1771-1839), an Italian who spent most of his productive life in Gennany and France, is remembered today as one of the major practitioners of opera semiseria. One of his most famous operas was *Camilla, ossia Il sotterano* (1799), whose plot bears an uncanny resemblance to the aforementioned Radcliffe gothic novel, *A Sicilian Romance*, as can be seen from the brief synopsis of the action, which virtually retells the same story. This semiserious opera makes heavy use of macabre settings, aberrant psychology, and jarring juxtapositions of the comic with the serious. The heroine Camilla has been imprisoned for seven years when the opera begins, forced to inhabit the underground vaults of a ruined castle in Naples owned by Duke Uberto, her husband by a secret marriage. The reason for Camilla's banishment is provided quickly: she has refused to reveal the identity of a man who once kidnapped and tried to seduce her, albeit unsuccessfully. After much confusion over false identities and forced confessions, Loredano and Cola, the Duke's nephew and servant, rescue Camilla and her son Adolfo. Loredano is himself forced to confess that he was the abductor and he clears Camilla's name so that she can be reconciled to her husband and son. Paër's version of the story utilized the same source as Dalayrac did for his opera of the same title (1791). But what is clear from these adaptations of *A Sicilian Romance* is how quickly British novels made their way onto Parisian stages.

Another example of an opera semiseria by Paër, *I Fuorusciti di Firenze* (1802), reveals yet another strain of the rescue opera, the "exile" or "outlaw" opera that would become particularly popular by 1830. In this work, Princess Isabella of Florence has been kidnapped by Uberto's *banditti* and imprisoned in a ruined Tuscan castle. His inveterate enemy Edoardo de Liggozzi, Isabella's husband, had exiled Uberto himself from Florence twenty years earlier. In the disguise of a shepherd, Edoardo attempts to rescue his wife, but is captured and forced to reveal his true identity. Rather than kill the pair, Uberto suddenly reveals that, twenty years earlier, he had left an infant daughter in Florence when he was forced into exile: Isabella. As one might expect, a happy ending is provided amid much sudden light relief. Such a work as *I Fuorusciti di Firenze* reveals how thoroughly the gothic had been sentimentalized or melodramatized by the turn of the century. By then, the use of the reunion between parent and child, a staple of stage melodramas also found in Pixérécourt's *Coelina*, had infiltrated opera.

But genres do not proliferate out of thin air. They evolve to serve specific ideological purposes, and theorists who have social, political, cultural, and aesthetic agendas in mind construct them. Diderot's dramatic theory inspired the development of the *drame bourgeois* otherwise known as *tragédie bourgeoise/domestique* or *drame sérieux* which significantly influenced Beaumarchais and Louis-Sébastien Mercier in France, and Lessing and the *Sturm und Drang* group in Germany (Ledbury, *Sedaine*, 3). In his *Discours sur la poésie dramatique* (*Discourse on Dramatic Poetry*, 1758), Diderot distinguishes between "two types of tragedy, *tragédie domestique* 'qui aurait pour objet la vertu et les devoirs de l'homme' (trans: whose subject would be virtue and man's duties), and *tragédie héroïque* 'qui a pour objet les catastrophes publiques et les malheurs des grands'" (trans: whose subject focused upon public calamities and the misfortunes of the great) (cited in Ledbury *Genre*, 219). His *tragédie domestique* used "an intense private space to symbolize society" and "never posed the relationship between the private and the public spheres as a problematic one." Many of the issues debated on the literary and philosophical page also applied to the opera stages. Diderot's *drame* especially influenced opéra comique from the late 1750s on, and it was this "fertile centre of dramatic experiment" (232–33) in the 1770s which in turn engineered melodrama, or what Peter Brooks calls, in *The Melodramatic Imagination*, a modern cultural discourse.

Theorizing about genre in eighteenth-century France "mutated from a discourse of hierarchy to a discourse of opposition" which associated the notion of genre with that of gender. Where "hierarchical structures of thought and behaviour were central to the mind-set of the court society ... [for] the encyclopédistes and other philosophes from Buffon to Diderot ... the importance of genre and generic categorisation [was] ... key to organising and understanding the complexity of nature and culture."[12] Innovations that interrogated the hierarchical system of genres and the aesthetic culture of the times encountered horror and fascination, and the possible creations were denounced by those working against the new forms as monsters in Claude-Henri Watelet's terms. Of course, the figurative monsters so vehemently remonstrated against were soon translated into literally horrifying figures. We would argue, in fact, that the gothic melodramas and the rescue operas were exegeses on the distrust of this very new genre, for they liberalized the fears and the very language used to combat the new genre.

Sedaine, who wrote the libretti for some of the most successful opéras comiques of the last third of the eighteenth century, modernized by hybridizing the genre in such works adapted from British plays as *Le Diable à quatre ou la double métamorphose* (opéra-comique, 1757),[13] and *Le Roi et le fermier*. The latter, first performed on November 22, 1762, was based upon Robert Dodsley's *The Miller of Mansfield*.[14] Sedaine's comedy aspired to a new kind of seriousness with its presentation of an egalitarian storyline. According to Ledbury, the play combines both the intimate sphere and public life; audaciously exploits royal presence; presents the irresistible characters of Betsy and Richard; and implicitly critiques court circles and the abuse of power (*Genre*, 100). Act I opens with Richard, the *intendant des forêts*, worried about Jenny, who has been absent since morning. When she does return, she explains that she has escaped from the castle of Lord Lurewel. However, since her flock, which was lured into the grounds as a device to snare her, is still trapped she now has no dowry and she worries that this will prevent her marriage to Richard. In Act II, which takes place in the forest, Richard meets the king, who has been separated from his courtiers and does not reveal his identity. Richard mistrusts him and treats him brusquely at first, but eventually invites him in to shelter from the storm. At the same time, Richard's gamekeepers arrest Lurewel. In Act III, over a joyful supper with the king, Richard tells Jenny's story. Lurewel is brought in, and after the king has revealed his identity, the former is sent away in disgrace and the king offers to resolve all difficulties by providing Jenny's dowry (Ledbury *Genre*, 100; n75). Thus Jenny, rather than being seduced as she is in the English version, escapes, while the beneficent and wise king, in contact with his people, sees the corruption and injustices of his courtiers and moves to correct and chastise them (102).

Sedaine worked through operatic reformulations with reconstructions of medieval stories such as *Aucassin et Nicolette ou les moeurs du bon vieux tem[p]s* (*comédie*, 1780) and *Richard coeur-de-lion* (*comédie*, 1786). As against Lionnel Gossman's argument that the introduction and use of the medieval during this period was a conservative move, it appears that the craze for medievalism allowed Sedaine and his contemporaries to explore new themes and stage possibilities. It enabled transformations in stage decor and satirical (and ironic) messages to underlie the retelling of narratives such as *Aucassin et Nicolette*. The staging of this anonymous late twelfth- or early thirteenth-century text, with its own extraordinary (parodic) intertextuality referencing Chrétien de Troyes's romances and earlier *chansons de geste*, including *The Song of Roland* and *La prise d'Orange*, aptly sustains Sedaine's argument in favor of genre hybridity. As *chantefable*, *Aucassin et Nicolette* alternated prose and assonanced verse and its performances, which sought to entertain rather than edify and instruct, were most likely musically accompanied. Prefiguring the form of opéra comique by almost six hundred years, the plot of this medieval tale anticipates those of the rescue operas. Its intrigue suggests that everything should be subordinated to love, including such chivalric attributes as honor and nobility. Indeed, Aucassin loves Nicolette, although she is a slave who has been baptized and is the godchild of the town's viscount, his father's vassal. His father refuses to let him marry her, however; and the father orders the viscount to send her away. The latter decides instead to seal her in his sumptuous palace. Utilizing both Nicolette's and Aucassin's refusal to obey their parents' wishes with regard to whom they are to marry, as well as keeping the anti-clerical and feminist messages of the medieval version, allowed for a spirited participation in the social and cultural upheavals of the 1780s from within the safe confines of a national literary treasure. This "revival", perhaps more than any other adaptation, signals how the use of these medieval texts encouraged change and presented the new parameters of opera performance under the guise of historicity.

Sedaine's 1770 prose tragedy, *Maillard ou Paris sauvé*, attempted to breach the "natural and immutable barrier between high and low genre" (Ledbury *Genre*, 198). Although the play's nationalism, its historical setting in the fourteenth century, and the entanglement of the domestic and political opposition between Maillard and Etienne Marcel place it within the tragic mode, the work is clearly a hybrid. *Maillard* contains several scenes that daringly reveal the intimate relations of the young bourgeois lovers, and the depiction of their child and the mother's breast-feeding pains disturb the *bienséances* of the genre (200–202). Furthermore, the almost choreographed spectacle, especially during the conspiracy scenes, together with such props as daggers thrust into a table, demonstrate Sedaine's familiarity with the conventions of opéra comique and with Shakespearean tragedies. Even Madame du Deffand, after having attended a private reading in 1770 of the first draft of the play, commented to Walpole that: "Cette pièce a plus de ressemblance à celles de votre Shakespeare qu'aucune des nôtres" (trans: "This play resembles more your Shakespeare's [plays] than any of ours") (cited in Ledbury *Genre*, 212).[15] Never publicly performed, *Maillard*'s consignment to obscurity reveals that the limits of tolerance for hybridity were quickly reached. However, the parodies that the *Maillard* debate fostered proliferated. They demonstrate that the prose tragedy was actually about the threat of genre anarchy (Ledbury *Genre*, 222–23), a literary anarchy that looked to dissolve boundaries and plotted out presciently the course of a civil and egalitarian society.

As a "pre-modern man of the theater," Sedaine did not succeed in breaking the concept of generic purity. However his experimentations, alongside the contemporary discourses as well as the borrowings from Italian and British pantomimic traditions, which David Garrick and Noverre so prized (Chéruzel, 67–72), generated the foundation for an alternative theatrical practice (see Marcoux). Sedaine's theatrical sense and understanding of the necessity of intimacy and for an *effet du réel*, coupled with irony, "provided a blueprint for those practitioners in theater, art, music-drama who, in the later nineteenth century, were responsible for what we now understand as the transition to modernism" (Ledbury, "Sedaine," 38).

Beethoven's *Fidelio*, perhaps the most famous of all the so-called rescue operas, is considered by many to be the final flowering and only masterpiece of the rescue-opera genre. It was based on Jean-Nicolas Bouilly's (1763–1842) libretto and Pierre Gaveaux's score,[16] and their version, an opéra comique, opened at the Théâtre Feydeau on February 19, 1798 as *Léonore ou l'amour conjugal*. This work was in its turn adapted by Mayr as *L'Amour le conjugal* (1805) and also by Paër as *Leonora* (1804). Each version skillfully combined elements of both "tyrant" and "humanitarian" operas. Bouilly's *Léonore* drew on recent French innovations with the imprisonment *topos*, the female singer in the male role, and the use of the rescue plot. Performed in the former ultra-royalist but pro-Italian opera Théâtre de Monsieur, with all its attendant social and political reputation, its composer played the role of Florestan, in an intrigue which engaged "French history by dramatizing a political crime at a sensitive juncture in the Directoire (1795–99)." "[H]istorically self-referential," it showed with very slight disguise "events that had occurred in recent life".[17] The *Léonore* libretto belongs to the Thermidorean reaction period after the end of the monarchy and of the revolutionary dictatorship (Charlton, *French Opera* IX, 57). *Fidelio* first played in 1805 as a three-act opera entitled *Léonore* as Napoleon invaded Austria. The 1814 definitive version bore the title of *Fidelio* and celebrated the triumph of liberty over tyranny and clearly marked Napoleon as the tyrant in Beethoven's eyes, and indeed the rescue opera played over and over again during the Congress of Vienna in 1815.

Originally set in Spain, the story concerns an imprisoned young woman, Leonora, who disguises herself as the boy Fedele. While living in the jail, she apprentices herself to the jailer Rocco, hoping to be able to use her position to free her husband Florestano, unjustly imprisoned for two years by the tyrant Pizzarro because Florestano had exposed the crimes of Pizzarro (and thus made himself a victim of unjust abuse of power). Pizzarro learns that his supervisor, Fernando, will arrive for a visit the next day, and he fears that his treachery will be discovered and punished. In desperation, he commands Rocco to prepare Florestan for his assassination, to be performed by the masked Pizzarro and witnessed by the devoted apprentice Fidele. But Fidele stalls long enough for Fernando to arrive and rescue her husband. Rocco is pardoned, and Pizzarro imprisoned. Even though Bouilly's politics bespoke of liberalism, his *Léonore* avoided explicit political allegorizing. Structured around motive and incident, it nevertheless portrayed the villain Pizzarro as a tyrannical monster. His cruelty, described by a chorus of prisoners in the dungeon, signified by analogy the excesses of 1793–94 rather than any commentary on the *ancien régime*, while the finale of the spectacle celebrated the return of justice and truth (Charlton, *French Opera* IX. 64–67).

Other works that anticipated *Fidelio* include Sedaine's *Comte d'Albert*, and his *Le déserteur*, which must have influenced Beethoven since it was "the most frequently performed stage work in Germany of any genre" (Charlton, *French Opera* IX; 54-55). Dalayrac's *Raoul, Sire de Crequi* also prefigured *Fidelio* politically and dramatically and its English adaptation at the Theatre Royal, Drury Lane in 1792 includes the cross-dressing of two women as soldiers who seek to liberate the brother to one of them. A copy of Paër's score for *Leonora*, discovered among Beethoven's effects after his death, reveals that he had certainly studied, and was influenced by, Paër's version of the famous tale. In Beethoven's version, however, there are a few changes, most notably in the emphasis on the group rather than the individual rescue of the husband. Again, the hero, Florestan, is captured by the villainous Pizzarro and held in a supposedly impregnable dungeon, while Florestan's wife Leonore disguises herself as a boy, as in the British version, in order to rescue her husband. The reconnaissance or reconciliation scene between husband and wife in prison stands as the high point of the work. And the rescuing troops arrive in the nick of time so that all can end happily.

Operas such as *Léonore* and *Fidelio* were essentially serious operas with happy endings—opera semiseries. Clearly this genre was popular and played a particularly influential role in reforming notions of exactly what an opera should look and sound like. As Scott Balthazar points out, such operas emphasized continuous action, formal complexity in structure, and a certain amount of dramatic and musical comedy (*NGD*, 1150). More importantly, however, they were one means by which the tropes of northern Romanticism spread throughout southern

Europe. What is perhaps most interesting to the contemporary literary critic, however, is the persistence of a female disguised as a male, or in a variety of androgynous costumes. Such a trope suggests the constructed nature of gender, while also revealing that gender, as well as identity, is a performance to be enacted for a variety of social and political reasons. The female performer asserted her rights both as an actor/singer/dancer and as a woman in the characters she embodied. Such a position comes close to the depiction of gender and identity in gothic as well as in sentimental novels of the period and points to the new feminine symbols associated with "nation" building.

**Conclusion**

In conclusion it is necessary to ask: why British citizens flock to a number of forgettable rescue operas before, during, and after the French Revolution? What was at stake in staging and viewing the performances? As we have suggested, the opera and its mutations/manifestations embodied a public space in which French and British citizens could vicariously experience the threats of violent political, social, and cultural revolution. But ultimately, we believe, the rescue operas were radically nationalistic for each nation, even though, ironically, they used the same tropes and told very similar familial and nationalistic scripts. Each country was trying to use the theater and the opera house to impose a form of nationalism on its emerging bourgeois populace. As Gerald Newman observes, Britain sought to see itself and its citizens in national and secular terms rather than in religious or tribal ones during the mid-eighteenth century. This shift was made possible, according to Newman, because of cultural, rather than political, activity, with one of the central figures being the "artist-intellectual," an individual who "both creates and organizes nationalist ideology" (56). Here, a composite figure begins to emerge: the adaptation and use of Handel as the artist and Shakespeare as the intellectual, a dual presence hovering as a protector over the domesticated landscape of British discourse. Benedict Anderson has also discussed the growth of secularism as allowing for a new sort of "imagined community," a country with a "national imagination" that would replace the religious construction of the medieval and renaissance communities (6, 36). There is no question that the institutionalization of the popular, hybridized opera during the eighteenth century was a central development in the growth of the new British "national imagination."

In contrast, French nationalism evolved in a radically different manner, with a revolution that accomplished very different ideological work than did the British revolution of the seventeenth century. At the conclusion of their brief experiment with a Commonwealth, the British welcomed back their king on their terms, and the country has not seriously contemplated violent social or political reform since. France's prolonged sojourn in feudalism created a combustible situation which ignited in 1789, and created a politically unstable and contested situation for most of the next century. Both countries staged hundreds of rescue operas, read dozens of gothic novels, and schooled themselves in the tenets of secularization, modernization, and nationalism. Taking their inspiration from northern European sources—Shakespeare, medieval literature and French and British history especially—these texts were written in the uncertainty that defines modernity. Through the rescue trope, they romanced the past, lured in spectators with terrifying scenes and rhetorical turns, even as they hybridized genre and denounced the injustices and arbitrariness of the throne. So great was the appeal of the rescue operas that their cultural residue, sentimentalism, and melodrama remain with us to this day.

## Notes

1   "But it is not to the orators of the revolution that the Romantics looked for instruction in rhetoric. They looked to the revolution itself, to that language made into History, that draws its meaning from events which are declarations. The Terror, as one knows, was not only terrible because of the executions; it was terrible because it proclaimed itself with this capitalization and made Terror the measure of history and the sign of modern times" (Blanchot, 520–21, cited in. Lebrun, 174; our translation).

2   Joseph Addison observed that the "absurdity of opera shows itself at the first sight," while he went on to note that "nothing is capable of being well set to music, that is not nonsense." Samuel Johnson called opera "an exotic and irrational entertainment," while Jonathan Swift spoke of "that unnatural Taste for Italian Music among us, which is wholly unsuitable to our Northern Climate, and the Genius of the People, whereby we are overrun with Italian Effeminacy and Italian Nonsense" (cited in Schmidgall, 32–3).

3   Contrast this definition of music with that proposed by Claude Lévi Strauss, who claimed that music is primarily an expression of the emotions, while Roland Barthes has stated that music is "inactual": that is, abstract and difficult to speak about because "language is of the order of the general, [while] music is of the order of difference." And in his own meditation about the meaning of opera, W.H. Auden echoes this definition: "Opera in particular is an imitation of human willfulness; it is rooted in the fact that we not only have feelings but insist upon having them at whatever cost to ourselves. Opera, therefore, cannot present character in the novelist's sense of the word, namely, people who are potentially good and bad, active and passive, for music is immediate actuality and neither potentiality nor passivity can live in its presence" (cited in Schmidgall, 20). So while Barthes emphasizes the inactual quality of music, Auden asserts the opposite.

4   Charlton's valuable essay "On Redefinitions of Rescue Opera" is the best on the subject, and includes six contradictory definitions of the term in an appendix.

5   The success of *Richard coeur-de-lion* raised the opéra-comique to new levels

and led to Sedaine's long-sought acceptance in the Académie Française (Ledbury, *Sedaine*, 284). Beaumarchais and Sedaine became collaborators, and the latter advised Beaumarchais on the *Mariage de Figaro*.

6 Naomi Schor states that "French Romanticism, Realism, and Naturalism all draw their impetus from the revolution: nineteenth-century literature in France is a protracted and therapeutic working through of the trauma of regicide and the shock of democratization" (144).

7 The first mention of "Marianne" to designate the Republic occurred in an Occitan song by Guillaume Lavabre entitled "La Garisou de Marianno" ("the healing/recovery of Marianne").

8 Pixérécourt's *Coelina*, generally considered the first melodrama, was based on François-G. Ducray-Duminil's extraordinarily popular novel *Coelina ou l'enfant du mystère* (see Gaspard, 128–29). Rahill provides this definition: "Melodrama is a form of dramatic composition in prose partaking of the nature of tragedy, comedy, pantomime, and spectacle, and intended for a popular audience. Primarily concerned with situation and plot, it depends on mimed action extensively and employs a more or less fixed complement of stock characters, the most important of which are a suffering heroine or hero, a persecuting villain, and a benevolent comic. It is conventionally moral and humanitarian in point of view and sentimental and optimistic in temper, concluding its fable happily with virtue rewarded after many trials and vice punished. Characteristically it offers elaborate scenic accessories and miscellaneous divertissements and introduces music freely, typically to underscore dramatic effect" (xiv).

9 This tale is reminiscent of François Thomas du Fossé's life story as recounted by Helen Maria Williams in her *Letters from France* (8 vols). His lover's father does not test him but his own father does. Baron du Fossé cannot accept that his heir will marry the daughter of a local farmer and issues a *lettre de cachet* with the aim of imprisoning him to prevent the marriage (see Mellor, 261–62).

10 The name "Camille" begins to function as a talisman from this time forward, with a beautiful, victimized woman named Camille rescued from out of a tunnel in no fewer than four popular "rescue operas" and melodramas of the period: Marsolier's *Camille ou le souterrain* (1791), Paër's *Camilla, ossia Il sotterraneo* (1799), Dalayrac's *Camille* (1791), and Le Sueur's *La caverne* (1793) Later, the female victim becomes a courtesan and, by 1852, Alexandre Dumas had composed the first version of his famous *La dame aux camélias*, adapted yet again toward the end of the century to great acclaim by the American playwright John Wilds as *Camille; or, the Fate of a Coquette*.

11 For the most thorough recent collection of this work, see Hale. The book assembles twenty-four tales, nineteen of which have never been published before in English, and provides Nodier's definition of the *frénétiques*: "[These writers] flaunt their atheism, madness and despair among the tombstones, exhume the dead in order to terrify the living and torment the imagination with scenes of such horror that it is necessary to look to the terror-ridden dreams of the sick to find a model."

12 Such theorists as Roger de Piles, the abbé Du Bos, Claude-Henri Watelet, and Voltaire associated the notion of genre with that of gender as they recast genre in oppositional terms. The opposition of genres structured eighteenth-century aesthet-

ic debates and disputes such as La Font's attack upon the Académie Royale de Peinture et de Sculpture in the 1740s or the long-running Italian/French opera dispute (which included the *querelle des bouffons*). La Fonts utilized the gender binary to criticize "Boucher's feminised mythologies" and to call for "a male and noble style" (Ledbury, "Sedaine," 14).

13   *Le Diable à quatre* was Sedaine's first drama written for public performance. It was based on the English play *The Devil to pay* performed at the Garrick theater, and translated in Claude-Pierre Patu's *Choix de petites pièces du théâtre anglais* (1756) as *La boutique du bijoutier* (See Ledbury, *Sedaine*, 87–88). Like Marivaux and Beaumarchais, Sedaine utilized carnivalesque role reversals and farcical violence, alluded to contemporary customs, the activities of the aristocracy, and satirized the clergy and the legal profession.

14   Sedaine consulted Patu's *Choix de petites pièces* and chose the Dodsley play in part because of its success on the British stage as an afterpiece in 1735 (Ledbury, *Sedaine*, 100).

15   *Maillard* was also a transposition of other English models, including the Restoration tragedy *Venice preserv'd* by Thomas Otway, which had been transposed by La Fosse into *Manlius*. Both had been used by Voltaire "to discuss tragic modes in drama in France and Britain in his *Commentaires sur Corneille*" (Ledbury, *Sedaine*, 212–13). Voltaire saw *Maillard* as "the final culmination of all the trends ... corroding the great traditions of French drama. He was convinced that it would open the floodgates to a form of practice that would destroy existing order" (213). Even Diderot found *Maillard*, a high tragedy set as an opéracomique, too much for his taste, and Grimm's lack-luster support implies the general loss of support of Sedaine by the philosophers (Ledbury, *Sedaine*, 220).

16   Gaveaux composed the reactionary song of the *jeunesse dorée Le Réveil du peuple* in the 1790s in order to counter the revolutionary *Marseillaise*.

17   See Charlton, *French Opera* IX, 51–67 & IX, 170–72.

**Works Cited**

Anderson, Benedict. *Imagined Communities: Reflections on the Origin and Spread of Nationalism*. Rev. edn. London: Verso, 1991.

Backsheider, Paula. *Spectacular Politics: Theatrical Power and Mass Culture in Early Modern England*. Baltimore: Johns Hopkins UP, 1993.

Balthazar, Scott. "Ferdinando Paër"; "Leonora"; "I Fuorusciti di Firenze"; and "Rescue Opera." In *The New Grove Dictionary of Opera* [*NGD*]. Ed. Stanley Sadie. London: Macmillan, 1992. 816–18; 1150; 316; 1293–94.

Bernard-Griffiths, Simone and Jean Sgard, eds. *Mélodrames et romans noirs 1750–1890*. Toulouse: PU du Mirail, 2000.

Blanchot, Maurice. *L'entretien infini*. Paris: L'Athenaeum-Gallimard, 1981.

Brooks, Peter. *The Melodramatic Imagination*. New Haven: Yale UP, 1976.

Charlton, David. "On Redefinitions of Rescue Opera." In *Music and the French Revolution*. Ed. M. Boyd. Cambridge: Cambridge UP, 1992. 169–188.

———. *French Opera 1730–1830: Meaning and Media*. Aldershot: Ashgate, 2000.

Chéruzel, Maurice. "David Garrick 1717–1779 Compagnon et ami de Noverre." In *Jean-Georges Noverre: Levain de la danse moderne.* Cahors: France Quercy, 1994. 67–72.
Cox, Jeffrey. "Romantic Drama and the French Revolution." In *Revolution and English Romanticism.* Ed. Keith Hanley and Raman Selden. New York: St Martin's Press, 1990. 241–60.
Didier, Béatrice. "Beaumarchais aux origines du mélodrame." In *Mélodrames et romans noirs 1750–1890.* Eds. Simone Bernard-Griffiths and Jean Sgard. Toulouse: PU du Mirail, 2000.115–126.
Dunkley, John. "The Representation of the Female in the Dramas of Sedaine." In *Michel Jean Sedaine (1719–1797): Theatre, Opera, Art.* Eds. David Charlton and Mark Ledbury. Aldershot, UK: Ashgate, 2000. 52–67.
Foster, Susan Leigh. *Choreography and Narrative: Ballet's Staging of Story and Desire.* Bloomington: Indiana UP, 1996.
Gaspard, Claire. "Coelina, de Ducray-Duminil à Pixérécourt: à l'aube de la 'littérature industrielle'." In *Mélodrames et romans noirs 1750–1890.* Eds. Simone Bernard-Griffiths and Jean Sgard. Toulouse: PU du Mirail, 2000. 125–144.
Hale, Terry. *The Dedalus Book of French Horror: The Nineteenth Century.* Cambridge: Dedalus, 1998.
Kennedy, Emmet, et al. *Theatre, Opera, and Audiences in Revolutionary Paris: Analysis and Repertory.* Contributions in Drama and Theatre Studies 62. London: Greenwood Press, 1996.
Lebrun, Annie. *Les châteaux de la subversion.* Paris: J.J. Pauvert-Garnier Frères, 1982.
Ledbury, Mark. *Sedaine, Greuze and the Boundaries of Genre.* Studies on Voltaire and the Eighteenth Century 380. Oxford: Voltaire Foundation, 2000.
———. "Sedaine and the Question of Genre." In *Michel-Jean Sedaine (1719–1797): Theatre, Opera, Art.* Eds. David Charlton and Mark Ledbury. Aldershot, UK: Ashgate, 2000.13–38.
Marcoux, J. Paul. "Guilbert de Pixérécourt: the people's conscience." In *Themes in Drama 14: Melodrama.* Cambridge: Cambridge UP, 1992. 47–59.
Mellor, Anne K. "English Women Writers and the French Revolution." In *Rebel Daughters: Women and the French Revolution.* Eds. Sara E. Melzer, and Leslie W. Rabine. Oxford: Oxford UP, 1992. 255–272.
Melzer, Sara E. and Leslie W. Rabine. Eds. *Rebel Daughters: Women and the French Revolution.* Oxford: Oxford UP, 1992.
Miles, Robert. *Gothic Writing 1750–1820: A Genealogy.* London: Routledge, 1993.
Newman, Gerald. *The Rise of English Nationalism: A Cultural History, 1740–1830.* New York: St. Martin's Press, 1987.
Noiray, Michel. "L'opéra de la Révolution (1790–1794): Un 'Tapage de Chien'?" In *La Carmagnole des Muses: L'Homme de lettres et l'artiste dans la Révolution.* Ed. Jean-Claude Bonnet. Paris: Armand Colin, 1988.
Rahill, Frank. *The World of Melodrama.* University Park: Penn State P, 1967.
Root-Bernstein, Michele. *Boulevard Theater and Revolution in Eighteenth-Century Paris.* Ann Arbor, MI, 1984.

Rosenblum, R. *Transformations in Late Eighteenth-Century Art*. Princeton, NJ: Princeton UP, 1967.
Schmidgall, Gary. *Literature as Opera*. New York: Oxford UP, 1977.
Schor, Naomi. "Triste Amérique: Atala and the Postrevolutionary Construction of Woman." In *Rebel Daughters: Women and the French Revolution*. Eds. Sara E. Melzer, and Leslie W. Rabine. Oxford: Oxford UP, 1992. 139–156.
Taylor, George. *The French Revolution and the London Stage, 1789–1805*. Cambridge: Cambridge UP, 2000.
Watt, James. *Contesting the Gothic: Fiction, Genre and Cultural Conflict, 1764–1832*. Cambridge: Cambridge UP, 1999.
White, Hayden. *Metahistory*. Baltimore, MD: Johns Hopkins UP, 1973.

Chapter Three

# Pursuing the Plerotic Sublime: Romantic Poetry and the Failure of Language

Richard A. Nanian

I begin with an assumption: reading and interpretation are metaphorical activities. To find correspondence between language and external reality is necessarily to believe in metaphor, to believe that something may be described and understood in terms alien to itself. If this assumption is valid, literary critics should be able to adopt and discard various metaphors at different times to suit their goals. The metaphor that currently dominates literary studies, undergirding all biographical, psychological, and cultural criticism, is that of the literary work as artifact.[1] Its implications are threefold. First, to identify any literary work as an artifact is to invest it with a questionable unity. It is a single thing, no matter how complex its internal structures, and should submit to any number of distinct but reconcilable judgments. Simultaneously, the artifact metaphor encourages the critic to see a literary work as fixed or static, and, as a result, dead. Living creatures—indeed, functioning systems of any kind—are not artifacts. The relationship between critic and literary work is thus of operator to operated upon; one is tempted to say coroner to corpse. Finally, the artifact metaphor is referential; an artifact has meaning only as a record of something else. Left behind, though seldom intended, as a historical record, it functions as such for those who come later. If one says, "This is an artifact," one effectively says nothing; the statement automatically begs the question, "Of what?"

The benefits of this metaphor should not be slighted. The suggestion that a literary work is stable and unified is comforting. Should it be otherwise, the very idea of reaching defensible and reproducible conclusions through a somehow scientific method of inquiry, analysis, and interpretation becomes problematic. And yet, this is a clue to the metaphor's limitations. Science demands reproducible results, independent confirmation, but an individual critic's conclusions are always idiosyncratic. No two critics, even those working within the same paradigm, will independently offer identical interpretations of a complex work. Meanwhile, referentiality is almost a moral quality, for it gives literature, and by extension the lives of literary critics, some relevance to the world. Little wonder, then, that arguments among literary critics so readily take on an ideological cast. The argument over the literary work becomes a smokescreen, because the real issue is something else, something more important.

Yet common readers (by which I mean those who are voluntary, neither paid nor compelled to read by institutions) should be forgiven if they find this metaphor unsatisfying. They do not experience literary texts as lifeless or silent artifacts. Whether the text in question is ancient or contemporary, the reader operates in a perpetual present. In Italo Calvino's marvelous aphorism: "Reading means approaching something that is just coming into being" (Manguel, 25).[2] Susan Sontag famously quarreled with the aims of literary criticism in "Against Interpretation," attacking a metaphor nearly identical with the one I have described here. "The modern style of interpretation excavates, and as it excavates, destroys; it digs 'behind' the text, to find a sub-text which is the true one" (6). Instead, she proposed, "The function of criticism should be to show *how* art *is what it is*, even *that it is what it is*, rather than to show what it means.... In place of a hermeneutics we need an erotics of art" (14). The subsequent failure of literary criticism to abandon Hermes for Eros is a failure of metaphor. Quite simply, the artifact metaphor will not support erotics. If an artifact is inert, referential, dead, any erotics with which it is associated turns into solipsism, fetishism, necrophilia. What we need, should we wish to accomplish Sontag's aim, is a different metaphor, one that presents the relationship between text and reader as dynamic on both sides.

Given that the artifact metaphor treats the literary text as an entity, as a noun, as matter, the most radical revision of that metaphor would be to see the text as a field, as a verb, as energy.[3] An energy metaphor would treat texts as dynamic processes rather than static entities, emphasize the temporal nature of the reading experience[4] as opposed to submitting a text to dissection, and articulate what a text presents to the reader instead of what it represents of external reality. Such a metaphor might well provide a vocabulary suitable to communicate the reading experience, but for it to do so, the energies of a literary text must be text-distinguishable, and then categorizable in some meaningful way. My attempts to develop an energy metaphor received a significant boost when I encountered the work of the poet and critic Elizabeth Sewell. In *The Structure of Poetry*, she offers the diagram shown in Figure 3.1. I call it a cognitive spectrum; to Sewell, it was "nothing more than a way I have adopted of looking at things." In her conception, language is capable of expressing a relatively narrow range of human cognition; logic, number, dream, and nightmare divide the rest. What determines our place along the spectrum she calls reference, by which she means the correspondence between our thought and the world, or what today we more often call signification.[5] As we move left on the diagram, our thoughts become more ordered: reference narrows so that thoughts and things correspond more precisely, until ultimately thought no longer requires any correspondence with external

## Pursuing the Plerotic Sublime

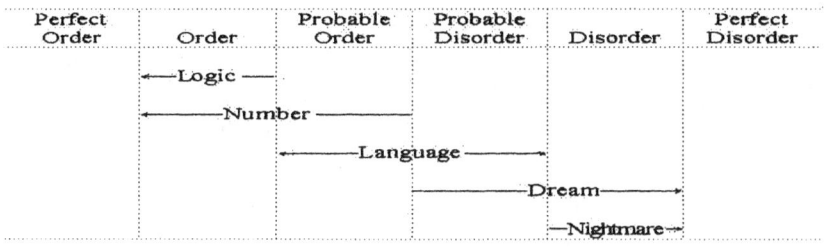

SEWELL'S COGNITIVE SPECTRUM

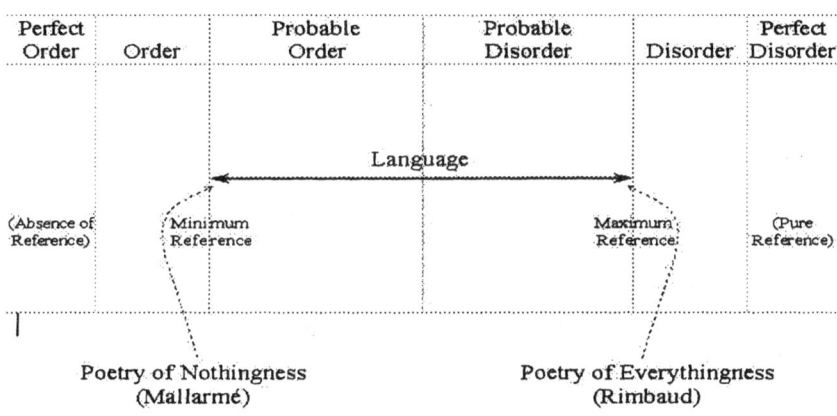

LANGUAGE AND THE RANGE OF REFERENCE

reality. For example, we can add two numbers successfully without knowing whether we add elephants or éclairs. However, one can still conceive a number in the abstract. Logic—if *a* then not *b*—requires virtually no reference at all. Conversely, as we move to the right, disorder prevails, and the correspondence between referent and world becomes less exact: reference broadens, multiplies, as when in a dream our minds find and follow connections between seemingly unrelated elements. When disorder becomes too dominant, the result can be terrifying chaos, or nightmare.

Pushed far enough towards either extreme, the mind encounters what might be called a cognitive break; we can think no further. Well before that cognitive break, however, there occurs a linguistic break, a point at which language fails. Sewell identifies Mallarmé and Rimbaud respectively as poets of "nothingness" and "everythingness," terms that refer to the limits of reference that can be expressed in language. The poetic values of nothingness and everythingness represent the attempt to achieve perfect order and perfect disorder through language. Because language only occupies the mixed middle ground of probability, that task is clearly impossible. With these perfect states necessarily remaining far beyond reach, Sewell argues that the poetry of nothingness and the poetry of everythingness—more accurately, though awkwardly, *the poetry of as-close-to-nothingness-as-language-can-get* and the reverse—confront the reader with the prospect of the infinite by approaching, as nearly as is possible for language, a condition of maximum or minimum reference, the points at which language ends and logic and nightmare begin. Language may in this way be made to suggest what is beyond its capacity to represent. To understand this point more clearly, one can imagine this scale of reference superimposed on Sewell's order/disorder spectrum[6] shown in Figure 3.2. Personally, I rather doubt that any poet can camp out permanently at such extremes. What interests me are the means by which poets can approach these two conditions. I am interested in the direction of travel—or the type of energy—rather than the destination. The movement towards order I call *kenosis*, from the Greek for *to empty*; the movement towards disorder I call *plerosis*, meaning *to fill* or, more accurately here, *overfill*.

As language approaches either order or disorder, it fails; yet language is most interesting at these points of failure. Either point of failure produces the sublime, a state ultimately surpassing language's ability to express. In the direction of kenosis, language fails as a fall into silence, but in the direction of plerosis, language fails as a climb into an inarticulate venting. The precedent for finding the sublime in two distinct directions can be found as far back as Longinus, who writes that sublimity "breathes the vehemence of frenzy and divine possession, and makes the very words inspired" (VIII, 14), but also that "the silence of Ajax in the book of the Lower World is great, and more sublime than any words" (IX, 14–15).[7] If Romantic poetry makes sense as an aesthetic category, and I think it does, it is because its greatest works convey a sense of passion, of exaltation, of divine frenzy to the readers.[8] If Romantic poetry can be described as plerotic poetry, it should be characterized by these effects: a tendency toward cognitive disorder (this does not mean a lack of formal structure) produced by the use of multiple and expanded signifiers, a rejection of number and logic in favor of dream and nightmare, and linguistic failure reached by way of a loss of articulation rather than a fall into silence.[9]

In the 1800 Preface to *Lyrical Ballads*, Wordsworth claims that his poems explore "the manner in which we associate ideas in a state of excitement" (x–xi). Here is immediate evidence of an inclination toward plerosis: the association of ideas is synonymous with reference, and any form of excitation naturally belongs to the right side of Sewell's cognitive spectrum. But these lines are merely prelude to his famous assertion that, "all good poetry is the spontaneous overflow of powerful feelings" (xiv). As plerosis is literally overfilling, a more plerotic claim is difficult to imagine, the change from *overfill* to *overflow* representing only a slight shift of perspective. Still, true plerosis is more than powerful feelings; it also carries with it an epiphanic quality, however transient. In this way, too, Wordsworth conforms to our expectation. Consider how in the 1802 Preface he writes not just of the importance of truth, but of its nature:

> no words, which his [the Poet's] fancy or imagination can suggest, will be to be compared with those which are the emanations of reality and truth.... Aristotle, I have been told, has said, that Poetry is the most philosophic of all writing: it is so: its object is truth, not individual and local, but general, and operative; not standing upon external testimony, but carried alive into the heart by passion; (xxxi–xxxii)

Although the poetry in this passage races ahead of both physics and physiology, the conception is striking enough to deserve our patience. Obviously, Wordsworth was no stranger to the metaphor of language as a field of energy. Words—or rather *some* words, those best suited to poetry—are not material constructs but *emanations*. How to tell the difference? Those that form the language of poetry issue exclusively from *reality* and *truth*, while those the poet's mind produces by definition issue from another source, namely the *fancy* or *imagination*. Reality and truth cannot speak directly, since speech requires a human voice, but are most accessible to those who are in the throes of some great passion: that is, in a state of excitement. Truth itself is *general* and *operative* neither as stated principle nor unreachable Platonic form, but only when *carried alive into the heart by passion*. Passion is thus the principle that unites the capacity for poetic language with the power to convey truth to the reader.[10]

We can see the practical results of Wordsworth's beliefs at the climax of "Tintern Abbey":

> And I have felt
> A presence that disturbs me with the joy
> Of elevated thoughts; a sense sublime
> Of something far more deeply interfused
> Whose dwelling is the light of setting suns,
> And the round ocean and the living air,
> And the blue sky, and in the mind of man:
> A motion and a spirit, that impels
> All thinking things, all objects of all thought,
> And rolls through all things. Therefore am I still
> A lover of the meadows and the woods,
> And mountains; and of all that we behold
> From this green earth; of all the mighty world

> Of eye and ear,—both what they half create,
> And what perceive; well pleased to recognise
> In nature and the language of the sense,
> The anchor of my purest thoughts, the nurse,
> The guide, the guardian of my heart, and soul
> Of all my moral being. (93–112)

This passage begins with the fusion of intellect and emotion: "Joy/Of elevated thoughts" connects the two directly. We are not told that his joy gives rise to elevated thoughts or that elevated thoughts make him happy, but that one is inherent in the other. In addition, his joy cannot be limited to the word's conventional definition, for it is the means by which a presence "disturbs" him. Indeed, we are told the presence does so prior to being told how, which gives "disturbs" primacy over "joy". The reader's conception of joy is forced to expand to accommodate Wordsworth's meaning here, a meaning nearly opposed to the common one. The result is a semantic overfilling that threatens the word's integrity. The lines that refer to "a sense sublime" and "something far more deeply interfused" are a trifle talky, more an attempt to label what I am calling plerosis than an example of it, but they at worst serve to reinforce the theme. Immediately afterwards, the poem's plerotic energy rebounds powerfully. Beginning in the extended metaphor that follows, readers are repeatedly compelled to expand their understanding of perfectly common words. The apparent contradictions pile up as quickly as they can be counted: "dwelling" is specifically material, but here is connected with "light," "ocean," "air," "sky," and "mind." Two of these locations are themselves described in unexpected ways: "round ocean" and "living air." Wordsworth unites materiality, action, and essence by identifying a "presence" as both "motion" and "spirit." He then reinforces this multiplicity by claiming that it both "impels" and "rolls through." To impel matter (the verb's direct objects are the overtly material "thinking things" and "all objects of all thought") requires solidity; to roll through material objects ("all things," an even broader category) requires permeability. A list of geographical features follows ("meadows," "woods," "mountains"), but no sooner has our attention been focused on external reality than Wordsworth draws us back to our own internal capacity for perception with "all that we behold" and "of all the mighty world of eye and ear." When he then suggests that eye and ear "half-create" what they "perceive," the multiplicity revealed over the previous dozen lines becomes the literal fusion of the internal's power over the external and the external's power over the internal. The human capacity for recognition then unites "nature and the language of the sense" (one of the aims suggested by the Preface) before, in a final extended implosion of semantic distinction, "anchor," "nurse," "guide," "guardian", and "soul" merge into one. And that's the point: the goal of plerosis is total linguistic convergence, a signifier that contains all reference and is impervious to particularization.

Alert readers will pause longer after "moral being" than at any of the other stanzaic breaks. Scarcely seven-tenths of the way through the poem, it has already reached its point of maximum plerosis. A falling off of semantic energy is inevitable; left to our own devices, we will be drawn back, however reluctantly, toward the center of the cognitive spectrum. Yet Wordsworth refuses to allow this return to normality to take its own course. Instead, he abruptly adopts a conversational mode, necessarily temporal and incompatible with any sublime (it would be an impoverished form of ecstasy that permitted chitchat), for which he must introduce another person. After the ecstatic effusion just experienced, what reader welcomes phrases addressed to Dorothy such as "Suffer my genial spirits to decay?" (113). That such a phrase is spoken in the negative (effectively "I would not suffer") matters not at all. It merely begins a whole series of apophases, as Wordsworth invokes all of the vexations from which he will henceforth supposedly be immune:

> neither evil tongues,
> Rash judgments, nor the sneers of selfish men,
> Nor greetings where no kindness is, nor all
> The dreary intercourse of daily life,
> Shall e' er prevail against us, (128–32)

Mentioning them summons them to the reader's mind. Wordsworth speaks of how Dorothy's "wild ecstasies shall be matured/Into a sober pleasure" (138–39), exactly as his own have, exactly as those of the poem have. The poem recapitulates his own maturation, and in so doing reproduces it in the reader. There is no more wild ecstasy, no more plerotic convergence of meaning; everything is perfectly safe, perfectly articulable. To see the change, one need only compare the prior use of "dwelling" with this later echo: "Thy memory be as a dwelling-place/For all sweet sounds and harmonies" (141–42). Replacing a metaphor with a simile is itself a step down from fusion to relation, but Wordsworth adds "-place" just so the reader not get the idea that "sounds" and "harmonies" occupy a literal dwelling. Similarly, although "what healing thoughts/Of tender joy" (144–45) superficially echoes the earlier "joy/Of elevated thoughts," these later "thoughts" are in fact only memories. No identity of or inherent connection between "thoughts" and "joys" is implied, and joy's power to disturb has been forgotten. At the last, when supposing his own death, Wordsworth hopes that his sister will remember him not as ecstatic or joyful or happy or simply enthusiastic, but as "unwearied in that service" (153). This is a kind of compound ebbing: the "un-" prefix forms a negation of a word that already denotes a loss of energy. A slight recovery follows, when he corrects himself with "rather say/ With warmer love—oh! with far deeper zeal! Of holier love," but zeal is not ecstasy, and holy love in hands other than those of someone like John Donne lacks plerotic punch. The fall from the heights of the previous stanza has been ineluctable and complete.

None of this results in a bad poem, of course. On the contrary, the manner in which the semantic energy of the poem mirrors the changes in Wordsworth himself is a stroke of genius. It is also an inescapable consequence of his determination to submit passion to reason by examining sublime experience only in the context of recollection. That he includes the fall away from the plerotic sublime in his poems is defensible, perhaps admirable, from one perspective: to do otherwise is arguably dishonest. But other poets ignore the impending return to normality, knowing that in so doing they postpone it only a moment; alternatively, they simply acknowledge it, perhaps sensing that the experience of being pushed beyond the mundane mid-range of cognition is part of what draws readers to poetry in the first place. Wordsworth dwells upon it, revealing a profound anxiety about exactly what he had wrought. As later poets pushed the bounds of plerosis further by eschewing the balance and security that placing sublime experience safely in the past provides, he looked on disapprovingly. In 1815, he writes:

> The appropriate business of poetry ... her appropriate employment, her privilege, and her *duty*, is to treat of things not as they *are*, but as they *appear*; not as they exist in themselves, but as they *seem* to exist in the *senses*, and to the *passions*. What a world of delusion does this acknowledged obligation prepare for the inexperienced! what temptations to go astray are here held forth for them whose thoughts have been little disciplined by the understanding, and whose feelings revolt from the sway of reason!—When a juvenile Reader is in the height of his rapture with some vicious passage, should experience throw in doubts, or common sense suggest suspicions, a lurking consciousness that the realities of the Muse are but shows, and that her liveliest excitements are raised by transient shocks of conflicting feeling and successive assemblages of contradictory thoughts—is ever at hand to justify extravagance and sanction absurdity. ("Essay Supplementary to the Preface" 471–72)

His warnings were prescient. A world of delusion did await. The disciplining of thought by understanding and of feelings by reason were on the wane. In some ways, "transient shocks of conflicting feelings and successive assemblages of contradictory thoughts" describes quite well the poetry that was to follow, the best of which was indeed often extravagant, though never, except to a hostile reader, absurd. What Wordsworth did not, possibly could not, acknowledge was that sometimes one delusion may be necessary to displace another, especially one to which we are accustomed and have given the name of reality; that disciplined thought is inevitably limited thought; that feelings under the sway of reason hardly deserve the name of feelings at all; and that conflict and contradiction may be not only unavoidable but extraordinarily beneficial, even—perhaps especially—when left unresolved.

Coleridge, too, was nonplussed by this tendency in Romantic poetry to abandon logical clarity at the most crucial moments. In the *Biographia Literaria*, Coleridge responds to Wordsworth's description of the role that "a vivid state of excitement" plays in poetic composition:

> it is indeed very possible to adopt in a poem the unmeaning repetitions, habitual phrases and other blank counters which an unfinished or confused understanding interposes at short intervals in order to keep hold of his subject which is still slipping from him, and to give him time for recollection ... But what assistance to the poet or ornament to the poem these can supply, I am at a loss to conjecture. (199–200; ch. XVII)

Coleridge's "blank counters" are plerotic markers, reflexive attempts to create a semantic construction capable of acting as a reference for that which has exceeded the mind's power to grasp and submit to analysis. His image of the subject slipping away only to be retained by the power of these semantic blanks is inspired, but he cannot imagine why, once time has passed and the experience has been assimilated by memory and reason, a poet would have any need of something that effectively announces a failure of articulation. His own experience in writing "Kubla Khan" might have taught him differently.

In "Tintern Abbey," Wordsworth had fused "thought" with "joy," and had referred enigmatically to a *something* that could have a "dwelling" constructed of the elements; he had claimed that some invisible force ("motion" or "spirit") had the power both to pass through and to affect matter; and he had recognized that perception and creation could be considered two sides of the same coin. Coleridge engages in this sort of thing as well, on a grander scale but more subtly, fusing opposites in the first two stanzas not by immediate juxtaposition but by a broader inclusion. Harold Bloom enumerates many of the poem's "contraries": "sun and moon, dome and cavern, light and dark, heat and ice, the voices of the dead speaking to the living," and it is indeed remarkable that Coleridge invokes so many opposites in a relatively short poem (219).[11] However, this collocation of contrary principles is only a prelude to the ultimate conflation of the ethereal and the material that Coleridge imagines when he claims that "deep delight" (transcendent pleasure, ecstasy) grants him the power to transmute music into literal solid matter:

> Could I revive within me
> Her symphony and song,

> To such a deep delight 'twould win me,
> That with music loud and long,
> I would build that dome in air, (42–46)

This is no mere suggestion of solidity, like Wordsworth's use of *dwelling*. Coleridge has already told us of what the dome consists: "walls ... towers ... gardens ... sinuous rills ... many an incense-bearing tree," even whole "forests" (5–10). To recreate the dome requires that he replicate all of its parts, man-made and natural. Nor does he stop with architecture and vegetation, for the next line—"That sunny dome, those caves of ice!"—is not an exclamation of awe that results from the force of the memory (after all, the crisis here results from the failure of memory) but, as the separation from "I would build that dome in air" by a comma reveals, a reiteration of his creative powers. The dome, the river, the plant life, and now the climate itself (sun and cold) are within his control through a literally unimaginable process. Within his control, that is, except that his powers of recollection fail him. He cannot recall the song, cannot fill in the blank counter. And for Coleridge, the necessity that his recollection of sublime experience remain irrational in order to reproduce the quality and intensity of that experience is what makes his poem fall short.

Moreover, the failure of language represented by extreme plerosis was as much moral and spiritual as aesthetic. Coleridge was terrified by the expansion and fusion of reference because it meant the transgression of boundaries. His works demonstrate that radical plerosis can lead explicitly to Sewell's realm of "Nightmare." When opposites appear together in Coleridge, the result is usually horror, as in "The Rime of the Ancient Mariner":

> *Her* lips were red, *her* looks were free,
> Her locks were yellow as gold:
> Her skin was as white as leprosy,
> The Night-mare LIFE-IN-DEATH was she, (190–93)

The usually skeletal depiction of Death has given way to lips and hair any 1950s Hollywood studio starlet would have envied. The skin "as white as leprosy" links what is conventionally a sign of health, beauty, and innocence to disease and corruption. Of Sewell's cognitive realms, nightmare offers the least resistance to the multiplication of reference and fusion of apparent opposites, and the greatest breakdown of boundaries. Most tellingly, having elected to name a figure of ultimate horror, Coleridge chooses a hyphenated term that fuses life and death into a single entity, because the fusion of two opposed principles is for him a greater source of horror than death alone would be (or is, considering that the poem's male Death appears conventional in every way). In this case, the LIFE-IN-DEATH profanes the promise of resurrection—Christ's and that which was promised to his followers.

Geraldine, the figure of horror in "Christabel," represents an even greater threat for Coleridge than the mariner's LIFE-IN-DEATH, but the source of the horror is the same: the power to transgress the boundaries between what are normally thought distinct categories. Most obviously, Geraldine disrupts the established order of familial relationships. The poem begins with Christabel leaving her father's castle for the express purpose of praying "For the weal of her lover that's far away" (30); the weal, and presumably the return. Once she prays, Geraldine appears immediately, and seemingly from nowhere:

> She kneels beneath the huge oak tree,
> And in silence prayeth she.
> The lady sprang up suddenly,
> The lovely lady Christabel!
> It moaned as near, as near can be
> But what it is she cannot tell.— (35–40)

The first reference we have for Geraldine is "it," without any antecedent. As the vaguest pronoun in the language, "it" is capable of the largest possible range of reference, yet remains specific because it is singular. Then, in the following line, "it" is repeated, and the uncertainty of the reference made explicit. Christabel "cannot tell" what it is, because Geraldine is an entity to whom may be attached any reference at all. More accurately and more ominously in this case, Geraldine may attach to herself any reference or combination of references she chooses.

Over the course of the poem Geraldine perverts the conventional family structure by taking the place of bridegroom, mother, and daughter. Appearing in response to Christabel's prayer, she usurps the place of the bridegroom. Upon reaching the castle she collapses, and "Christabel, with might and main! Lifted her up, a weary weight,/Over the threshold of the gate" (130–32). Having already assumed the position of her betrothed, Geraldine now becomes the bride and turns Christabel into the husband, not just by the act of carrying Christabel over the threshold, but because of an implied physical change as well: the "lovely lady" is now credited with "might and main," or heroic, masculine strength. Coleridge thereby suggests that Geraldine not only possesses the capacity to transgress boundaries and to fuse opposites within herself, but that this capacity is infectious. Transgression begets transgression; fusion begets fusion.

Christabel's mother enters the poem. Although dead, she is not a figure of horror to Coleridge because she cannot fully cross the boundary between death and life, and thus does not blur reference. Only Geraldine, with her presumably supernatural perception, is aware of her. She wills the mother there at midnight because her ghostly arrival confirms this as the day of Christabel's marriage. With an effort, Geraldine overcomes the mother's spirit, and Christabel, seeing her guest momentarily drained, offers Geraldine her mother's own wildflower wine. Multiple transpositions follow rapidly, as Christabel briefly acts like a mother nursing a sick child, using a potion made by her mother from ingredients taken from Geraldine's home, the natural world outside the bounds of the castle. The mother's brief appearance having announced this as Christabel's wedding day, Geraldine becomes her bridegroom in terms that are probably as explicit as could be expected to see publication in 1816. She "lay down by the maiden's side!/And in her arms the maid she took" (262–63). In the conclusion to Part I, Coleridge also reiterates that she has usurped the place of Christabel's mother:

> And lo! the worker of these harms,
> That holds the maiden in her arms,
> Seems to slumber still and mild,
> As a mother with her child. (300–01)

The blurring of the sexual and the maternal is now complete, and nature itself is "jubilant" at the transgression because boundaries, for Coleridge, are a function of Christian civilization, not nature (308). As the poem continues, no boundary proves safe. By the end of Part II, Geraldine is on her way to becoming wife, daughter, or both to Sir Leoline. Meanwhile, apparently snake-like in her true form, she also transforms Christabel into a crawling, hissing creature.

At which point, Coleridge abandons the poem. One may only speculate what, if anything, he had in mind for Part III. Perhaps Leoline's friend Roland would have appeared and saved the day, but if we assume he is the same general type as Leoline—the noble, elder warrior—that is doubtful. If their puissance, honor, and rectitude are no help, Christabel's innocence and beauty provide no protection, the mother's spirit is powerless, and all of the more powerful natural and supernatural forces are arrayed on Geraldine's side, only one possibility is left: Leoline's bard Bracy. His music, he has already claimed, can act with the force of exorcism: "I had vowed with music loud/To clear yon wood from thing unblest" (528–29). For a poet to cast a bard as the eventual hero is predictable. However, Coleridge has already shown that Geraldine is immune to the power of song, because she has one further ability—one that perhaps terrified Coleridge most of all.

Geraldine's ultimate power is to silence, to cause a failure of language. When Christabel tries to speak, she is "O'ermastered by the mighty spell" (620)—the only time Geraldine is given an expressly magical ability. As the emblem of transgression, Geraldine represents the power to overwhelm the capacity for logical expression, which depends upon clear boundaries between signifiers. She even manages to transgress the boundary between text and author, for her power to shatter language's integrity is so strong that it works on its creator, who cannot conceive a way to end the poem happily. Instead, he gives us an autobiographical epilogue in which "pleasures flow in so thick and fast upon the heart" that they lead him to "words of unmeant bitterness" (662, 664). He considers, maybe for the first time, that simply to juxtapose conflicting ideas and multiple references may be aesthetically pleasing: "Perhaps 'tis pretty to force together/Thoughts so unlike each other," although "pretty" is hardly Olympian praise (667–67). He thus reluctantly admits that logical resolution, and certainly that which accords with specific philosophical or moral precepts, however comforting, might not be necessary. But while he may accept this principle in theory, he could not follow it in his own poetry, and spent his career abandoning, amending, and apologizing for his greatest achievements.

That from which Coleridge shrank was embraced by Keats, whose Negative Capability, "when a man is capable of being in uncertainties, Mysteries, doubts, without any irritable reaching after fact & reason" is essentially a defense of plerotic poetry (193). The poet must not only ignore the question of objective verification ("reaching after fact"), but also abandon the attempt to assimilate experience to logic ("reaching after ... reason"). If the poem thus created is successful, the reader will follow suit. For Keats, the reason why Coleridge tended to abandon his greatest works, producing fragments instead of whole poems, was his inability to accept the ambiguity that is the result of expanded signification—an inability he also projected onto the reader. In arguing for Negative Capability, Keats rejects the necessity of the return from sublime noesis to ordinary rationality that in some way undercuts plerosis in the works of both Coleridge and Wordsworth.

Many of the techniques commonly associated with Keats's poems serve either to multiply reference or in some other way increase the level of semantic energy far beyond language's usual range. For example, readers have long observed that by, using past participles as adjectives, he invests nouns with dynamism, matter with energy. In barely the first quarter of "The Eve of St. Agnes," we hear of "frosted breath ... sculptur'd dead ... aged man ... carved angels, ever eager-eyed,/Star'd ... hair blown back and wings put cross-wise ... brain, new stuff'd ... wing'd St. Agnes ... honey'd middle of the night ... hallow'd hour ... throng'd resort ... buzz'd whisper ... hot-blooded lords ... aged creature ... ivory-headed wand ... [and] palsied hand" (6–97). In a particularly virtuosic twist, Keats enlists his readers in the technique by instructing them to apply such a construction to themselves, "let us wish away,/And turn, sole-thoughted" (41–42). These examples ignore those occasions when Keats devotes an entire participial phrase to the same purpose, such as the "Emprison'd in black ... Fix'd on the floor ... not cool'd by high disdain ... Hoodwink'd with faery fancy ... Buttress'd from moonlight ... hid from the torch's flame" (15–93). The effect here is not quite as concentrated, but still noticeable. In both types, note how often the participle is formed from a word that was not conventionally a verb in the first place; certainly "sculpture," "star," "honey," "throng," "palsy," and "buttress" are more familiar as nouns. Nouns are thus made to become verbs in order to act as adjectives. Keats overrides the distinctions between parts of speech and so creates a kind of plerotic grammar.

Keats's famous synaesthesia is also inherently plerotic. Often, he will string together a series of adjectives devoted to different senses. "He found him in a little moonlight room,/Pale, lattic'd, chill, and silent as the tomb" (112–13): "pale" is visual, "chill" is tactile, "silent" is aural. In five words, Keats has managed give the room associations with three senses without sacrificing any of the text's dynamism. He has also squeezed another of those wonderful descriptive participles, "lattic'd," into the line for good measure, and while "pale" and "lattic'd" are both visual, one represents color and the other pattern. To similar effect, he will modify a noun commonly associated with one sense with an adjective connected to another: "soft amethyst," "warmed jewels" (221, 228). But his greatest synaesthetic achievement may be a passage justly famous as the most intense description in English of taste ever accomplished:

> he forth from the closet brought a heap
> Of candied apple, quince, and plum, and gourd
> With jellies soother than the creamy curd,
> And lucent syrops tinct with cinnamon;
> Manna and dates, in argosy transferr'd
> From Fez; and spiced dainties, every one,
> From silken Samarcand to cedar'd Lebanon. (264–70)

Part of the effect here is achieved by simple abundance, yet lists by themselves do not generate plerosis. The intensity of the flavors mentioned is a factor, yet few readers pause to imagine each flavor distinctly. The true brilliance of this passage is the physical—the *physiological*—effect reading the words aloud (or silently, if one allows one's mouth to move) has on the reader. A stunning variety of vowel sounds occurs here, and the sequence produces an astonishing effect: the rapid alternation between those which stretch our mouths side-to-side and those which stretch them front-to-back contorts them in ways that reproduce the motions one makes when savoring a particularly flavorful delicacy—they literally make us salivate. Sound is thus transmuted into taste, creating a conflation of senses. Finally, Keats adds one more bit of grammatical legerdemain: the choice of *soother*, which exists as a noun in English but not as a comparative (presumably meaning "more soothing"), stresses normal language's insufficiency to convey the experience while it renders the line more compact.

The downside of plerosis is that sublime experience cannot be assimilated to the rational mind, and thus language, which depends upon some degree of order, cannot truly convey it. Plerosis is an energy that throws us toward the sublime but cannot carry us there. Inevitably, the most plerotic language ends in retreat, either because the poem ends, or because it continues and language is an inherently limited and somewhat rational structure. Language articulates, and articulation is the enemy of plerosis, as Walt Whitman knew. His answer—and like Alexander's hacking through the Gordian knot, it obeys the letter of the law but arguably violates the spirit—is to claim that articulation is overrated:

> Speech is the twin of my vision.... it is unequal to measure itself.
> It provokes me forever,
> It says sarcastically, Walt, you understand enough.... why don't you let it out then?
> Come now I will not be tantalized.... you conceive too much of articulation. (31)[12]

Speech is the twin of his vision, can actually match it, provided he is not tantalized into articulation. And so he sounds his "barbaric yawp" (55)[13]—the ultimate plerotic cry, the frenzy of possession, the single word signifying all he thinks and feels, the universal signifier, which of course also denotes the entire poem. No further development of plerosis is is possible, and Whitman himself spent the rest of his life retreating from his unnamed 1855 masterwork by imposing various forms of order on what had been gloriously disordered: titling it, cutting or modifying particularly problematic lines, and most notably dividing the whole into more easily digestible sections by means of various numbering schemes. Perhaps he hoped that these would make the poem more accessible, and would therefore help it become what he had intended: a new American gospel. It did not, but as is always the case with plerosis, what matters is the achievement, not the inevitable retreat.

Multiple and expanded signifiers, a preference for dream and nightmare over number and logic, and linguistic failure reached by way of a loss of articulation rather than a fall into silence: these techniques are all means to the same end, an end that helps define Romanticism as an aesthetic category. Perhaps this brief sampling of plerotic techniques offers some fruitful and intriguing readings, and suggests some of the potential benefits of a critical method based upon reading the text as energy rather than as artifact.

## Notes

1 The major exception to the current dominance of the artifact metaphor is deconstruction, which, while not eliminating referentiality, changes the direction

of the reference. Artifactual criticism focuses on a text to render a judgment about something extrinsic to it; deconstruction uses literature as a means to observe the operation of the language within. While a reader's experience should in some way reflect the operation of language within a text, the inappropriateness of deconstruction for my purposes stems from Derrida's war on the metaphysical concept of presence, an agon which may be considered the cornerstone of his philosophy and is, in my view, responsible for much of its perceived (and sometimes very real) opacity.

2   This is Alberto Manguel's translation of a line from Calvino's *If on a winter's night a traveler*, which he uses as the head note to the second chapter of *A History of Reading*. In the original Italian, the line reads, "leggere è andare inconttro a qualcosa che sta per essere e anchora nessuno sa cosa sarà" (*Se una notte*, 71). William Weaver translates the same line as "Reading is going toward something that is about to be" (72). Weaver's translations of Calvino are deservedly renowned, but in this case I prefer Manguel's; the quadruple present participle underscores the point. The line is spoken by the character Ludmilla, Calvino's ideal reader, and continues (in Weaver's translation), "and no one yet knows what it will be."

3   The idea of language as energy has a long history, of course. Most notably, the theories of Giambattista Vico depend upon a dynamic view of language.

4   Stanley Fish uses a nearly identical phrase in his early essay "Literature in the Reader" in order to define his critical approach: "The concept is simply the rigorous and disinterested asking of the question, what does this word, phrase, sentence, paragraph, chapter, novel, play, poem, *do?*... The basis of the method is a consideration of the temporal flow of the reading experience, and it is assumed that the reader responds in terms of that flow and not to the whole utterance" (26–27). Both the question and the method held great promise, but Fish soon turned most of his attention towards explaining how interpretations are accepted or rejected by "interpretive communities."

5   Sewell actually divides all the qualities of language between reference and what she calls "sound-look"; however, in my judgment this division ultimately proves untenable, for reasons beyond the scope of my purposes here.

6   Sewell notes that this diagram should be viewed as a Mercator projection: the extremes meet. Perfect Order and Perfect Disorder are therefore identical states, but this state lies beyond the human capacity to imagine. She calls it "a vanishing point for the mind" (53).

7   A full bibliography of literature on the sublime would itself be a major project. After Longinus, those authors who have most influenced my own conception of the sublime—whether because I incorporated or rejected their ideas—include John Baillie, Joseph Priestley, Edmund Burke, and Immanuel Kant. More recent relevant authors include Jean-François Lyotard, Michel Deguy, and Jean-Luc Nancy. Although not normally considered a theorist of the sublime, William James's four characteristics of mysticism in *The Varieties of Religious Experience* (ineffability, noetic quality, transiency, passivity) are, in my view, perfectly applicable to sublime experience. However, my greatest debt is to Ihab Hassan, whose influence on my thought—both through seminal works such as *The Literature of Silence* and *The Dismemberment of Orpheus*, and through many

hours of patient instruction and generous conversation—defies my ability to measure.

8   Every discussion of the sublime's relationship to Romantic poetry owes something to Thomas Weiskel's *The Romantic Sublime*. Weiskel was the first to found a theory of the sublime upon the principle of a divided self, and to argue that sublimity is an other-than-fully-conscious state. "Instead of the achieved stasis, the *discordia concors* of ideal and real, there is oscillation, movement over the widening gap between two terms, culminating in the withdrawal of consciousness from the sensible world. In the sublime moment, dualism is legitimated and intensified.... the sublime splits consciousness into alienated halves" (48). This quotation begins with Kant's definition of sublime experience as a rapid alternation (oscillation) and ends with Freud's concept of alienation, but the transition is not a happy one. Kant and Freud both divide the mind between discrete and equally metaphorical entities; unfortunately, Weiskel's substitution of consciousness for the imagination (these are the respective entities described as being in motion) requires more than a little slippage. To equate the two is something of a paradox, because it is difficult to see how imagination, divorced from reason and perception, can be considered a conscious process, let alone consciousness itself. Weiskel also distinguishes between the "idealist" and the "naturalized" sublimes by associating the former with depth and the latter with height (24–5). Although his division of sublime experience is not identical with mine, I find his argument valid and, for purposes other than my own, productive.

9   Kenotic poetry—poetry that drives us towards silence instead of frenzy— exists as well, and includes the work of poets such as Wallace Stevens, T.S. Eliot, and most obviously Emily Dickinson, whom Hart Crane insightfully addressed as "O sweet, dead Silencer."

10   Gerald Bruns has called this idea of language "*Energeia* ... the power by which a speaker's utterance moves an audience not to delight only but to understanding" and described it as central to Romantic thought: "What is significant about Wordsworth's Preface ... is that in it the concept of language as energy becomes the ground for a rejection of the ancient concept of literary language" (45, 49).

11   Bloom's reading of "Kubla Khan" is typically incisive, but strangely ignores the ultimate incapacity and failure that crowns the poem. Bloom finds the conclusion a paean to the powers of "the poetic imagination" and a casting of the poet as "the reincarnation of the young Apollo" (220). The passage is conjectural, with "would" hanging heavily over the whole paragraph, but nowhere does he acknowledge that the speculation in the poem is empty of promise. Christian Coleridge does not believe in the first Apollo, let alone a reincarnation. The imagination to which Coleridge refers is the "the repetition in the finite mind of the eternal act of creation in the infinite [and transparently Old Testament] I AM," and the finitude of the human mind inevitably confers certain limitations (*Biographia*, 167). Coleridge would not think the greatest poet, much less himself, capable of the kind of creation that "Kubla Khan" describes.

12   I am quoting and citing by page number the 1855 untitled version of what Whitman named "Poem of Walt Whitman, an American" in 1856, "Walt Whitman." in 1860, and finally "Song of Myself" in 1881, but for ease of reference I will provide here the section and line numbers corresponding to the final

version of the poem. These lines (with changes) appear in Section 25, lines 7–10.
13   Section 52, line 3.


**Works Cited**

Bloom, Harold. *The Visionary Company*. Rev. ed Ithaca: Cornell UP, 1971.
Bruns, Gerald. *Modern Poetry and the Idea of Language: A Critical and Historical Study*. New Haven: Yale UP, 1974.
Calvino, Italo. *If on a winter's night a traveler*. Trans. William Weaver. New York: Wolff-Harcourt, 1981.
———. *Se una notte d'inverno un viaggiatorre*. Torino: Einaudi, 1979.
Coleridge, Samuel Taylor. *Biographia Literaria: or Biographical Sketches of My Life and Opinions*. Ed. George Watson. London: Everyman-Dent, 1975.
———. "Christabel." *Poems*. Ed. John Beer. London: Everyman-Dent, 1993. 260–78.
———. "Kubla Khan." Ed. Beer. 205–07.
———. "The Rime of the Ancient Mariner." [1828]. 215–55.N.L. Fish, Stanley. "Literature in the Reader." *Is There a Text in this Class? The Authority of Interpretive Communities*. Cambridge: Harvard UP, 1980. 21–67.
Keats, John. "The Eve of St. Agnes." *Complete Poems*. Ed. Jack Stillinger. Cambridge, MA: Belknap-Harvard UP, 1982. 229–39.
———. "To George and Tom Keats." 21, 27(?) December 1817. Letter 45. *The Letters of John Keats 1814–1821*. Vol. I. Ed. Hyder Edward Rollins. Cambridge, MA: Harvard UP, 1958. 191–94.
Longinus. *On the Sublime*. Trans. A. O. Prickard. 1906. Oxford: Oxford UP, 1926.
Manguel, Alberto. *A History of Reading*. London: HarperCollins, 1996.
Sewell, Elizabeth. *The Structure of Poetry*. New York: Scribner, 1952.
Sontag, Susan. "Against Interpretation." *Against Interpretation and Other Essays*. New York: Delta-Dell, 1966. 3–14.
Weiskel, Thomas. *The Romantic Sublime: Studies in the Structure and Psychology of Transcendence*. Baltimore: Johns Hopkins UP, 1976.
Whitman, Walt. *Leaves of Grass* [1855, 1856, 1860, 1867, 1871–72, 1881–82, 1891–92]. *The Walt Whitman Hypertext Archive*. Ed. Ed Folsom and Kenneth M. Price. 2003. <http://www.whitmanarchive.org/archive1/works/leaves>. Accessed 3 September 2004.
Wordsworth, William. "Essay, Supplementary to the Preface." [1815] *Selected Poems and Prefaces*. Ed. Jack Stillinger. Boston: Houghton, 1965. 471–81.
———. "Lines: Composed a Few Miles Above Tintern Abbey, on Revisiting the Banks of the Wye During a Tour, July 13, 1798." Ed. Stillinger. 108–11.
———. "Preface to Lyrical Ballads." [1800]. *Lyrical Ballads: An Electronic Scholarly Edition*. Eds. Bruce Graver and Ron Tetreault. <http://www.rc.umd.edu/editions/LB/html/Lb00-1.html>. Accessed 17 August 2004.
———. "Preface to Lyrical Ballads." [1802]. *Lyrical Ballads: An Electronic*

*Scholarly Edition.* Eds. Bruce Graver and Ron Tetreault. <http://www.rc.umd.edu/editions/LB/html/Lb02-1.html>. Accessed 17 August 2004.

# Chapter Four

# Half-asleep on Thresholds: Fragile Boundaries in Coleridge's "Fears in Solitude"

## Onita Vaz

In the half-lyrical, half-topical poem "Fears in Solitude," Coleridge employs the real threat of French invasion—the imperative for the composition of the poem—as a metaphor for the recreative power of the secondary imagination and the epistemological instability of generic categories. The poem demonstrates the secondary imagination's ability to dissolve the conceptual boundaries that purportedly divide private lyric utterance and public political discourse by delicately balancing the historical pressures of the day with the Romantic desire for imaginative activity. Instead of conflicting voices vying for supremacy in "Fears in Solitude," we are confronted by the paradoxical coexistence of competing categories always vulnerable to infiltration.

Coleridge's description of the secondary imagination, articulated in the *Biographia Literaria* almost twenty years after the initial publication of "Fears in Solitude," recalls the thematic and formal tactics employed by him to deftly maneuver between these categories in the poem. He writes that the poetic imagination "dissolves, diffuses, [and] dissipates, in order to re-create; or where this process is rendered impossible, yet still at all events ... struggles to idealize and to unify" (I, 304).[1] The esemplastic imagination is, therefore, "vital" (I, 304) and exploits categorical distinctions in order to facilitate recreation. Likewise, the progression of "Fears in Solitude" also depends on the exploitative and invasive power of the secondary imagination. The title of the poem itself invokes the metaphor of invasion: the tranquility of solitude is infiltrated by the insecurity of fear. Hence solitude, that aesthetic imperative which induces reflection, is no longer inviolable. And this is precisely the argument of the poem, in my view. The penetration of solitude by fear, of tranquility by insecurity, is what generates the creative process and it is this penetration which allows solitude to be resurrected in the space of the poem.[2]

This space for emotional solitude created in and through the poem, however, is also not free of fear; the newly created lyric space is ruptured by the knowledge of a real threat to the nation's borders. In fact, this is the very threat that propelled poetic creation in the first place. Coleridge specifies the circumstances under which he wrote "Fears in Solitude" by appending to the title the following:

"Written in April 1798, during the Alarm of an Invasion." There had been an actual, but unsuccessful, invasion by over a thousand Frenchman on the English coast near Fishguard in February 1797; the real goal of the French force had not been the Welsh coast, but an attack on the commercial center of Bristol. The attempted invasion and the subsequent disclosure of French plans laid bare England's geographic vulnerability, and fears of another invasion were only exacerbated by Napoleon's invasion of neutral Switzerland in January 1798.[3] In this state of affairs, the physical borders of the nation that enable the Romantic poet the possibility of solitude are also at risk. This fear of invasion is figured in the poem through shifts in theme and language. The "small and silent dell" (2)—an obvious synecdoche of England—affords the poet a "quiet spirit-healing nook" (12). This "green and silent spot, amid the hills" (1) is profuse with luscious nature; the healthy hills, the "swelling slope," the "gay and gorgeous covering" of the "never-bloomless furze," which "now blooms most profusely" (4–7) provide the poet with the ideal setting in which he can contemplate "better worlds" (26).[4]

The stability of this meditation-inducing space (described in the first verse paragraph), where the Romantic poet finds "religious meanings in the forms of nature" (24), is undermined by the very next verse paragraph which completely displaces joyful reflection by a melancholy disquisition on guilt and the horrors of invasion. Indeed, the Coleridgean and Wordsworthian thematic is usurped by the intrusion of political realities. The "green and silent spot, amid the hills," seemingly secure from the harsh world, is incapable of preserving the poet in a state of reflective calm, for now

> ... he must think
> What uproar and what strife may now be stirring
> This way or that way o'er these silent hills—
> Invasion, and the thunder and the shout,
> And all the crash of onset; fear and rage,
> And undetermin'd conflict. (34–39)

The poem moves from concrete images of abundant and fruitful nature to the idea of a possibly ravaged nation. Not only is the physical space of solitude threatened on the figurative level, both as an aesthetic concept and as an impetus to aesthetic creation, but it is also vulnerable on the very literal plane of an invasion of the land. This jarring sense of displacement is further evidenced by the lack of a logical transition from the description of the natural landscape to the depiction of the invaded land; the turn, instead, is abrupt, yet matter-of-fact. Coleridge writes:

> [the poet] dreams of better worlds,
> And dreaming hears thee still, O singing-lark,

That singest like an angel in the clouds!

My God! it is a melancholy thing
For such a man, who would full fain preserve
His soul in calmness, yet perforce must feel
For all his human brethren—O my God!
It is indeed a melancholy thing,
And weighs upon the heart, that he must think
What uproar and what strife may now be stirring
This way or that way o'er these silent hills. (26–36)

The opening verse paragraph, which sets up the poem as a typical Romantic treatise on the poet's consciousness, is usurped by the poet's own inevitable recognition of historical exigencies and his nation's guilty conscience. The space that affords solitude and the solitude which in turn induces "meditative joy" (23) in the individual are all casualties of guilt and fear of invasion. The geographic and conceptual boundaries that define the dell, the solitude and even the Romantic poet as integral entities are no longer distinctive or inviolable.[5] Instead of simply being the agent that "struggles to ... unify" and reconcile differences, the secondary imagination must also react to these dissolving lines.

Coleridge argues in the *Biographia* that imagination "reveals itself in the *balance* or reconciliation of opposite or discordant qualities" (my italics; II, 16). There is no reconciliation of opposites in "Fears in Solitude"; what Coleridge masterfully accomplishes instead is a balancing act through which he presents disparate or discordant ideas as paradoxical yet necessary complements of each other.[6] He marks the tension between these fragile boundaries through the shifting rhetoric of his text. Coleridge's private reflection on nature, for instance, is contaminated by the language of public discourse and national guilt: a lyric meditation on the natural and moralizing landscape suddenly gives way to a changed tone and vocabulary; the lark which sings like an angel is drowned out by "the thunder and the shout,/And all the crash of onset" not merely of a military invasion, but of public discourse as well. The languid mood of the opening paragraph is overtaken by the brisk tone and the prosaic vocabulary of the political arena:

... Meanwhile, at home,
All individual dignity and power
Engulph'd in Courts, Committees, Institutions,
Associations and Societies,
A vain, speech-mouthing, speech-reporting Guild,
One BENEFIT-CLUB for mutual flattery,
We have drunk up, demure as at a grace,
Pollutions from the brimming cup of wealth. (54–61)

"We have been too long/Dupes of a deep delusion!" (160–61), mutters Coleridge, because, according to him, the English "all make up one scheme of perjury" (79), and use language as a tool of misconception.[7] The poet's own private meditation is thrown off-course by the knowledge of a public rhetoric that is unconnected to honesty, sensitivity, or even thought. "The poor wretch," remarks Coleridge,

> who has learnt his only prayers
> From curses, who knows scarcely words enough
> To ask a blessing from his Heavenly Father,
> Becomes a fluent phraseman, absolute
> And technical in victories and defeats,
> And all our dainty terms for fratricide;
> Terms which we trundle smoothly o'er our tongues
> Like mere abstractions, empty sounds to which
> We join no feeling and attach no form! (109–17)

The "empty sounds" to which neither feeling nor form attach are in direct contrast to the poem itself in which the poet meditates on sin and its consequences. Conscious of the fact that "we have offended" (42), Coleridge indicts his countrymen for "bartering freedom and the poor man's life/ For gold, as at a market" (63–64). He prays that retribution will not come in the form of an invasion, to "make us know/ The meaning of our words, [and] force us to feel! The desolation and the agony/ Of our fierce doings" (127–30). Coleridge had voiced such sentiments before; for instance, in *Conciones ad Populum*, published in late December 1795, he lays out his theory about the cause of the Terror:

> It was a truth easily discovered, a truth on which [Pitt] has proceeded, that valour and victory would not be the determiners of this War. *They* would prove finally successful whose resources enabled them to hold out the longest. The commerce of France was annihilated. ... Immense armies were to be supported.... The Guillotine became the Financier-General.—That dreadful pilot, Robespierre, perceived that it would at once furnish wind to the sails and free the vessel from those who were inclined to mutiny.—Who, my Brethren! was the cause of this guilt, if not HE, who supplied the occasion and the motive? (*Lectures 1795*, 74)

Although Coleridge lays the blame for Robespierre's reign of terror squarely at Pitt's feet, that is not all the evidence against the "fierce doings" of the British. In the same lecture, Coleridge recites a list of devastations caused by British policies (both its imperial policies and its domestic and international tactics in the ongoing Napoleonic War), and warns his audience that "the four Quarters of the Globe groan beneath the intolerable iniquity of this nation!" (58). Coleridge's accusation against the British public is that there is no reflection in the public sphere, no sense of moral dilemma at the nation's own imperial policies, and even no recognition of the similarity between the repressive tactics of the British government and the terror campaign of the French. In his first political lecture early in 1795, Coleridge warns his audience that "the Example of France is indeed a 'Warning to Britain.' A nation wading to their Rights through Blood, and marking the track of Freedom by Devastation" (6). Three years later, he finds such judgments still lacking in the public sphere. Since reflection is of vital urgency, Coleridge cultivates it in his own private poetic utterance.

Although the space of public language itself has been contaminated by a lack of feeling and "dainty terms for fratricide," Coleridge also strives to balance this opposition, as Paul Magnuson notes, by using the public rhetoric as a defense against the accusations of atheism and sedition brought against him by the government and the oppositional press. The poem, in which a private meditation is displaced by a reflection on national guilt, enters the public arena as a personal and public pledge of a Christian and a patriot. Magnuson reads this as a dialogic move in which there is "no distinction between an aesthetic language" and an ordinary political language. Magnuson continues that "in dealing with the dialogic relations of lyric poetry and political journalism, [his own] dialogic method differs from the theory of Bakhtin, who places primary emphasis upon the multiplicity of voices within a single work" ("The Politics of 'Frost at Midnight,'" 190). Even though Magnuson is accurate in reading Coleridge's poems in the context of the political and journalistic discourses of the day, and sees no opposition between the two, it is also important to recognize that "Fears in Solitude" does, in fact, register the Bakhtinian polyvocal "multiplicity of voices in a *single* work" (my italics). Although Coleridge blends lyric language with ordinary language in the poem, I do not believe this suggests that there is "no distinction" between the two, as Magnuson implies. Indeed, in some of his annotations of the poem, Coleridge himself foregrounds the generic shifts in "Fears in Solitude." In one instance, he remarks that certain lines are really "*Prose* that in a frolic ... put on a masquerade Dress of Metre, & like most Masquerades, blundered in the assumed character" (*Poetical Works* I, 469). Coleridge's incorporation of the language of masquerade in his own poem and his rejection of the rhetoric of the "fluent phraseman" imply a validation and an elevation of his own lyric utterance to which feeling is attached; it is this necessary contradiction between the two voices that Coleridge upholds in the poem, and it is through his own reflective language that he manifests the vacuousness of public discourse.

His own reflections lead him into the bosom of his family at the end of the poem; this move enables him to shun the vices of the nation by retreating into a private society to "indulge/Love, and the thoughts that yearn for human kind"

(232–33). This concluding move paradoxically suspends, and perhaps even negates, much of what has preceded it. To elaborate this point, I will enlist the help of one of Coleridge's earlier poems, "Reflections on Having Left a Place of Retirement." Here Coleridge recalls a previous occasion when he climbed a "bare bleak Mountain" (30) from which he viewed the vast prospect below him. He writes:

> It seem'd like Omnipresence! God, methought,
> Had built him there a Temple: the whole World
> Seem'd *imag'd* in its vast circumference.
> No *wish* profan'd my overwhelmed Heart.
> Blest hour! It was a Luxury—to be! (38–42)[8]

The luxury of mere existence ("to be") is unsullied by any knowledge of lack; the poet feels whole and exuberantly complacent. This sense of satisfaction in life is vehemently denounced in the very next verse paragraph in which Coleridge poses a moral question; "Was it right," he asks,

> While my unnumber'd brethren toil'd and bled,
> That I should dream away the trusted Hours
> On rose-leaf Beds, pamp'ring the coward Heart
> With feelings all too delicate for use? (44–48)

Uncomfortable with the implication, Coleridge writes, "I therefore go, and join head, heart, and hand,/Active and firm, to fight the bloodless fight! Of Science, Freedom, and the Truth in CHRIST" (60–62). The inaction of complacent existence, even though it reminds the poet of God in nature, is a luxury that cannot be indulged, because it necessitates the forgetfulness of human suffering: the "unnumbered brethren" who toil and bleed. This prerogative Coleridge refuses on moral grounds. The knowledge of incompleteness or loss is essential for the poet; it obligates him to choose action—albeit philosophical and intellectual—over "feelings all too delicate for use."[9]

In "Fears in Solitude," Coleridge is indeed roused from a "rose-leaf bed" (where he may be "pampering the coward heart") into a reflection on national guilt that makes up the majority of the 233-line poem. Coleridge calls the menfolk to arms in the event of an invasion—"Stand forth! be men! repel an impious foe" (140), he urges. But he also exhorts them to humility so as to forestall retribution for their own nation's sins. However, this call to action appears to be mitigated at the end of the poem, where the mind luxuriates in the domesticity of family and in the rather abstract and impotent yearning for humankind. The consciousness of guilt which disturbed the poet's meditation does not appear to have resulted in a purposeful response, as it did in "Retirement," but in a passive desire for sympathy. Although Coleridge discredits those who make it sound "As if the soldier died without a wound" (118), it appears that he too contributes to this "crime" of language. In his final aesthetic and moral move in the poem, Coleridge seems to barter the reality of history for the luxury of "feelings all to delicate for use."

This crisis is extended to the uneasy relationship between solitude and activity in "Fears in Solitude"; it is solitude which frames meditation and the call to action, while the move out of solitude into society necessitates a tame and domesticating gesture. The more ardent call to patriotism has led the poet to seek the very shelter of the "dear Cot" he apparently rejected in "Retirement" as the site of complacency. By this move the poet implicitly denies, or perhaps even rejects, the subject matter of the body of the poem: national guilt and the threat of invasion. The virtual exclusion of the majority of the poem's subject from its conclusion manifests the problematic nature of the aesthetic enterprise when confronted by historical exigencies. The pressing nature of political and historical circumstances requires a morally responsible gesture on the part of the poet—something that Coleridge tries to achieve in "Retirement." Nevertheless, the luxury of the imaginative task promises a more rewarding fulfillment. If the Romantic imagination is to be allowed to fashion the materials it encounters it must not be weighed down by history. Coleridge partially circumvents this ethical problem by aestheticizing history and making it the subject of the poem, thereby allowing for the simultaneous existence of political realities and aesthetics. Thus when "Fears in Solitude" reaches its finale, the poet's allegiance is with his "solitary musings," not with the historical imperative of the day. As Jean-Pierre Mileur suggests, "the process of recovery" in the conversation poems "is governed by a principle of exclusion" (35). Hence the recovery of patriotism, and imaginative and intellectual regeneration, is gained via the exclusion of the political and the social. This move is effected by a retreat into a symbolic nation—the family. For Coleridge, however, any "principle of exclusion" is itself false, for exclusion denotes the existence of discrete categories, a concept he eschews. The family then becomes the microcosm of the nation, and Coleridge's meditations do not, in the final analysis, prove "too delicate for use." The cultivation of familial love and communion becomes the proper antidote to the immorality of public action and the "empty words" of public political discourse. The family becomes the space that can enable the possibility of change in the nation, and a transformation of its discourse. [10]

This shift from nation to family, from historical realities to "solitary musings," is not a "lyric turn," as Clifford Siskin would contend. He remarks that much of the literature of the Romantic period "veers from the generic and historical to the natural and transcendent, metamorphosing all analysis into claims of Imaginative vision" (12).[11] Although the various shifts in "Fears in Solitude" do register this move from the generic/historical to the natural/transcendent, the invocation of "thoughts that yearn for humankind" is not a swerve from the historical. As Nicholas Roe has demonstrated, the emphasis on "solitary musings" is instead a considered response to contemporary political realities, and, in my estimation, one that foregrounds the concept of difference. Coleridge's shifting attitudes to the French Revolution after the Reign of Terror and the unambiguous actions of imperial France were grounded in the realization that the hopes pinned on the Revolution would not be realized. [12]

Coleridge, the radical lecturer from Bristol, and author and editor of the mostly political journal *The Watchman*, retired from public life after the failure of the journal in May 1796. Having had enough of the repressive and vituperative nature of the public square for the time being, he moved to Nether Stowey in December 1796. The course of domestic and international politics had led Coleridge to conclude much earlier that political mechanisms were inept at effecting social change; he gradually transferred the site of hope to the poet's mind, to the possibilities afforded by the imagination, as Roe suggests.[13] Once at Stowey, Coleridge was able to devote more time to his creative enterprises. Much of the next two years were spent in the company of Wordsworth; this time together proved aesthetically stimulating to both.[14] Roe comments that, despite the creativity, this "rural life ... appears as an emblem of political and intellectual isolation" ("Coleridge, Wordsworth, and the French Invasion Scare," 146). What is also clear, however, is the constant infiltration of political realities into many of Coleridge's poems written during his retirement: "The Destiny of Nations: A Vision," "Fire, Famine and Slaughter: A War Ecologue, with an Apologetic Preface," "France: an Ode," "Fears in Solitude," and even "Kubla Khan," to name but a few. [15]

This incursion of the political into the lyrical is best described by Roe's assessment that the figure of Robespierre was a critical element in the formulation of Coleridge's early ideas about the imagination. Coleridge's first definition of the imagination emerges in his 1795 lecture on the slave trade:

> ... we are progressive and must not rest content with present Blessings. Our Almighty Parent hath therefore given to us Imagination that stimulates to the attainment of *real* excellence by the contemplation of splendid Possibilities that still revivifies the dying motive within us, and fixing our eye on the glittering Summits that rise one above the other in Alpine endlessness still urges us up the ascent of Being, amusing the ruggedness of the road with the beauty and grandeur of the ever-widening Prospect. Such and so noble are the ends for which this restless faculty was given us—but horrible has been its misapplication. (*Lectures 1795*, 235–236)

Although this passage is a harbinger of the famous bifurcated definition of imagination in the *Biographia*, Roe observes that the "seminal significance of this passage ... lies in its immediate implications for Coleridge rather than in anticipating his position twenty years later" ("Imagining Robespierre," 172). Coleridge believed that Robespierre had been true to the original tenets of the Revolution, but was unfortunately also adept at using them to justify terrorism. This was the "misapplication" of imagination as described by Coleridge, who saw Robespierre as the "distorted reflection of [his] own political and philosophical positions" ("Imagining Robespierre," 169). Therefore, "by redeploying the dying revolutionary motive to progress in the 'restless faculty' of the imagination," argues Roe, "Coleridge found his own solution to the dilemma confronting a whole generation caused by the complete failure of the French Revolution" ("Imagining Robespierre," 172). Coleridge's disillusion with the inability of "constituted power" (163), as he puts it in "Fears in Solitude," to effect progressive change is instrumental in shaping an alternative site of transformation.[16]

The shift between the political and the lyrical exemplified in the poem is indicative of Coleridge's response not only to the complex figure of Robespierre, but also to the contemporary political climate in Britain. Just as Robespierre's terrorism decimated the hopes of the Revolution, the political and public arena in Britain has been defiled by a repressive and corrupt government; the only possibility of purification and atonement for national sin, and the best opportunity for the resumption of the "dying revolutionary motive to progress" is the cultivation of the poetic imagination. Perhaps it is "Fears in Solitude" and not "The Rime of the Ancient Mariner" (completed a month before) that is the poem of "pure imagination," as declared by Robert Penn Warren. The invasion of lyric utterance by political realities in "Fears in Solitude" not only reflects Coleridge's own personal journey in and out of public and private domains, but in doing so also evidences the work of imagination, that "restless faculty" so accurately described by Coleridge at his first try.

Shifting in and out of these various discourses, Coleridge manages to keep them all in flux, precisely because he is aware of the vulnerability of states of certainty and security, an awareness epitomized in the line suggesting the fragility of national sovereignty: "Peace long preserv'd by fleets and perilous seas" (88). This image of the vulnerable British nation is another register in which "discordant qualities" are balanced in the poem. Coleridge describes the evils wrought by the British people; he calls them a "selfish, lewd, and effeminated race,/Contemptuous of all honourable rule" (62).[17] His admonition ranges from the particular manifestations of national sin, such as slavery and the suppression of free speech, to a delineation of the professions that contribute to the depraved state of the body politic:

> College and wharf, council and justice-court;
> ... the briber and the bribed,
> Merchant and lawyer, senator and priest,
> The rich, the poor, the old man and the young;
> All, all make up one scheme of perjury. (75–79)

The depiction of the particularized atrocities of a nation recedes with the invocation of a Britain where familial ties and high principles bind the poet to an ideal Nation:

> ... O dear Britain! O my Mother Isle!
> Needs must thou prove a name most dear and holy
> To me, a son, a brother, and a friend,
> A husband, and a father! who revere
> All bonds of natural love, and find them all
> Within the limits of thy rocky shores. (177–82)

As Magnuson asserts, the British landscape becomes the "location of national pride" ("The Shaping of 'Fears in Solitude,'" 209), and also the teacher and moralizer of the poetic sensibility. Coleridge declares that it is "from thy lakes and mountain-hills,/ Thy clouds, thy quiet dales, thy rocks and seas" that he has

> drunk in all [his] intellectual life,
> All sweet sensations, all ennobling thoughts,
> All adoration of the God in Nature,
> All lovely and all honourable things. (185–90)[18]

Coleridge presents these two versions of Britain as coexistent because the space of the idealized Nation is itself threatened by the equally vulnerable position of a people who have sinned. The only available course of action to prevent the real from invading the ideal is to return to the domestic hearth, which is capable of maintaining "bonds of natural love" that will, according to Coleridge's logic, eventually spill over into the nation. The concluding paragraph of "Fears in Solitude" invokes this idea: the poetic imagination, which was dislocated from nature at the beginning of the poem when forced into a meditation on communal guilt, is reunited with nature and the synecdoche of the nation—the family.[19] Nature and politics coexist in Coleridge's mind as shifting domains not constrained by discrete borders.

This move is also depicted in the structure of the poem—the meditation on guilt is framed by opening and concluding verse paragraphs firmly planted in physical nature. M.H. Abrams, discussing the greater Romantic lyric, argues that the division of subject and object is diluted in these conversation poems, so as to "make it eligible for resolution by the Romantic dialectic of thesis-antithesis-synthesis" (219). This sustained interaction between mind and nature, in which "the elements lose their separate identities" (219), is ironically not present in "Fears in Solitude," except in the two paragraphs in which nature is objectified as the idealized Nation. The meditation on guilt is disconnected from the speaker's interaction with nature, except for the fact that it is arbitrarily framed by stanzas that represent the Romantic dialectic. This gesture then literally shapes the coexistence of two separate voices within the space of the poem itself. Abrams, however, suggests that the poem "exemplifies the sustained dialogue between mind and landscape," (223) and quotes the following lines from the final verse paragraph of "Fears in Solitude":

> ... the mighty majesty
> Of that huge amphitheatre of rich
> And elmy Fields, seems like society
> Conversing with the mind, and giving it
> A livelier impulse and a dance of thought! (217–21)

The fact that the subject and the object only appear to lose their separate identities in these lines, however, is the very reason why the reconciliation supposedly achieved by Coleridge is problematic within the context of the poem, and does not fulfill Abrams's model of "thesis antithesis-synthesis." After all, the "huge amphitheatre of rich/ And elmy Fields" only "*seems* like society/ Conversing with the mind" (my italics). The first verse paragraph of the poem is explicit in noting that it is the mind that gives meaning to the natural landscape it perceives:

> And [the poet], with many feelings, many thoughts,
> Made up a meditative joy, and found
> Religious meanings in the forms of nature! (22–24)

By the end of the poem this communion is no longer valid. The mind does not bring within its intellectual, aesthetic, and moral ken the nature that is before it, which it then transforms by the power of imagination; instead, nature is presented as an entity separate from the mind. In the opening gambit of the poem, the mind "found/Religious meanings in the forms of nature," but by the end of the poem—quite unsatisfactorily for the Romantic reader—nature only "seems" to converse with the mind. The poet's mind—that once supreme subject—no longer has full interpretive power over nature, and the Romantic desire for an organic whole, repeated in Abrams's own theorizing of the greater Romantic lyric, is not fulfilled in "Fears in Solitude."[20]

The balance achieved in "Fears in Solitude" is not the result of synthesis, as suggested by Abrams, but is enabled by the necessary and seemingly contradictory elements bound into the thematics and rhetoric of the poem. In Coleridge's preface to the discussion of the imagination in Chapter Thirteen of the *Biographia* he cites Kant's notion of opposites, which are of "two kinds": "either logical, i.e. such as are absolutely incompatible; or real without being contradictory" (I, 298). It is the latter idea—opposites that are real without being contradictory—on which Coleridge relies, years earlier, in "Fears in Solitude." Coleridge's argument in the poem is that a reconciliation of opposites in which "the elements lose their separate identities" is not essential for a successful communion between mind and nature; the interaction can also be achieved when these "opposite or discordant qualities" are balanced or juxtaposed.[21] The arbitrary collusion between subject (mind) and object (nature) and the coexistence of two equally valid entities (mind and nature) evidence the arbitrariness of categories and borders themselves. That both possibilities are shown to be true within a poem later defined as the greater Romantic lyric speak to the fact that the poem defies the neat reductivism of an Abrams-like gesture.

"Fears in Solitude" does not register vacillation, however. The poem depicts the poet's imagination constantly hovering on thresholds, because the plasticity of boundaries demands just such a response from the secondary imagination. Hence the mind reflecting on nature cannot but be impinged upon by society, which in turn must be infringed upon by the consciousness of the individual, which engenders even more shifting distinctions. These fragile boundaries, always susceptible to invasion, are finally best represented by the condition of "half-sleep" in which the poet is suspended before his dreams are shattered by the intrusion of sympathy and outrage for his guilty nation. The poet hovers on the threshold between sleeping and waking, for it is only in that borderline state that he can paradoxically be fully awake and aware of the potential of his imagination.[22] Eventually the main threat of military invasion is diluted in the poem. It has a pervasive presence, however, at the level of a metaphor for the secondary imagination; for the poem itself is dependent on the invasive, or on the contrary, the recreative, power of the discourse of Romantic imagination.

### Notes

1  In Chapter Fourteen of the *Biographia*, Coleridge also describes the secondary imagination as a "synthetic and magical power" (II, 16). I will return to Coleridge's idea of the unifying capacities of the imagination later in my discussion.

2  Karl Kroeber, for instance, argues that Coleridge's mistitling of "Fears in Solitude" as "Fears of Solitude" in the June 8, 1809 edition of *The Friend* exposes

more than just an inadvertent slip. The change, according to Kroeber, "reveals socio-political forces impinging upon a poetic development" (359) that left Coleridge severed from the "language of communal feelings" (372). Also see C. R. Watters's "A Distant 'Bourn' Among the Hills: Some Notes on Coleridge's 'Fear in Solitude' (1798)," for a discussion of how the "moral deadening" of Coleridge's England is connected to a "deadened response to language itself" (90).

3  See Nicholas Roe's "Coleridge, Wordsworth, and the French Invasion Scare" for a detailed analysis of why the fear of another French invasion was not without cause. (A later version of this article is published in Roe's *Wordsworth and Coleridge: The Radical Years*.)

4  All quotations from "Fears in Solitude" are cited by line number from *Poetical Works* I, 468–77.

5  Coleridge recalls a conversation he had with John Thelwall, the well-known radical, who had visited him in July 1797: "We were once sitting in Somersetshire in a beautiful recess. I said to him—'Citizen John! this is a fine place to talk treason in!' 'Nay! Citizen Samuel!' replied he, 'it is a place to make a man forget that there is any necessity for treason!'" (*Table Talk* I, 180–81). Citizen Samuel's comment is noteworthy as it shows him grappling with the inevitable recognition that even the "beautiful recess" cannot exclude contemporary political forces, a theme he treats fully in "Fears in Solitude."

6  So much attention has been given to the imagination's capacity for reconciling opposites, thanks in no small part to Coleridge's emphasis on organic unity, that the notion of balance as a crucial element of the secondary imagination has gone almost unattended. See Norman Frumm's "Ozymandias and the Reconciliation of Opposites" for an incisive discussion of Coleridge's refusal to reconcile art and nature, which "stands on its head the whole point of Schelling's theory of art, which *reconciles* subject and object (mind and nature)" (56). (I will revisit this point about the reconciliation of subject and object.)

7  Kroeber's argument about language is instructive here. He contends that Coleridge's creation of the spot in "Fears in Solitude" is "exemplary of how by transforming the phenomenal into the linguistic one can retain and intensify the strengthening experiences of delight in nature." Kroeber maintains that Coleridge sees "his society's misuse of language as cause, not merely symptom, of a breakdown in such interenrichments, which should be the essence of social existence" (366).

8  *Poetical Works* I, 261–63. Coleridge termed this poem "*Sermoni propriora*" (a description added to the 1797 publication of the poem), while he called "Fears in Solitude" "*Sermoni propior*," indicating that the poem is "a sort of Middle thing between Poetry & Oratory" (469). See 260–61 for an analysis of the differing terminology. Also see note 9 below for the original title of "Retirement" in which Coleridge foregrounds the heterogeneous tone of the poem.

9  J.C.C. Mays cites March–April 1796 as the probable date of composition, so that Coleridge's desire "to fight the bloodless fight," as stated in the poem, intersects with his work on *The Watchman*, which saw its opening number published on March 1, 1796. But when Coleridge actually published the poem (titled "Reflections on entering into active life. A Poem which affects not to be Poetry") later that October, *The Watchman* had come to an end after "more than a year's

continuous activity in public and political affairs" (116). Although Coleridge devotes most of his attention to his poetry after this, his desire to avoid "feelings all too delicate for use" can be seen in the constant incursion of politics into his poetry; in December 1796, for instance, he published the decidedly political poem "Ode on the Departing Year" in the *Cambridge Intelligencer*.

10  Kelvin Everest also argues that the poem "confirms for Coleridge the potential of his retirement, the confidence and the social example that it can yield" (279). Also see Roe's *The Radical Years* for the relationship between Coleridge's evolving ideas and William Frend's concept of "universal benevolence" (211–216).

11  *The Historicity of Romantic Discourse* gravitates around the assiduous practice of revision among the Romantics. Siskin argues that revision effaces difference, and so presents all change as developmental (114, 120); he identifies the tendency of many unrevised texts to also "exhibit [such] revisionary behavior" (109). Romantic texts are not the only ones susceptible to the "transcendence of difference" (120), according to Siskin; Romantic criticism, past and present, also follows a similar trajectory.

12  See Roe's *The Radical Years* for a thoroughly engaging analysis of Coleridge's early radical leanings and his shifting political allegiances.

13  Roe believes that this strategic transference, which occurred "as early as June 1795," "was to sustain Coleridge through years when Wordsworth—who had made a parallel reinvestment of hope in Godwin's philosophy—suffered a crisis of despair." Wordsworth's ability to wrest free of Godwinian rationalism was, therefore, dependent on Coleridge's influence on him during the extended period of time they spent in the West Country; this "revivifying influence flows through Wordsworth's poetry of spring 1798," says Roe ("Imagining Robespierre," 172–173; a version of this article also appears in *The Radical Years*).

14  For Coleridge's part, he was furiously at work on his drama *Osorio*, and poems such as "This Lime-Tree Bower my Prison," "The Rime of the Ancient Marinere," and "Christabel," to name just a few. Roe theorizes that Coleridge's subsequent "creative paralysis" can be linked to the French invasion of Switzerland in January 1798 and the threatened attack against Britain. This "moment of disillusion," exemplified in the March–April compositions of "Fears in Solitude" and "France: An Ode," registers Coleridge's final break with Revolutionary idealism, and "stands at the threshold to Coleridge's declining creativity in the years following" (*The Radical Years* 2–3, 268). I have to concur with Mays, however, who cites the variety of Coleridge's verse and the quantity of his output to argue that Coleridge never had a "fractured" poetic career (*Poetical Works* I, lxxix, xcvii, xcii), and since Coleridge never attempted to duplicate a poem like "The Rime of the Ancient Mariner" in later years, it is wrong to assume that he failed as a poet (xciii). I also think it is essential to keep in mind that many of Coleridge's famous poems were revised during those years of supposed creative failure. "The Eolian Harp," for instance, begun in late 1795, was not given this title until winter 1815–1816, and the passage on the "one Life," on which hinges the notoriety of the poem, was only included shortly before the poem's publication in *Sibylline Leaves* (1817).

15  The small matter of "bread and cheese" (*Letters* I, 227, 320) was never far

from his mind, and even while at Stowey, Coleridge occasionally contributed to various journals (Holmes, 133, 143, 175–176). On the hunt for modes of self-sustenance, he turned down a Unitarian ministry when offered an annuity by Josiah Wedgwood. But Coleridge did not fully extract himself from the public arena; in late 1799 he went to London to work for the *Morning Post*, once again demonstrating his constant and restless migration between these two spheres.

16  "France: An Ode," first published in the *Morning Post* in April 1798 as "The Recantation," is an earlier embodiment of the same theme articulated in "Fears in Solitude." Coleridge further foregrounds this idea when he appends an "Argument" to "France: An Ode" when the poem is published in the *Morning Post* on 14 October, 1802; he describes the last stanza of the poem as "an address to Liberty, in which the Poet expresses his conviction, that those feelings, and that grand ideal, of freedom, which the mind attains by its contemplation of its individual nature, and of the sublime surrounding objects ... do not belong to men, as a society, nor can possibly be either gratified, or realised, under any form of human government; but belong to the individual man, so far as he is pure, and inflamed with the love and adoration of God in Nature" (*Poetical Works* I, 464).

17  When Coleridge published a version of "Fears in Solitude" in *Sibylline Leaves*, he omitted the line "selfish, lewd, and effeminated race." For this and other revisions to the poem, consult the Variorum Text of *Poetical Works* (II, 593–606). Mays uses the *Sibylline Leaves* version as copy text.

18  "France: An Ode" and "Frost at Midnight," published in the 1798 quarto edition along with "Fears in Solitude," also invoke the pedagogic role of nature. Also see note 16 above for the repetition of the phrase "adoration of the God in Nature" in "France: An Ode."

19  Coleridge's designation of the family as the space of national revitalization is complicated by his own unhappy marriage. Mere months after composing the poem, Coleridge was hardly at his "lowly cottage" in Stowey, as Holmes observes (198), and in September Coleridge went to Hamburg with the Wordsworths; it was only in July of 1799 that Coleridge returned home to Stowey.

20  Roe observes that in the last movement of the poem nature "offer[s] no assurance of guardianship or rest," and that even the "analogy of landscape and ... society" lacks redemptive value because Coleridge has already established the "degenerate" nature of society (*The Radical Years*, 266). "Coleridge's indulgence is self-deception," remarks Roe, "but it arises from a need to believe in the beneficent influence of nature to moral good that the poem has significantly failed to answer." Because "Coleridge's political, philosophic, and religious beliefs had been involved as a progressive and mutually sustaining whole," Roe believes that "'Fears in Solitude' marks a disabling inversion of this ideal" (267). I would argue, however, that the poem, with its many juxtapositions, demonstrates Roe's theory about the redeployment of revolutionary ideals in the realm of imaginative activity, and, rather than "mark[ing] a disabling inversion" of Coleridge's previous ideas, the poem registers the interdependency of these two sets of belief.

21  "A Soliloquy of the Full Moon, She Being in a Mad Passion" (*Poetical Works* I, 691–694), written in late April 1802, shortly after "A Letter to...," foregrounds just this relationship between the Romantic poet and nature. Although Coleridge assumes the voice of the moon, it is only to criticize the voices of "those mutter-

ing! Spluttering! Ventriloquogusty/ Poets"—himself and Wordsworth among them—who change the moon into whatever they desire. Despite all these transformations at the hands of poets, the moon declares its own distinct subjectivity by asserting, "I am I myself I, the jolly full Moon."

22 In "Effusion XXXV, Composed August 20th, 1795, at Clevedon, Somersetshire" (later titled "The Eolian Harp"), Coleridge employs the same motif to describe his mind at work: "... like birds of Paradise, I ... hov'ring on untamed wing" (*Poetical Works* I, 233). Also see Coleridge's 1811 lecture on Milton in which he again invokes the same concept to describe the imagination (*Lectures 1808–1819: On Literature I*, 311).

**Works Cited**

Abrams, M.H. "Structure and Style in the Greater Romantic Lyric," *Romanticism and Consciousness: Essays in Criticism*. Ed. Harold Bloom. New York: Norton, 1970.

Bakhtin, M.M. *The Dialogic Imagination: Four Essays*. Ed. Michael Holquist. Trans. Caryl Emerson and Michael Holquist. Austin: University of Texas Press, 1981.

Coleridge, Samuel Taylor. *Biographia Literaria*. Eds. James Engell and Walter Jackson Bate. 2 vols. *The Collected Works of Samuel Taylor Coleridge*. Vol. 7. Princeton, NJ: Bollingen Series 75 for Princeton UP, 1983.

———. *Collected Letters of Samuel Taylor Coleridge*. Ed. E. L. Griggs. 6 vols. Oxford: Clarendon Press, 1956.

———. *The Friend*. Ed. Barbara E. Rooke. 2 vols. *The Collected Works of Samuel Taylor Coleridge*. Vol. 4. Princeton, NJ: Bollingen Series 75 for Princeton UP, 1969.

———. *Lectures 1808-1819: On Literature*. Ed. R.A. Foakes. 2 vols. *The Collected Works of Samuel Taylor Coleridge*. Vol. 5. Princeton, NJ: Bollingen Series 75 for Princeton UP, 1987.

———. *Lectures 1795: On Politics and Religion*. Eds. Lewis Patton and Peter Mann. *The Collected Works of Samuel Taylor Coleridge*. Vol. 1. Princeton, NJ: Bollingen Series 75 for Princeton UP, 1971.

———. *Poetical Works*. Ed. J. C. C. Mays. 3 vols. *The Collected Works of Samuel Taylor Coleridge*. Vol. 16. Princeton, NJ: Bollingen Series 75 for Princeton UP, 2001.

———. *Table Talk*. Ed. Carl Woodring. 2 vols. *The Collected Works of Samuel Taylor Coleridge*. Vol. 14. Princeton, NJ: Bollingen Series 75 for Princeton UP, 1990.

———. *The Watchman*. Ed. Lewis Patton. *The Collected Works of Samuel Taylor Coleridge*. Vol. 2. Princeton, NJ: Bollingen Series 75 for Princeton UP, 1970.

Everest, Kelvin. *Coleridge's Secret Ministry: The Context of the Conversation Poems 1795–1798*. Sussex: The Harvester Press, 1979.

Froman, Norman. "Ozymandias and the Reconciliation of Opposites." *Coleridge's Theory of the Imagination Today*. Ed. Christine Gallant. New York: AMS

Press, 1989.
Holmes, Richard. *Coleridge: Early Visions.* London: Penguin Books, 1990.
Kroeber, Karl. "Coleridge's 'Fears': Problems in Patriotic Poetry." *CLIO* 7 (1978): 359–73.
Magnuson, Paul. "The Politics of 'Frost at Midnight.'" *Romantic Poetry: Recent Revisionary Criticism.* Eds. Karl Kroeber and Gene W. Ruoff. New Jersey: Rutgers UP, 1993.
———. "The Shaping of 'Fear in Solitude.'" *Coleridge's Theory of the Imagination Today.* Ed. Christine Gallant. New York: AMS Press, 1989.
Mileur, Jean-Pierre. *Vision and Revision: Coleridge's Art of Immanence.* Berkeley: University of California Press, 1982.
Roe, Nicholas. "Coleridge, Wordsworth, and the French Invasion Scare." *The Wordsworth Circle* 17 (Summer 1986): 142–148.
———. "Imagining Robespierre." *Coleridge's Imagination: Essays in Memory of Peter Laver.* Eds. Richard Gravil, Lucy Newlyn and Nicholas Roe. Cambridge: Cambridge University Press, 1985.
———. *Wordsworth and Coleridge: The Radical Years.* Oxford: Clarendon Press, 1988.
Siskin, Clifford. *The Historicity of Romantic Discourse.* Oxford: Oxford UP, 1988.
Warren, Robert Penn. "A Poem of Pure Imagination: An Experiment in Reading." *Selected Essays.* New York: Columbia UP, 1958.
Watters, C.R. "A Distant 'Bourn' Among the Hills: Some Notes on Coleridge's 'Fears in Solitude' (1798)." *Charles Lamb Bulletin* 59 (July 1987): 85–89.

Chapter Five

# Romantic Drama and the Discourse of Criminality

Marjean D. Purinton

In *Principles of Penal Law* (1802–1805), Jeremy Bentham writes

> A scaffold painted black, the livery of grief—the officers of justice dressed in crape—the executioner covered with a mask, which would serve at once to augment the terror of his appearance, and to shield him from ill-founded indignation—emblems of his crime placed above the head of the criminal, to the end that the witnesses of his sufferings may know for what crimes he undergoes them: these might form a part of the principal decorations of these legal tragedies; whilst all the *actors* in this terrible *drama* might *move in solemn procession*—serious and religious music preparing the hearts of the *spectators* for the important lesson they were about to receive. (1:549, emphasis added)

Bentham's description of a public scene of punishment reads like stage directions, his discourse marking the theatricality and spectacle of crime and punishment. For Bentham and other penal reformers of the Romantic period, criminal punishment necessitated educational, exemplary, preventative, and therefore performative aspects in order for it to serve the public good. The function of criminal punishment as well as criminal activity was to have an effect on the audience similar to that of tragedy. In *On Murder Considered as One of the Fine Arts* (1827) Thomas De Quincey writes that the final purpose of murder as a fine art "is precisely the same as that of tragedy in Aristotle's account of it; viz 'to cleanse the heart by means of pity and terror'" (8:47).

Romantic culture was fascinated with criminality, its occurrences, its deterrents, its consequences, and the late eighteenth and early nineteenth centuries witnessed a period of transition and change in the culture's attitudes about and responses to crime. As the political, industrial, and socio-religious revolutions of the period destabilized aristocratic power, generated population growth and urban migration, and fostered economic and spiritual meliorations, criminal activity soared. It was no longer containable under the laws and administration of predominately rural justices of the peace. By the mid-eighteenth century, legal paternalism began to deteriorate in London and in the rapidly growing provincial industrial or commercial towns. By the early nineteenth century, England was experiencing multiplying criminal indictments at a rate much greater than the growth in population as well as increasing regulation as it moved from an "unpoliced" to a "policed" society.

Social historians such as Peter King, John M. Beattie, and Norma Landau have demonstrated how the eighteenth-century "bloody code" gave way to Romantic penal regimes that sought the reformation of criminals through imprisonment rather than enough the presumed deterrence of public executions.[1] Jeremy Benthan, in fact, questioned the efficacy of the very theatricalized scene he described as social education, for public punishments in England had, in his opinion, evolved from tragedy to farce. He writes:

> A capital execution has no solemnity. The pillory is sometimes a scene of buffoonery ... Burning in the hand, according as the criminal and the executioner can agree, is performed either with a cold or a red-hot iron; and if it be with a hot iron, it is only a slice of ham which is burnt: to complete the farce, the criminal screams, whilst it is only the fat which smokes and burns, and the knowing spectators only laugh at this parody of justice. (1.550)

The enactment of public punishments had, in Bentham's opinion, mutated into comical sideshows, negating the exemplary and deterrent functions of social education that such punishments were meant to represent. In *A Treatise on the Police of the Metropolis* (1795), Patrick Colquhoun argues that the present system of justice has not had the effect of preventing crimes with publicly staged death penalties "since even the dread of this Punishment has, under the present circumstances, no effect upon guilty associates, that it is no uncommon thing for these hardened offenders to be engaged in new acts of the theft, at the very moment their companions in iniquity are launching, in their very presence, into eternity" (31). In short, theatricalized punishments were not working.

There was a gradual failure of the common law tradition (the individualistic law ideology of Blackstone and others) as it proved inadequate in the face of social and economic growth and failed as a unifying principle in the face of revolutionary challenges. The new bourgeois community increasingly identified the urban poor as a criminal class, and it sought support for the disciplining and management of criminals. According to Patrick Colquhoun, increased criminal activity can be attributed to "[t]he enlarged state of Society, the vast extent of moving property, and the unexampled wealth of the Metropolis, joined with the depraved habits and loose conduct of a great proportion of the lower classes of the people" (3). In the face of these sociological realities, Colquhoun, Bentham, and others initiated efforts to establish new poor laws, new punishments, professional police forces, and penitentiaries. The "meritorious performance" of criminal behaviors, as De Quincey terms it, would be removed from public stagings and located instead behind the closeted chambers of state institutions (8:16).

Consequently, the psychology and pathology of criminality became the focus of journalism and literature during the Romantic period. Bentham's treatises, *The State of Prisons* (1777) and *Panopticon: On the Inspection House* (1791), include studies on the problem of criminal behavior. William Godwin's novel, *Caleb Williams; Or Things as They Are* (1794), exposes crime as an error that demands reform rather than retribution. In *A Treatise on the Police of the Metropolis*, Colquhoun defines an urgent need for "a new science" of police that would achieve the "prevention and detection of crimes." Beginning in 1827, the murder mystery *Richmond: Scenes in the Life of a Bow Street Runner* enjoyed popular circulation. That same year, De Quincey's essay, *On Murder Considered as One of the Fine Arts*, parodied popular fascination with the criminal mind as his persona details proceedings of the Society for the Encouragement of Murder and relates the preoccupations of its Murder-Fanciers.

It was Romantic drama, however, that was the genre and the locus uniquely suited to the exposure and exploration of the discourses of criminality and to express the movement from public display to private attention. As we have seen, criminality took on theatricality in the forms of public trials and public punishments; criminal activities notoriously occurred at theaters during productions. Conversely, Romantic drama made spectacles of crime and its consequences. Joanna Baillie directly connects her theater theory with public executions in the "Introductory Discourse" to the 1798 *Plays on the Passions* when she points to both as pedagogical devices that feature "parts of a criminal's behavior" and that force audiences "to press forward to behold what we shrink from, and wait with trembling expectation for what we dread." For Baillie and other playwrights, Romantic theatre constituted a public site where cultural concerns with criminality could be staged and debated. While criminal and detective elements appear in obvious and circumspect forms in Romantic drama, I am particularly interested in the ways in which these dramas reflect and promote the discourse of criminality that shaped the period. Frequently, the dramas displace their engagement with contemporary criminality historically and geographically, and especially represent criminality as political conflict. These displacements often take manifest forms of anti-French, anti-German, anti-Catholic, anti-Semitic statements popular in the English drama of the period.

This displacement occurs in Robert Jephson's 1779 tragedy *The Law of Lombardy*, in Frances Burney's 1794 tragedy, *Edwy and Elgiva*, and in James Boaden's 1795 gothic play, *The Secret Tribunal*. The particular law at the center of the conflict in Jephson's tragedy subjects women to a mortal penalty:

> All women nobly born (be their estate
> Single or husbanded) who to the shame
> Of chastity, o'er-leap its thorny bounds
> To wanton in the flowery path of pleasure. (2.6.23)

The rigid French ordinance respecting the chastity of women resonates in the spirit of England's marriage law of 1753, the Hardwick Act, that legalized a double standard of gendered behaviors rendering women objectified property in the marriage contract. Colquhoun asserts in *A Treatise on the Police of the Metropolis*, "In short, the property of the woman is the measure of the crime ..." (48). English marital law sought to preserve the nation, as it claimed, for it protected the mothers and wives, the guardians and preceptors of English culture. Similarly, Lombardy's law subjugated women under the guise of national security. A senator explains the law's logic of application:

> Tis rehears'd
> That the wild licence of our countrywomen,
> O'erleapt all modest bounds. Sweet prudency
> (That ruby of the sex) had been cast by
> For casual wantonness, till our name abroad
> Became a by-word, and confusion, strange,
> Disturb'd domestic peace. (3.6.33–34)

Princess Sophia is accused and convicted of violating this harsh edict. Act Five of the play actually includes a scaffold scene for Sophia's public execution similar to that described by Jeremy Bentham in his *Principles of Penal Law*. While Sophia does not blame those who enforce the law, she nonetheless asserts that being shunned and neglected, being believed to be cheap and vile, are sharp penalties for the woman who profanes her honor, but death "turns the clear stream of justice into blood, / And makes such law more curs'd than anarchy" (5.9.68). She encourages her mute spectators to mark her words but to forget her example. The epilogue of the play urges theatergoers that the blame for criminality here lies not entirely on "weak woman" (74), but that is exactly what penal codes of past and present seek to do. Bentham's *Principles of Penal Law*, for example, includes an entire section on criminality and the regulation of female prostitution. Colquhoun estimates in 1795 that 50,000 women of varying social ranks lived by prostitution in the metropolis (340).

Burney's tragedy, *Edwy and Elgiva*, similarly involves criminality associated with marital law displaced onto an Anglo-Saxon setting. Because Elgiva is a second or third cousin of Edwy, ecclesiastical, not civil, law prohibits their marriage—a union that would significantly alter efforts by Dunstan, the abbot of Glastonbury, to seize power under the guise of convent reformation. But Edwy and Elgiva are secretly married, a crime according to Britain's law. Edwy assures Elgiva that the canon law prohibiting their marriage is "but a prejudice,/An ord'nance of the Pope, and not from Heaven" (1.5. 43–44), and he believes that he can convene a synod and have their secret marriage confirmed in spite of the law. His trusted advisor Aldhelm, bishop of Winchester, is not convinced that Edwy can overturn this unjust law, and warns Edwy that divorce might lead to tumult and rebellion. As in Jephson's play, laws governing the passions and marriage are linked to national security and peace. It is, of course, Elgiva who bears the stigma of the law's labeling power as she is called a "pernicious concubine" (2.10.17), a "courtesan" (2.10.14), and a "lawless lover" (3.4.14). Romantic-period audiences would no doubt see parallels between Elgiva and the contemporary Queen Caroline affair. Caroline of Brunswick's marriage to her cousin George, later King George IV, in 1795 created considerable controversy about its potential effects on the nation.

Dunstan manipulates a spectacle that can impassion the crowd, thereby criminalizing theatricality to achieve his own political ends. Astutely, he recognizes that the crowd can be duped. He tells Octo, "The crowd require illusion, not conviction./Entic'd by Terror, caught by Ambiguity,/Weakly beguil'd and eagerly amaz'd" (3.1.2830). He adds that the crowd functions much like spectators at the theater and that they can be moved "by calling forth their passions, and their interests,/By raising fears unnam'd, and Hopes mysterious" (3.1.32–33). Dunstan's use of spectacle dramatizes Romantic-period ambivalence about the efficacy of public punishments as a deterrent. Writing in *Principles of Penal Law*, Bentham observes: "… it may be said … that these real representations, these terrible scenes of penal justice, will spread dismay among the people, and make dangerous impressions. I do not believe it" (1:550). In *A Treatise on the Police of the Metropolis*, Colquhoun adds that executions should "be exhibited as seldom as possible …" for by being often repeated, "they lose their effect upon the minds of the People" (6). He maintains that the exhibition should be rendered as "terrific" and "solemn" to the eyes of the people as possible, for "the terror of the example operate[s] as the means of prevention" (453). For Baillie, the spectacle of a public execution has the power to excite fear and dread of criminal behavior and extreme passions that would result in such a horrible death.

The prologue and epilogue of *Edwy and Elgiva*, like the epilogue of *The Law of Lombardy*, remind us that contemporary issues of criminality are, in fact, being displaced and enacted onto scenes of historic and geographic distance. Speaking the epilogue to Burney's tragedy, Sarah Siddons asks:

> What had these ancient pontiffs in their mind

> When they made Laws to shackle all mankind
> In matrimonial Vows? now with permission
> To wed or this or that; now Prohibition
> To take or one or t'other; while good sense
> And Piety alike receiv'd offence
> Since all was arbitrary, changing, vague,
> Fram'd, one would think, but to Perplex and plague. (47–54, 89)

Siddons rejoices that Britain is no longer shackled by such arcane laws: "O in these happier days, enlighten'd times,/When superstition fabricates no crimes" (57–58, 89). The irony is, of course, that "enlightened" penal codes are as artificial and arbitrary as those rendered by Anglo-Saxon superstition, when, as the prologue proclaims, "In those dark ages when the dread command/Of Druid Superstition rul'd the land" (1–2, 13). Similarly, the epilogue of Jephson's play begins:

> Of all the Gothic laws I ever heard,
> The Lombard Law was sure the most absurd:
> What! could the monsters mean to make us die,
> But for a little harmless gallantry?
> Were such a barbarous custom now in fashion,
> Good Lord! it would unpeople half the nation
> Were British law-makers such rigorous churls,
> They'd hardly leave a head to wear false curls. (74)

The "barbarous customs" of Lomabard are being replaced with British legislation of criminal behavior that is, the play suggests, as absurd and "gothic" as those of France's past.

James Boaden's gothic play *The Secret Tribunal* begins with a prologue written by a lawyer, John Litchfield, Esq., that indicts German law-makers for their secretive efforts to check criminal activities, resulting in a tyrannical judiciary that can be bribed or whimsically angered:

> What time the policy of *German* Rule
> Fetter'd the native freedom of the soul;
> When SUPERSTITION held her sanguine state,
> And dealt, at will, the rapid blow of fate;
> The world beheld all pledge of safety gone,
> And even MONARCHS TREMBLED ON THE THRONE.
> JUDGES, with functions unconfin'd and *free*,
> At midnight issued many a dark decree. [n.p. ii]

If Jephson's and Burney's tragedies question the efficacy of public punishments as deterrent for criminality, Boaden's play points to the risks of moving punishments away from public scrutiny and into the dark, clandestine chambers of secret tribunals. Like Jephson's and Burney's plays, the prologue to *The Secret Tribunal* protests that what the play enacts does not happen in contemporary Britain: "Open as day *our* Courts judicial move, / And RICH or POOR their *equal* influence prove" [n.p. iii]. The play takes place in Wirtemberg in Suabia where a struggle between brothers for the crown results in one woman being murdered and another being made patsy (a disposable object in the scheme) for the crime, while politically desperate Ratibor tries to usurp his brother's royal inheritance. The play's hero makes the tragic mistake of trusting a judicial system that is corrupt and sinister. He voices his plan:

> To wait citation.
> When the dark summons of the secret judges,
> Calls me to answer for the imagin'd treason,
> Immediately I will present myself
> And hurl confusion upon Ratibor. (3.2.38)

He vows to meet these "dark avengers" (4.2.51) and the Minister of Vengeance. Similarly, Ida, the play's heroine, naïvely trusts her fate to the hands of the judicial system. She embraces the opportunity to answer her accusers, even though they meet secretly and no one knows where. If those accused before the secret judges are found guilty, "they are never heard of more" (4.1.48). Ironically, the duke assures us that "no partial judgment can be fear'd/From men enlighten'd, sanctified to truth" (5. 1 .60).

The tribunal spectacle of Boaden's play is as arresting as Bentham's scaffold scene in *Principles of Penal Law*. The stage directions read: "*At the upper end is a luminous Cross of a deep red, and over this, surrounded by Clouds, an Eye, radiated with points of fire. A Throne adorned with trophies in gold, upon a ground of black velvet*" (5.1.59). The play's epilogue reminds us, like those of Jephson's and Burney's plays, that we are witnessing dreadful scenes of justice no longer practiced in Britain:

> SUCH the dread scenes of a benighted age
> Now only known in the historic page:
> Thence by our Poet drawn, but to display
> Old ENGLISH justice in unclouded day. (71)

Boaden's play makes visible and public the potential of harsh and unfair justice rendered behind closed doors, perhaps a warning to contemporary theater-goers about what it could mean to move criminal punishments into private spaces. The epilogue concludes with haunting questions:

> But are these institutions quite destroy'd?
> SECRET TRIBUNALS, are they now employ'd?
> THOUSANDS. Yes, while we sink in soft repose,
> Our Judges eyes no gentle slumbers close. (71)

At a time when the writ of habeus corpus had been suspended, and when the Treason and Sedition Acts had just been passed in the wake of French revolutionary fears, Britain's concerns about secret tribunals are reasonable and grounded.

The last two plays treat criminality in different ways from those by Jephson, Burney, and Boaden just examined. George Colman the Younger recast William Godwin's novel *Caleb Williams* into a play entitled *The Iron Chest* in 1796. In an open court, a jury, rather than the secret tribunal staged by Boaden's play, has acquitted Sir Edward Mortimer of murder, even though he is actually guilty of the crime—something that Wilford, his secretary, comes to realize after he secretly sees incriminating evidence against Sir Edward. Sir Edward is head keeper of the forest, one of those judges, claims Wilford, "who, in their office, will never warp the law to save offenders: but his private charity bids him assist the needy, before their necessities drive them to crimes which public duty must punish" (1.1.12). It is ironic that Sir Edward is in a position to pass judgment on the criminality of the rural poor with crimes such as deer-stealing prompted by their hunger, when he is himself guilty of killing a man. Sir Edward trumps up charges of theft against Wilford who, he fears, may reveal his secret criminality. Wilford takes solace in knowing that an English court will find him innocent of the crime for which he has been charged, for unlike the principal characters of Jephson's, Burney's, and Boaden's plays, he is not to be judged before secret and antiquated judicial systems. He rationalizes, "This charge is to be open;—in the eye of the world; of the laws.—Then why should I fear? I am native of a happy soil where justice guards equally the life of its poorest and richest inhabitant" (3.2.109–110). However, Captain Fitzharding disagrees, noting the strength of the case of the robbery charge against Wilford and adding, "Yet accidents / Sometimes combine to cast a shade of doubt/Upon the innocent" (3.2.118). Colman's play conflates generic tensions accompanying the transformation of the novel into drama with criminal transgressions so as to suggest that such generic transformations are themselves criminal.

Perjury, a false accusation, is similarly central to the criminality in Baillie's 1812 tragedy *The Stripling*. Based on an actual event that had taken place in Glasgow, the drama presents a young man, whose father is in prison, about to be tried for a capital offence, forgery. Like Sir Edward in Colman's play, the fate of the accused, a man named Arden, depends on the testimony of one person—John Robinair, who had lured Arden into the expensive, extravagant, and dangerous habit of gambling. Arden falls deeply in debt, and faced with financial ruin, he commits the forgery in order to buy time to raise money. He then defrauds an elderly relation, Fenshaw, who would have probably named Arden as his heir within a few years. Robinair goads, and probably blackmails, the old man to prosecute Arden for the stolen one thousand pounds, a crime punishable by death according to English law. Colquhoun states, "by the Laws of England, there are above one hundred and sixty different offences which subject the parties who are found guilty, to death without benefit of Clergy" (5). The House of Commons eventually reduced the number of capital crimes in the 1820s as the new penal regime of criminal reformation began to replace the "bloody code" (Philips, 69). Arden's son, Robert, determines to eliminate the one person who could give evidence against his father. As a result, Arden's life is spared, but Robert is executed for the murder of Robinair, the principal witness against his father.

Robert is indicted for the murder of John Robinair because he left his hat at the scene of the crime. The justice of the peace explains how a criminal comes to leave such telling evidence: "When men commit such deeds, they do so in a state of mind which renders them incapable of perceiving what circumstance will excite or prevent suspicion; and they are as often detected from caution as from oversight" (5.1.566). This inattention on the part of the criminal is precisely what De Quincey's persona in *On Murder Considered As One of the Fine Arts* attributes to the arrest in 1812 of the perpetrator of the infamous Williams murders—murders that were committed in 1811. Both Williams and Robert Arden failed "in the art of murder" with their bungling of incriminating evidence. At that passionate moment of murder, Baillie's character, only fifteen years old, may not have had his wits about him: "the mind in that state may be cunning; but it is a cunning which betrays oftener than conceals" (5.1.566). But Baillie's play leaves us with little sense of justice having been rendered, for it is Robinair, its actual villain, who feeds upon Arden's attraction to the gaming houses. According to Colquhoun, the gaming houses were especially fascinating allurements:

> by means of splendid entertainments, and regular suppers, with abundance of the choicest wines, so as to form a genteel lounge for the dissipated and unwary ... Thus drawing into this vortex of iniquity and ruin ... the thoughtless and opulent part of Society; who too easily become a prey to that idle vanity which frequently overpowers reason and reflection; and the delusion of which is seldom terminated till it is too late. (140)

Arden gets caught up in the spirit of the times, driven to Romantic white-collar crimes, which are known, claims Colquhoun, "to advance in proportion to the excessive accumulation of wealth" that characterized the early nineteenth century and contributed to its increasing crime rate [n.p.4]. The word that Baillie selected as the title of her play, "stripling," suggests associations with the "strip" or lash of punishment often administered in public exhibitions. While such public punishments were less frequent by 1812, due to the implementation of new penal codes, Baillie's tragedy stages in public space a theatricalized exemplum about the treatment of criminality with which the Romantic period had become so engaged and concerned.

### Note

1  See King, *Crime, Justice, and Discretion in England, 1740–1820* John M. Beattie, *Policing and Punishment in London, 1660–1750* and Norma Landau, "Introduction," 1–16.

### Works Cited

Baillie, Joanna. *The Stripling: A Tragedy in Prose*. 1812. *The Dramatic and Poetical Works of Joanna Baillie, Complete in One Volume*. 2nd edn. London: Longman, Brown, Green, and Longmans, 1851. 551–569.

Beattie, John M. *Policing and Punishment in London, 1660–1750: Urban Crime and the Limits of Terror*. Oxford: Oxford UP, 2001.

Bentham, Jeremy. *Principles of Penal Law*. 1802–1805. *The Works of Jeremy Bentham*. Vol. 1. New York: Russell & Russell, 1962. 365–580.

Boaden, James. *The Secret Tribunal: A Play in Five Acts*. 1795. *The Plays of James Boaden*. Ed. Steven Cohan. New York: Garland, 1980. 1–72.

Burney, Frances. *Edwy and Elgiva: A Tragedy*. 1788–1795. *The Complete Plays of Frances Burney*. Vol. 2. Ed. Peter Sabor. Montreal: McGill-Queen's UP, 1995. 10–89.

Colman the Younger, George . *The Iron Chest: A Play in Three Acts*. 1796. *The Plays of George Colman The Younger*. Vol. 2. Ed. Peter A. Tasch. New York: Garland, 1981. 1–127.

Colquhoun, Patrick. *A Treatise on the Police of the Metropolis; Considering a Detail of the Various Crimes and Misdemeanors By which Public and Private Property and Security are, at present injured and endangered: And Suggesting Remedies For Their Prevention*. 1795. 7th edn. London: Cadell and Davies, 1806.

De Quincey, Thomas. *On Murder Considered As One of the Fine Arts*. *The Collected Writings of Thomas De Quincey*. 1827. Vol. 8. London: A&C Black, 1897. 9–124.

Jephson, Robert. *The Law of Lombardy: A Tragedy*. 1779. *The Plays of Robert*

*Jephson*. Ed.Temple James Maynard. New York: Garland, 1980. 1–74.

King, Peter. *Crime, Justice, and Discretion in England, 1740–1820*. Oxford: Oxford UP, 2002.

Landau, Norma. "Introduction." In *Law, Crime and English Society, 1660–1830*. Cambridge: Cambridge UP, 2002.

Philips, David. "Policing." In *The Oxford Companion to the Romantic Age: British Culture 1776–1832*. Ed. Ian McCalman, John Mee, Gillian Russell, Clara Tuite. Oxford, Oxford UP, 66–73.

# Part 2
# Women Writers and Romantic Constructions of Power

Chapter Six

# Towards Constructing a "Poetics of Space" for the Sentimental Novel: A Topo-analysis of Charlotte Smith's *The Old Manor House*

Nancy Metzger

Charlotte Smith's biographer Loraine Fletcher has identified *The Old Manor House* as a key text pioneering the metaphorical use of the manor house to reflect socio-political relationships and trends in society, a metaphor subsequently adapted by later novelists. For example, Fletcher claims that "the estate, its history and undetermined future, are codes for England or that the hierarchy of characters is representative of English society" (Fletcher, 5). Other critics, such as Joseph Bartolomeo, have also recognized the politically confrontational nature of Smith's novels, identifying their liberal politics at the time of the French Revolution, or, like Kathryn R. King, who discusses the implications of writing and sewing as means by which women exerted their creative powers within restrictive social roles, have focused on gender relations in *The Old Manor House*. This analysis, like Fletcher's, will focus on the centrality of Rayland Hall in *The Old Manor House* by using Gaston Bachelard's *The Poetics of Space* as a paradigm by which to explore how domestic space is used symbolically. I will also seek to historicize some elements of Bachelard's paradigm which are nostalgically conservative, although this conservatism suits a sentimentalist mode.

Gaston Bachelard's *The Poetics of Space* utilizes as its key figure the house and the different parts and elements of a home as the basis of a structural and metaphorical analysis of how space is depicted in fiction. Because the domestic sphere is the primary focus in the sentimentalist novel, so that the house itself is fundamental in the unfolding of the novel, Bachelard's paradigm makes an efficient tool to use in revealing the intimate domestic relationships at the heart of Charlotte Smith's *The Old Manor House*.

In *The Poetics of Space*, Gaston Bachelard states: "it [is] reasonable to say we 'read a house,' or 'read a room,' since both room and house are psychological diagrams that guide writer and poets in their analysis of intimacy" (38). Bachelard conducts his topo-analysis in *Poetics* on the basis that there are resonances implicit in oneiric, or dream-like, images that evoke universal psychological and emotional responses. For example, the image of a lighted candle in a window conveys a sense of waiting, anticipating, and watching, as well as a homing focus and a homey comfort that welcomes the traveler. Because the sentimental is attempting to evoke the emotional response that Bachelard claims is *possible to evoke* through the use of oneiric images of space, his *The Poetics of Space* provides a useful paradigm by which to examine the depiction of home in Charlotte Smith's *The Old Manor House*. This paradigm parallels the domestic imagery that Smith utilizes in portraying the domestic environment of *The Old Manor House*. Key parallels to examine include outside versus inside space; the significance of doors and windows in bridging these spaces; the prominence of locks and locked caskets; and how American and England can be symbolic in Book III of the same outside (wild) versus inside (domesticated) space that holds true for the other three books. Finally, I will analyze how components of Bachelard's background, including gender and class, influence his own sentimentalist view of the domestic sphere. Although there are places where the details of *The Old Manor House* fail to mesh with Bachelard's overall paradigm, examining the parallels may still illuminate key traits at the heart of the sentimental novel.

While the sentimental greatly depends both on portraying a heightened sense of feeling, as is evident in Orlando's and Monimia's fervent emotional responses, and on evoking feelings of compassion, tenderness, and sympathy in the reader, through pity felt for the setbacks experienced by the main characters, *The Old Manor House* also functions as a property romance, centering on the problem of who will inherit Rayland Hall and conflicts between Orlando's duties to Mrs. Rayland, his benefactor, and Monimia, his beloved. At the beginning, Orlando Somerive is a younger son but, on account of his charm and good looks, is favored to inherit Rayland Hall from his elderly cousin, Mrs. Rayland, when she dies. Since his older brother proves dissolute, and Orlando has four sisters to help provide for, gaining, and staying in, Mrs. Rayland's good graces is vital to his and his family's future. Therefore, Orlando spends most of his time at Rayland Hall, where he also meets and falls in love with Monimia, the orphaned niece of Mrs. Lennard, Mrs. Rayland's companion. Since Orlando has no occupation, it is decided that he should become a soldier, and he sails out to fight against the rebels in America. When he returns to England, he discovers that both Mrs. Rayland and his father have died, his family has relocated to London, and Monimia has disappeared, leaving no means to trace her whereabouts. After a struggle to make money and to find Monimia, whom he marries, Orlando is contacted by Mrs. Lennard, who has since married and is now Mrs. Roker. She approaches Orlando to let him know where Mrs. Rayland's real will is hidden, thus enabling Orlando to gain title to Rayland Hall and return there with Monimia, his wife. In *The Old Manor House*, Rayland Hall is central to most of the plot as the location of most of the action in the first part of the novel, as an object of longing while Orlando is away, and as the inheritance which seals the resolution of the plot.

One element of the oneiric imagery of "house" that Bachelard explores on a broad level in *The Poetics of Space* is the "dialectics of outside and inside." Bachelard begins with the claim that "the dialectics of outside and inside is supported by a reinforced geometrism, in which limits are barriers" (215). The first task of these barriers becomes "[t]o make inside concrete and outside vast" (215). The lack of such clearly erected barriers to establish a "vast Outside" and a "concrete Inside" results in a dizzying nightmare that "is the result of a sudden doubt as to the certainty of inside and the distinctness of outside" (218). This confusion, resulting from a lack of barriers to define inside versus outside space, correlates with the concrete detail of the interiors of Rayland Hall versus the vastness of the estate's grounds.

In the context of a home, the interior space is described in more concrete detail, while the parks surrounding it are treated in less detail in order to convey their vastness. Moreover, the concreteness of the inside space not only makes it easier for the reader to picture, but also demonstrates the greater control that the inhabitants of the house, particularly Mrs. Rayland, can exercise "inside" the house. Most obviously, Mrs. Rayland controls the choice of who will inherit Rayland Hall, and still exercises enough control over the activities within the house to keep a large staff occupied in maintaining the comforts and stature of her ancestral home. However, since she is old and suffers from gout, she is mainly housebound, and therefore *not* able to exert control over the "vast outside" space of the estate grounds. Rather, Orlando, the presumed heir, who rambles freely over them, as does Stockton, the new, young merchant-owner of neighboring Carloraine Castle. Stockton and his friends, symbolic of the rising, moneyed, middle class, hunt on Rayland Estate without permission or conscience about their trespass.

In contrast to this vast "outside space" which is easily trespassed, the concrete nature of Rayland Hall's "inside" space represents Mrs. Rayland's continuing power as the current owner of the estate. While Orlando is the best positioned to defend Mrs. Rayland's dictums about "preserves" on the estate, even the house servants, such as Patterson who is involved in using Rayland Hall to store smuggled goods, are subverting the control Mrs. Rayland *should be able to* exert over the "inside space" of her own home. Such anarchic activities both outside and inside the house signal the breakdown of control in the domestic order, as well as the breakdown of the old social order in England. The resulting anxiety parallels Bachelard's conception of the "dizzying nightmare" that "is the result of a sudden doubt as to the certainty of inside and the distinctness of outside" (215). Mrs. rayland's inability to maintain control over her ancestral home and estate symbolizes the loss of control of the aristocratic upper class in the face of challenges from the new middle class.

Given the strong dialectics between outside and inside, doors are very important as the means to negotiate the space between the outside and the inside. According to Bachelard, "the door is an entire cosmos of the Half-open. In fact, it is one of its primal images, the very origin of a daydream that accumulates desires and temptations: the temptation to open up the ultimate depths of being, and the desire to conquer all reticent beings" (222). Thus, the significance of doors as thresholds holds true, not only for their implicit ability to either close in "inside" spaces, or become barriers that define "outside" spaces, but also psychologically as barriers that preserve the integrity of privacy.

Doors feature most prominently in Smith when they are locked, as a means to create an "inside space" and shut others out, keeping other people artificially in an "outside" space, as well as keeping them psychologically at arm's length. Similarly, windows mediate a barrier between inside and outside space. Although Bachelard does *not* take up the issue of windows extensively, the commonalities and distinctions between doors and windows provide some striking insights. One vital difference is that, rather than creating "an entire cosmos of the Half-open" (222) as a door does, a window maintains a physical barrier that can not be trespassed bodily, while creating an opening through which an observant gaze can penetrate. Thus, both doors and windows provide some sort of passage, or hinge, between outside and inside spaces; however, while a door allows for a physical passage, serving as a throughway from one type of space to another, a closed, glassed window prohibits such passage. Yet, windows always, whether open or closed, provide for the passage of the gaze. In particular, there are many instances of Mrs. Lennard, Mrs. Rayland's companion, gazing out of windows—indeed, she attempts to exert power beyond the confines of the inside space the two women chiefly inhabit, sometimes for herself and sometimes on behalf of Mrs. Rayland. However, the effect tends to be rather ambiguous. While watching for Monimia's and Betty's late return from an outing, Mrs. Lennard *cannot* punish Monimia for her tardiness until she returns within the confines of the house—the inside space—although once Monimia comes inside, Mrs. Lennard *does* punish her by locking her in her turret room again. Similarly, when Orlando's father comes to Rayland Hall to talk with him, and the two men are speaking in the stableyard, Mrs. Lennard, who "saw them from one of the windows" (157), reports to Mrs. Rayland on Mr. Somerive's presence, and he is subsequently invited inside. However, Mr. Somerive first has to enter at least the artificial confines of the stable yard before the ladies can exert the power that they wield within "inside" spaces.

In certain situations, only fear of the gaze, symbolized by the windows, is necessary to cause anxiety. On the first occasion that Orlando goes up to meet Monimia in her room and bring her down to the library, she expresses worry that her aunt might catch them. She protests, "I have recollected that one of the windows of my aunt's closet up stairs looks this way. If she should be in it, if she should see us!" (71). But Orlando assures her that Mrs. Lennard would not sit in her window, in the dark, watching out. However, on a later occasion, it becomes apparent that Mrs. Lennard *does* watch out the windows at night, since she scolds Monimia, saying, "How is it, then, [...] that light is sometimes, aye, and very lately too, seen from your window, at hours when your own candle is taken away?" (197). Thus, windows provide an opportunity to attempt to extend one's power beyond the confines of the inhabited "inside" space and to exert influence in the broader "outside" space, although, the effective means to actually *control* the "outside" space is minimal. Beyond the suppression of some actions as a result of fear of the gaze, and fear of detection, power can not be exerted until its victim obliges by returning to the confines of the "inside" space, within which Mrs. Rayland and Mrs. Lennard reign supreme, or, if not supreme, than nearly so.

Doors, in that regard, are much more successful, both at averting the gaze and at creating an internal space that provides a haven safe from outside influence—or so they are meant to. Indeed, one of the major tropes of *The Old Manor House* is locked doors. Mrs. Lennard is continually locking Monimia away in her turret room to keep her away from Orlando. However, Orlando finds a second, boarded-up entrance—through a concealed door, up a low staircase and through a passage that winds up "to the top of the turret" (63), to a door located behind the head of Monimia's bed. In her attempt to reveal the door, Monimia must cut the glazed linen covering it (63–64), the sexual implications of which have been noted by other critics. In this way, not only is Orlando able to gain access to Monimia's "inside" space of the turret room, but she is also able to use this secret passageway to leave the locked turret room in order to meet him regularly in the library. This failure of the locked door, or the deception that it is secured, enables the romance between Orlando and Monimia to develop.

Subsequently, on the night of the tenants' dinner, Monimia slips out of her locked turret room to Orlando's study (219) to meet him and be introduced to his sister Selina for the first time. While Monimia is in the study, many people come by and try to enter, including Orlando's father, and his brother Philip with Betty. Monimia's ability to successfully keep them all locked out preserves the sanctuary of not only her "inside" space in the study, but also the private space of relationship that she shares with Orlando. This private "inside" space of relationship prefigures the "inside" space of the home that they will ultimately create together and share as husband and wife—ultimately, a new haven of home.

Bachelard equates "inside" space not only with the interior haven of home and the psychological space of an individual, but also with the interior of personality; therefore, Monimia's success at keeping Orlando's diverse family members locked *out* also serves to keep his developing relationship with her private. As a result of the social pressures, both from his father's concern that Orlando may indulge in an inappropriate relationship with a servant-girl and from Orlando's own concerns that Mrs. Rayland's gaining knowledge of their relationship would cause him to lose any chance of inheriting Rayland Hall, it is vital to Orlando and his future that he keep hidden, "inside" himself, his relationship with Monimia. The only person let into the room, and likewise in on the secret, is his sister Selina, by the lovers' mutual consent.

The issue of locks and locked doors serving to preserve secrets is taken up by Bachelard specifically in regard to chests and small caskets. While I have turned a broad part of this discussion toward looking at what is kept, or not kept, hidden behind locked doors, there also is in fact a hidden, locked casket containing the will that ultimately is responsible for Orlando and Monimia gaining title to Rayland Hall after Mrs. Rayland's death. Bachelard discusses how oneiric images of chests "condense cosmic wealth in a slender casket. If there are jewels and precious stones in the casket, it is the past, a long past, a past that goes back through generations [...] The casket contains the things that are unforgettable, *unforgettable* for us, but also unforgettable for those to whom we are going to give our treasures" (84). No precious jewels turn up in the padlocked tin box that has been hidden down a secret passage, reached via going through Mrs. Lennard's old closet; however, since it *does* contain Mrs. Rayland's will, which guarantees that Rayland Hall comes into Orlando's possession, its contents are worth as much as any jewels. Moreover, since the will passes on the legacy of the Rayland past to Orlando, who will take on the Rayland name, it symbolizes both the *unforgettable* nature of Rayland Hall in Orlando's experience, and the treasure that Mrs. Rayland passes on to her distant relatives.

With regard to wardrobes, a different type of closed container, but one which Bachelard associates closely with caskets, Bachelard states: "[i]n the wardrobe there exists a center of order that protects the entire house against uncurbed disorder. Here order reigns, or rather, this is the reign of order" (78). The casket that contains Mrs. Rayland's will is not only similar to such enclosed spaces, but is reached after going through Mrs. Lennard's old closet to a secret passageway; the restoration of the "reign of order" represented by finding the will after going through the closet, a wardrobe-like space, to locate the casket clearly shows the symbolic nature of closets as centers of order. While there are many more such features of the house itself that could be examined at great length, one section of *The Old Manor House* that initially seems problematic is Volume III, in which Orlando leaves not only Rayland Hall, but also England altogether, in order to fight the revolutionaries in colonial America.

As Loraine Fletcher explains in her analysis of *The Old Manor House*, Rayland Hall serves as an extended metaphor and as the imageof the critique Smith would make of England's decaying social order. If one follows Fletcher's argument, that Rayland Hall is representative of England, with nearly all the different social echelons being portrayed, from the robbers in the basement to the reigning aristocrat in Mrs. Rayland, then the surrounding estate over which Mrs. Rayland likewise exercises control is parallel to the extended territory of England—namely, England's colonies, and specifically, America. Just as Mrs. Rayland is unable to adequately control who enters or leaves the grounds of her estate, England is finding it historically difficult to control her North American colonies, which are in the throes of political rebellion. Given this historical context, after Orlando joins the army, expecting only local assignments in the neighborhood of Rayland, and certainly within England, he instead gets shipped off to fight in the war against the rebelling colonies. In this expanded metaphor, England represents the "inside space" of "domesticity," since it is long established and functions under its own set of social and political codes; in contrast, America is linked to idea of "outside space," whose chief attribute is its "vastness"—a quality America is well-suited to represent, especially during the 1770s, when so much of it was still uncharted. Moreover, this sense of "vastness" is clearly conveyed by Orlando's extensive treks through the limitless forests he must traverse before being able to re-connect with British troops, after he has fallen in a battle. These parallels demonstrate that the construction of "space" in *The Old Manor House* is consistent throughout, whether on the macro level of nations (inside/domesticated/England versus outside/undomesticated/America) or whether on the micro level of intimate workings of Rayland Hall and the relationships between individual characters. Significantly, despite the seeming break in the text when it diverges to follow Orlando's soldierly exploits in America, the same overall structure and tropes are still functioning and providing unity throughout the book.

Although all of these images seem to be illuminated by viewing them through the paradigm of Bachelard's *Poetics of Space*, one of the problems that remains derives from the idyllic nature of the home that Bachelard describes. Bachelard seems to construct his understanding of the house as haven and "inside" space versus "outside" space from a nostalgic, even rosy-glassed, vision of home. But note how nostalgia is paralleled by Orlando's visions of home. For example, when he views Rayland Hall for possibly the last time before departing to be a soldier and sail to America, the narrator describes thus: "[Orlando] stopped on the top of [a high down], and, turning his horse's head, fixed his eyes on the seat of all his past happiness, of all his future hopes, and thought how much he probably had to suffer before he should revisit it again, how probable it was that he should never see it more!" Also, upon his return from America, when Orlando travels to West

Wolverton in search of his family and finds the family home sold, and his sisters and mother gone, he is invited inside by the new owner. The narrator describes: "Every object [Orlando] saw was a dagger to his heart. As Philip had sold to Stockton every thing as it remained at his father's death, a great part of the furniture was the same. Startled at every step he took by the recollection of some well-known object, he entered the parlour more dead than alive" (409). While such nostalgic descriptions of Orlando's view of home not only resonate with a sentimentalist mode, but also and provide substantial parallels to Bachelard's conception of home, this vision of home is, at least in part, possible because for both Orlando, the character, and Bachelard, the man, home exists as a comfortable sanctuary that comforts, at least partly, because it requires no work on their part to create or maintain it—work being the preserve of servants and/or women.

Such golden-haloed, hallowed views of home seem to be predicated on the idea that even the smallest space—"the corner; which implies the larger construct of home—is a haven that ensures us one of the things we prize most highly—immobility" (Bachelard, 137). I doubt whether many women, when they think of home, would *naturally* associate home with 'immobility'—or, for that matter, associate a 'corner' with havens and repose. My sense from Monimia's typical household tasks—which are often Cinderella-like in their breadth and the length of time required—is that Monimia, like many women today, would probably view a corner with dread, as a harbor for dust waiting to be removed, rather than as a harbor of peace for herself.

Bachelard also has an idealized image of house work. For example, he meditates on "women's construction of the house through daily polishing," and considers, "what a great life it would be if, every morning, every object in the house could be made anew by our hands, could 'issue' from our hands" (69); I rather doubt that Bachelard would be so enthusiastic if it were actually his own hands from which the house, and every object in it, were being "constructed anew" through the "daily polishing" *he* had to perform. If we consider Monimia to be in the position of having to carry out such housewifely duties, we do not get a very strong sense that she would associate home with immobility. Instead, as first a servant in Rayland Hall, and second as a wife to Orlando, she is often the person responsible for the daily polishing, rather than Mrs. Rayland, who escapes such work because of her upper-class status, or Orlando, who escapes this work because of his gender and position as husband and head of the household.

Although Bachelard claims that even "in this prison [of a corner, of a trap] there is peace" (145), Monimia does not seem able to enjoy much rest. Indeed, even she has married Orlando and they have moved into their own home, she is compelled to take work in to support them, prior to Orlando finding and claiming the will and thereby Rayland Hall. The sewing that Monimia takes in again keeps her enclosed in "inside" space, with scarcely more freedom to leave than when she was physically locked in her turret room by Mrs. Lennard. Monimia has little opportunity to explore the vastness of London while, in contrast, Orlando is able to continually enlarge his social circle in the city. Thus, Orlando is enabled to indulge in a nostalgia for "home as haven" because, for him, fit can function as such, rather than as a workplace or as a prison.

If Bachelard valorizes home and internal space as a haven and an opportunity to withdraw, then the positive connotations associated with this are predicated on the inhabitant traveling in the vastness of outside space, so that, in contrast, retiring to home becomes haven-like—but, what if the opposite is true? What must home evoke for the person who is locked into the house, and even into her room, so that she is never allowed the opportunity to explore the external space, the vastness of it? One implicit assumption seems to be that home equals haven when it can be withdrawn to *by choice*—when it is *not* the chief place of employment and cause of work. Other critics, such as Judith Fryer in her book *Felicitous Space*, explore the issue of the different ways in which women inhabit, and write about, domestic space. Writers have also been inspired to argue against Bachelard's idealistic construction of the home. For example, Sandra Cisneros began writing *The House on Mango Street*, which portrays the life of a poor girl raised in a third-floor flat located in the ghetto, in reaction to "a heated graduate discussion of Gaston Bachelard's *Poetics of Space*" (Doyle, 12). In discussing Cisneros' book as a response to Bachelard's *Poetics*, Julian Olivares recognizes that Bachelard describes a "poetics of space" from the perspective of an upper-class man, clearly only one standpoint of many, and one that is indeed privileged in its experience of home.

Although Bachelard's *Poetics* has this shortcoming of representing the standpoint of a privileged, upper-class, white male, when used to examine the same type of standpoint in a character, it is very useful. Thus, Orlando's nostalgic view of Rayland Hall and West Wolverton very much parallels Bachelard's analysis of such spaces because the character Orlando occupies the same type of social space as the critic Bachelard.

Another problem that arises in trying to apply Bachelard's *Poetics of Space* is that the tone of Rayland Hall's domestic sphere is itself far from this idealized vision of "home as haven" that Bachelard privileges. In fact, one could describe Rayland Hall as cold and impersonal, quite the antithesis of Bachelard's conception of such domestic space. This coldness in the domestic space is parallel to the coldness of Mrs. Rayland, symbol of a failing aristocratic line who, as a spinster, has denied herself both the consummation of marriage as well as the fulfillment of family life, which creates the crisis of inheritance at the heart of the novel. The coldness of Rayland Hall thus correlates with the coldness of familial relations, both in Mrs. Rayland's lack of immediate family and in her coolness to her extended family, as evidenced in her distanced relations with her cousins, the Somerive family. Thus, Orlando's marriage with Monimia and their claiming of Rayland Hall not only valorizes the rise of the middle class in its encroachment on traditionally aristocratic domains, both social and propertied, but also promises to revitalize the estate from being merely productive, to being reproductive, as symbolized by the birth of their son, thus likewise vindicating the new bourgeois cultural values inherent in the domestic and the familial. Moreover, since Smith has been shown to be critiquing the older, aristocratic order and supporting the rise of the new middle classes through the use of Rayland Hall as an emblem of social disorder, such a depiction of the old social order as cold and sterile in contrast to the vitality of the rising, bourgeois class as warmly domestic and fruitful further undergirds Smith's overall stance in relation to England's contemporary social stresses.

Since the sentimental novel relies on portraying in characters and evoking in readers such emotions as tenderness and compassion, nostalgic images of the home serve as a successful means to evoke emotion in the reader. Even in places where the paradigm fails to mesh, as in the decided lack of warmth in the portrayal of Rayland Hall under Mrs. Rayland's authority, the dissonance between the expectation and the reality of how warm a home should be is just as, or maybe more, powerful in conveying Charlotte Smith's critique of the failing aristocratic social order. Thus, the sense of safety and comfort—which the oneiric image of home invokes in the reader, contrasted to the prison-like conditions of Rayland Hall that Monimia experiences—evokes an even greater measure of empathy for Monimia's problems. This sharp contrast, between warm, homey expectation and the cold, sterile depiction of Rayland Hall, can be re-established at the resolution of *The Old Manor House* as the site for warm and familial domestic space. The reader's fervent hope in response to Monimia's pathetic plight as "prisoner" in the hall, that she and Orlando will be united in order to establish a more ideal home, is realized in the final act of Orlando being able to return with Monimia and their son to Rayland Hall, thus creating a satisfying, emotional conclusion to *The Old Manor House.*

**Works Cited**

Bachelard, Gaston. *The Poetics of Space.* Trans. Maria Jolas. Boston, MA: Beacon Press, 1994.
Bartolomeo, Joseph F. "Subversion of Romance in *The Old Manor House.*" *Studies in English Literature, 1500–1900* 33 (Summer 1993): 645–57.
Doyle, Jacqueline. "More Room of Her Own: Sandra Cisneros's *The House on Mango Street.*" *MELUS* 19 (Winter 1994): 5–35.

Elliott, Pat. "Charlotte Smith's Feminism: A Study of *Emmeline* and *Desmond*." *Living by the Pen: Early British Women Writers*. Ed. Dale Spender. New York: Teachers College Press, 1992.

Fletcher, Loraine. *Charlotte Smith: A Critical Biography*. New York: St. Martin's Press, 1998.

Fryer, Judith. *Felicitious Space: The Imaginative Structures of Edith Wharton and Willa Cather*. Chapel Hill, NC: University of North Carolina Press, 1986.

King, Kathryn R. "Of Needles and Pens and Women's Work." *Tulsa Studies in Women's Literature* 14 (Spring, 1995): 77–93.

Olivares, Julian. "Sandra Cisneros' *The House on Mango Street, and the Poetics of Space*." *The Americas Review* 15 (Fall–Winter 1987): 160–70.

Schofield, Mary Anne. "'The Witchery of Fiction': Charlotte Smith, Novelist." *Living by the Pen: Early British Women* Writers. Ed. Dale Spender. New York: Teachers College Press, 1992.

Smith, Charlotte. *The Old Manor House*. Ed. Jacqueline M. Labbe. Ontario: Broadview, 2002.

Chapter Seven

# The Second Soul-less Sex? Mary Wollstonecraft and the "Mahometan"

Carolyn A. Weber

> Thus Milton describes our first frail mother; though when he tells us that women are formed for softness and sweet attractive grace, I cannot comprehend his meaning, unless, in the true Mahometan strain, he meant to deprive us of souls, and insinuate that we were beings only designed by sweet attractive grace, and docile blind obedience, to gratify the senses of man when he can no longer soar on the wing of contemplation. (*VRW*, 5:88)[1]

In her response to Milton's Eve in the second chapter of her *Vindication of the Rights of Woman*, Mary Wollstonecraft draws on a popular dispute in her time over whether or not Islam denied women souls, as well as an afterlife.[2] Wollstonecraft's reference reveals her knowledge of soul theories, no matter how misconstrued, especially as they pertain to Eastern cultures. It also expresses her fear that Western patriarchal society will dismiss women as "soul-less," and therefore insignificant creatures (like the "creature" of her daughter's Frankenstein). Her comment implicitly connects education with the soul, or, to put it more precisely, the lack of an education with the state of being "soul-less." It is at once a remark inherently ingrained by social class, and yet framed within an ideology aimed at social freedom, particularly for women. For, in the tone of the latter, having a soul also means owning true independence, as well as "humanity."

Wollstonecraft's primary concern in her second *Vindication* therefore lies with the "ensouling" of women. Her act of writing extends this issue to the realm of expression, even craft, thus linking dignity and transcendence not only with the female soul, but also with the female artist's legacy of immortality through art. Wollstonecraft's entire argument consequently responds to a strategic allusion in the very second paragraph of her introduction. She almost immediately associates "Mahometanism" with the predominant Protestant British male ethic; that is, she uses Mohammedanism as a metaphor for British patriarchy at large, an oppressive system which denies women the inherent dignity of a soul, and therefore not only undermines their capacity for the transcendent experience, but also forfeits their "immortality":

> In a treatise, therefore, on female rights and manners, the works which have been particularly written for their improvement must not be overlooked; especially when it is asserted, in direct terms, that the minds of women are enfeebled by false refinement; that the books of instruction, written by men of genius, have had the same tendency as more frivolous productions; and that, in the true style of Mahometanism, they are treated as a kind of subordinate beings, and not as a part of the human species, when improvable reason is allowed to be the dignified distinction which raises men above the brute creation, and puts a natural scepter in a feeble hand. (*VRW*, 5:71)

Wollstonecraft's evocation of the Mohammedan deserves careful attention, as it has both political and spiritual repercussions for gendered notions of transcendence, immortality, and the soul in the Romantic period. It also reveals how discourses of "religious" scandal became a vogue power-play dynamic among Romantic writers, and a form of subversion and sympathy for women writers in particular.

It is important to first qualify just how Wollstonecraft is approaching the term "Mahometan" as this helps to explain her relatively liberal and misinformed use of it. For many writing in Wollstonecraft's time, the various sects of Eastern religions appeared "blurred," and knowledge being perpetuated about them was often severely misinformed. For instance, numerous dictionaries and religious compendiums of the period either do not yet have entries for various Eastern sects, or they misrepresent them by our modern standards. For example, Mohammedans are often recognized as following a caste system, and Hindus are primarily defined by their vegetarianism. Moreover, many popular travel narratives and missionary records of the period, while often sympathetic or partially defensive of the East, present confused or censored renditions of religious rites, behaviors, and beliefs.[3] Some misconceptions and exaggerations bordered on what we would now deem the comical, if they were not so simultaneously alarming. For instance, the frontispiece to a London 1824 volume entitled *China: Its Costume, Arts and Manufactures* bears an illustration with the inscription "Mahometan Woman & Son." Such a prefatory picture to a volume on local customs and the economy of the Chinese misleadingly implies China to be primarily Mohammedan in its national religion.

Wollstonecraft's working knowledge of the term "Mahometan" therefore may have been unwittingly tainted by precisely her own research, and certainly would have been shaped by the many notions circulating in European society at the time. Such misinformed terminology aside, however, Wollstonecraft may have been purposefully evoking colloquial associations with the term to suit her popular audience, as will be explored shortly in relation to her dialogue with Burke and the Hastings trial. Wollstonecraft's specific use of the word "Mahomet," as opposed to other sects often referred to at the time, such as "Hindoo" or "Brahmin," would have been more powerful in terms of arresting the audience's attention. Its derivation from "Mohammed" sets a "foreign" savior-figure in juxtaposition with the British (nationalist) Christ, so central to Burkean discourse and evocative of the political tension involving Richard Price and the Dissenters that helped inspire her first *Vindication*. Furthermore, the name implies the "Imposter," a popular British title given to the Eastern prophet in Wollstonecraft's day. "Mahomet," for instance, is the last entry among predominantly famous lunatics in M. Aiken's *Memoirs of Religious Imposters, from the Seventh to the Nineteenth Century*.[4]

Wollstonecraft's use of the term "Mahometan," and all its specific as well as diffuse associations, reveals a complex appeal to both sympathy and shock in her call for women's equality. Wollstonecraft's "Mahometan strain" complicates the field of Romantic orientalism by presenting a discourse that at once operates within, and yet challenges, Said's concept of orientalism as presenting distinct gendered notions of the "other." In Wollstonecraft's framework, the Western patriarchy is not portrayed as omnipotent in contrast with a more sexually unbridled and yet ultimately impotent or effeminate Eastern patriarchy. Furthermore, while she does present Western women as eager to be dominated and unable to think for themselves, these critiques are contrasted with the liberated woman's potential. The English woman is thus "orientalized" by an extension of sympathy, but not "orientalized" in terms of the Saidian association with subservience. Both the Western and the Eastern "phallus" is presented not as something to be feared or revered, but as an oppressive tool to be removed, or an obstacle to be overcome, both for the good of the individual (female and male) and therefore for all of society and the future of the nation. Wollstonecraft's appeal to the East suggests that the West is in fact not strongly, manfully, or truthfully free. In fact, such projected and perpetuated "manliness" (a system whose lifeblood women are equally responsible for sustaining, especially in their cultivation of an insubstantial "womanliness") lies at the root of the problem in attaining a radically true egalitarian democracy. In this sense, Wollstonecraft's orientalism seems more ambiguous, and holds repercussions for studying the presentation of, or appeal to, the "exotic other" by the "domestic other" in feminist discourses. I am reminded here of Marilyn Butler's revisioning of Said's *Orientalism* in her discussion of imaginative literature in English on the East following the 1790s. Whereas Butler identifies this orientalism as "intellectually ambitious," however, I would add it is also "ambiguous," especially once it enters the sphere of evoking gendered constructions of the "other" within self-consciously political gendered discourses.[5]

Several avenues exist through which Wollstonecraft would have gained at least a colloquial knowledge of the term "Mahometan." The Britain of her age perpetuated a desire to imitate what was considered a more sophisticated French culture. Eighteenth-century France was undergoing what Raymond Schwab would term an "oriental renaissance" comparable to the earlier "classical renaissance." It would be marked by Antoine Galland's famous "translation" of the multi-volumed *Arabian Nights Entertainment* and the consequent popularity of the genre of the "oriental tale," in whose development, as Butler has noted, "accuracy to modern Middle Eastern realities played a minimal part" (396). This fascination would only be fed by the French Revolution, and would increase reactions to British empiricism as trade and governing relationships with "exotic" colonies become more publicized and politicized. The British craved knowledge of the East, but it was a knowledge that lay in tension between "truth" and "fiction" as contextualized within the wider European rage with comparative religion and mythology. The period from the 1780s to the 1820s saw a sharp rise in conscientious oriental scholarship, seen, for example, in the popularity of Sir William Jones's Asiatic Society of Bengal (which rose in competition to the Society of Antiquaries, consisting of a London circle of liberal Francophiles). Yet it also hosted the era of the long allegorical poem in imaginative dialogue with the East. Within her own personal circle, however, Wollstonecraft's relationships with Mrs. Inchbald and Henry Fuseli offer examples of possible sources for Mahommedism. Mrs. Inchbald's extensive theater repertoire included a scandalous play based on the life of Mohammed.[6] It is also possible that Henry Fuseli's use of the vampiric pose was influenced by various beliefs about Mohammedism circulating at the time.[7]

For the scope of this discussion, however, I will focus on a popular source for knowledge of the Mohammedans in Wollstonecraft's lifetime: the East India Company. But what, I will argue, renders her reference to Mohammedans particularly loaded is how Wollstonecraft uses such verbal and spiritual allusions in her fight for the female cause to evoke, engage in, and draw upon the trial of Warren Hastings, as headed most predominantly in terms of memorable oration by Edmund Burke. On one hand, her analogy between the "Mahometan" spiritual system and the British social system is a tactic that not only highlights the irony of the relationship between church and state, but which also builds support for alleviating the oppression of women in Britain through a sympathetic identification with "other" oppressed colonies. On the other hand, however, her seemingly casual dropping of such an "Anti-Christ" name provides the shock value necessary in cultivating the passionate attraction of her argument. Wollstonecraft is, after all, entering a political forum based on a thinly-masked emotional ethos, as epitomized in the discourse of such contenders as Price, Paine, and Burke, and played out even more theatrically in the famous court debates of the period. But the effects of the shock value are designed to go even further: Wollstonecraft appeals to a nationalistic sense of what is "right and just" and British "duty." She does this by assuming *and* appropriating the nationalistic patriarchal discourse, so representative of the exact forces against which she claims women, and all of society, must labour against to reform, and that is so symbolically embodied—especially to Wollstonecraft—in a political figure such as Burke.

Warren Hastings's ambiguous figure, in contrast, offers Wollstonecraft a fascinating culmination point on which to stand, yet again, against Burke and his symbolic orthodoxy. For while Hastings's motives and actions "typified tyranny and plunder" in the eyes of his political accusers, he also had a reputation for being popular, well-liked, and good-natured. Much of the public, while pitted against him, also found themselves drawn to him, not unlike Fanny Burney, for instance, who would find him "so mild, so gentle, so extremely pleasing in his manners" (Moon, 328–29). The cognitive dissonance was contagious, and only served to fuel the emotionalism of the courtroom politics. Even Thomas Babington Macaulay found himself at a loss to reconcile his preconceived notion of Hastings's character with the actual reputation that he had left behind him in Bengal (Macanlay, "Warren Hastings"). In his famous rendition of the trial, Macaulay would write that Hastings "looked like a great man, and not like a bad man" ("The Impeachment of Warren Hastings," 4). Some public opinion swayed so far as to construct the impeached ruler who had worked himself up the ranks of the East India Company as a well-intentioned "underdog," a devoted employee of the crown who was now being "raped" by the system, whether it be the Whigs, external political enemies to the Company, or envious traitors from within the Company. In fact, public sympathy grew for Hastings in ironic direct proportion to his financial devastation incurred by the long, drawn-out trial; almost a decade later, he emerged penniless, but more popular than ever. In spite of the horrific crimes against humanity brought against him in the form of charges of exploitation, exhortation, and violence against the Indian people, many of his policies and actions could also be read as sympathetic toward the same people while balanced as a compromise in duty to the British Crown. He was praised by many for having brought the Company's government in Bengal safely through the critical years of war, saving it from bankruptcy and chaos. Although his extension of British dominion over the whole of India could be seen as powered by selfish greed and the desire to gain favor with the Crown, it also resulted in acts that could be interpreted as having been done in the interest of preserving India's dignity, to at least the extent possible given the colonial situation (for example, retaining the nominal status of Indian rulers who had survived, but reducing their role to that of mere puppets). Hastings claimed that he desired none of these things, but that after thirteen years of unrest and rule in Bengal, the establishment in India of an essentially British administration, though far from perfect, was inevitable. Wollstonecraft surely must have felt much political, if not personal, empathy with a portrait such as Moon paints of Hastings:

> In [Hastings's] view, British rule suffered from "many radical and incurable defects," could not be lasting, and was of questionable benefit to Britain herself. The most that wise policy could achieve was to minimize its evils, to make the best of such temporary advantages as it offered and "to protract that decay which sooner or later must end it." (Moon, 4)

In such ways, Hastings represented the radical who threatened British strongholds by challenging the "mythos" of the East fabricated and upheld by the British, and even cultivated as a certain imaginative propaganda. Hastings claimed a genuine interest in the Indian civilization dating from his early days at Kasimbazar. For instance, upon his return to England in 1765, he tried to implement the study of Persian at Oxford. Although his attempt was unsuccessful, it did draw the attention of Dr. Johnson, who later encouraged him in a letter to continue contributing to, and expanding upon, the "acts and opinions of a race of men, from whom very little has been hitherto derived" (Moon, 350). Significantly, Jonathon Scott would dedicate as a "token of grateful respect" his translation of the *Arabian Nights* to Hastings, the 1800 edition of which Byron had in his library. The trial of Hastings was a timely backdrop and incentive for Wollstonecraft's interests. His charge with "high crimes and misdemeanours" would be so controversial because of the "relativity" of justice such circumstances raised; tensions played out, particularly between Hastings and Burke, were centered on a "politics of sympathy" that oscillated between not only the domestic and the "other," but also government interests and individual, and so universal, human rights.

Keeping all this in mind, how is Wollstonecraft's seemingly passing reference to the "Mahometan" even remotely indicative of her construction of women and their immortality? By "immortality" in this discussion, what is meant is a "social immortality" in addition to a purely spiritual one. The two might be argued to be necessarily connected. But in her implicit analogy between British orthodoxy, or the English Church, and the "Mahometan strain," Wollstonecraft is taking the Romantic impulse to secularize the spiritual even further by arguing that the same system which claims that we are each capable of having a soul that can be educated and thereby "saved" deprives women, in reality, of both an education and therefore a true "soul," in terms of both spiritual and social significance. For when women's artistic and political productivity is curbed, so are their legacies or "immortality."

"It is time to effect a revolution in female manners—time to restore to them their lost dignity—and make them, as a part of the human species, labour by reforming themselves to reform the world" (*VRW*, 5:45). In her rousing call to arms, Wollstonecraft links cause with effect in a way that dissolves any arbitrary distinctions between the public, or larger social, and private or domestic spheres: that is, she asserts that the education and reform of each individual woman will have universal consequences. This seemingly at first private act—the education of each woman, whether mother, sister, wife or spinster—will evolve into a power that will dismantle the currently destructive system ftom within:

> If men be demi-gods—why let us serve them! And if the dignity of the female soul be as disputable as that of animals—if their reason does not afford sufficient light to direct their conduct whilst unerring instinct is denied—they are surely of all creatures the most miserable! and, bent beneath the iron hand of destiny, must submit to be a *fair defect* in creation. But to justify the ways of Providence respecting them, by pointing out some irrefragable reason for thus making such a large portion of mankind accountable and not accountable, would puzzle the subtilest casuist. (*VRW*, 5:45–46)

As Wollstonecraft's rejoinder to *Paradise Lost* indicates, the fact that women have been reduced to animals from a social want of cultivating reason is the result of a system whose injustice, hypocrisy, and own irrationality would confound even the arch-enemy of the great English epic.

But Wollstonecraft's concern does not end with the ameliorative effects on our social system for subsequent generations. Her argument holds consequences for the female writer in particular, and her "educated" soul, which will not only affect our intellectual inheritance, but is the channel through which the female artist will gain her own "immortality." These are recurring themes throughout much of Wollstonecraft's writing. For instance, in her *Advertisement to Mary*, Wollstonecraft explains that writing is a spiritual process, one that should come from the soul and reflect its source: "Those compositions only have power to delight, and carry us willing captives, where the soul of the author is exhibited, and animates the hidden springs" (*Works: Mary*, 1:3). For Wollstonecraft, the text is a metempsychosal template, which is inhabited by the soul of the author. It then follows that the author must cultivate a worthy soul, if what is to be written should bear any worth. Body and spirit become increasingly double-edged in terms of their relation to writing as a metaphor in itself for the soul's journey/development. The body of a text takes on a spirit of its own, as infused into it by the author. Thus, the education of the individual (especially the author) during life's journey is what constitutes the true value of that individual (and thus, a text)—this education creates the "soul" that so differentiates us from the animals, and which animates our intellectual heritage. Such views hold consequences for shifts in attitudes toward parenting during that period that extend beyond dialogues with Rousseau or the popular manners and educational handbooks for the young. Rather, they bind creation with procreation, highlighting the emerging social, and even nationalistic, importance of an "educated" mother. The ramifications of this set up the domestic space as a powerful headquarters for the future of a race; they also set mothers in positions of spiritual importance in terms of their children's education—a position traditionally held by the father as the "religious" epicenter and teacher of the family.

Repeatedly throughout her *Vindication* Wollstonecraft highlights the unenlightened woman's "soul-lessness" by associating her with the brute. In one example, she sympathetically connects women with animals in terms of their mutual exploitation and cruel handling by men: "This habitual cruelty," she argues, "is first caught at school, where it is one of the rare sports of the boys to torment the miserable brutes that fall in their way. The transition, as they grow up, from barbarity to brutes to domestic tyranny over wives, children, and servants, is very easy" (*VRW*, 5:172). Fittingly, as a former schoolteacher, Wollstonecraft identifies the actual condoning and systemization of such male behavior by connecting it with unchecked youth and school, and furthermore suggests its perpetuation into less "physical" and yet therefore even more essential, and thus more disturbing, social "institutions" (such as marriage). Consequently, Wollstonecraft's cry for "humanity to animals," as based on her assertion that "it is not at present one of our national virtues," suggests an encoded critique of British society's treatment of women, and a call for reform in manners not only in the education of one another, but also in our care for one another. Like Burke's argument that "[o]ur liberty is as much in danger as our honour and our national character" in his speech on the fourth day of impeachment at the Hastings trial (Thursday, May 7,1789), Wollstonecraft appeals to a sense of national character and pride (*WEB*, 10:450).[8] Education is the most fundamental way of raising women's souls from the brutish to the divine. Wollstonecraft situates—and thereby attempts to further justify—her *Vindication*'s call for the "legitimacy" of women's souls through education within a nationalistic petition.[9]

Susan Wolfson argues that "for all its transcendental reference, the idea of 'soul' had substantial socio-historical resonance" (33–68). With this in mind, Wolfson examines gendered (and ungendered), as opposed to "sexed," notions of the soul held by Romantic writers: "In male-authored texts, classical paradigms and the linguistic precedent of the feminine anima of Latin endorse gendering the soul as feminine ... For women writers, moreover, the sexed soul is inherently unstable. Their texts both disclose the contradictions of gendered definitions and reflect the ambivalence of their own desires" (34, 37). On the one hand, these female writers wrestle with the burden of contradiction and alienation within their very own identity construction. On the other hand, this very alienation offers a position from which to query the idea of a determining sexual identity in the soul (57) and, I will add to the argument, social and spiritual ramifications for "immortality" as well as the soul as "character" based on gendered distinctions in socializing, education, and production.

Andrew Elfenbein argues that what is so interesting about the eighteenth century is that neither "masculinity" nor "femininity" was a fixed category. Rather, gender definitions varied in each discourse, as authors adapted them to differ from, as well as to complement, one another. Elfenbein uses this debunking of a simple homo/hetero binary in eighteenth-century writing to contextualize his observation that "For Wollstonecraft, the topic that encouraged the most experimentation with sex and gender roles was that of genius" (228). The concepts of "genius" and the "soul" share a distinct and complicated history; but I raise the issue of genius because it was one of great importance to Wollstonecraft, as the nurturing and cultivation of genius was inexorably tied to the recognition, value, and even immortality of one's soul. As Elfenbein points out, eighteenth-century audiences were fascinated by examples of "natural" genius, and Wollstonecraft was no exception. As a governess in Ireland, she read Hugh Blair's lectures on genius and taste (*MWL*, 138). [10] Blair distinguishes between the two: whereas genius involves production, taste involves consumption (1:52). In the face of her anxiety about women's inability to produce because of various social pressures and restrictions, however, genius loses its emphasis on productivity. What proves most attractive to Wollstonecraft, rather, is the notion that genius was potentially free from restrictive gender associations.

In her novel *Mary, a Fiction*, when the invalid Henry tries to convince the heroine that she should one day be reconciled with her husband, Mary cries that it would be death to her soul to do so (*Works: Mary*, 1.67). In one way, Wollstonecraft is subscribing to her age's belief that because of his/her "divine" gifts, a genius had certain dispensations, and therefore existed outside conventions, such as marriage, which were believed to stifle such a unique spirit. As Elfenbein supports, Wollstonecraft repeatedly throughout her writings connects the soul and genius through liberation. This form of liberation is what I believe lies at the heart of her call to and for women in her second *Vindication*. Wollstonecraft fictionally depicts the powerful climax that finally attaining a "true soul" brings for a woman in her novel *Maria, or the Wrongs of Woman*. The scene occurs after Maria vows to leave her husband upon learning, significantly, that he is planning to sell her body. With her removal of her wedding ring, she undergoes her "awakening":

> "Was it possible? Was I, indeed free?" ... How I had panted for liberty—liberty, that I would have purchased at any price, but that of my own esteem! I rose, and shook myself; opened the window, and methought the air never smelled so sweet. The face of heaven grew fairer as I viewed it, and clouds seemed to flit away obedient to my wishes, to give my soul room to expand. I was all soul ... (*Works: Maria*, 1:152)

The fact that Wollstonecraft illustrates the true birth of the soul in sexually climactic terms that frees one from not only marriage, but all such gender restrictions, foreshadows Coleridge's famous observation on the androgyny of the mind that Virginia Woolf would later revisit (interestingly, Coleridge regarded Wollstonecraft as a "genius"). It also recalls Wollstonecraft's recurring biblical allusions to the irrelevance of gender distinctions in the hereafter. It could be extended, then, that for Wollstonecraft educating the sexes equally, and the equality, in turn, that this would produce, is a necessary preparation for the (ironically ungendered) immortal state of our souls.

If liberty is a necessary prerequisite for the legitimacy of the soul, then oppression can only lead to spiritual, as well as intellectual and physical, degradation. Wollstonecraft's opening to Chapter Four of her second *Vindication* suggests that it was written against Burke in its association of the present, as of yet unreformed, British social system with the oppression of women:

> That woman is naturally weak, or degraded by a concurrence of circumstances, is, I think, clear. But this position I shall simply contrast with a conclusion, which I have ftequently heard fall from sensible men in favor of an aristocracy: that the mass of mankind cannot be anything, or the obsequious slaves, who patiently allow themselves to be driven forward, would feel their own consequence, and spurn their chains. Men, they further observe, submit everywhere to oppression, when they have only to lift up their heads to throw off the yoke; yet, instead of asserting their birthright, they quietly lick the dust, and say, let us eat and drink, for to-morrow we die. Women, I argue from analogy, are degraded by the same propensity to enjoy the present moment; and, at last, despise the freedom which they have not sufficient virtue to struggle to attain.

I argue that just as Wollstonecraft wrote her first *Vindication* (1790) in response to Burke's *Reflections on the French Revolution*, so her second *Vindication* (1792) was largely shaped by Burke's impeachment and the subsequent trial of Warren Hastings (1787–95), who was the first governor-general of India from 1774 to 1784.

Hastings resigned in 1784 and returned to England, where his longtime political enemies, Edmund Burke and Sir Philip Francis, the latter whom he had wounded in a duel in India, charged him with high crimes and misdemeanors. Hastings was impeached in 1787; the trial, begun in 1788, ended with acquittal in 1795, despite the bitter prosecution of Burke, Francis, Richard B. Sheridan, and Charles James Fox. The early years of Hastings's trial paralleled a pivotal and loaded time in Wollstonecraft's own life. After traveling to Lisbon to be with her best friend, Fanny Blood, who would die shortly thereafter in childbirth, Wollstonecraft returned to London to find the school that she had set up with her sisters failing.

As a result, she undertook a brief stint as a governess in Ireland (from which she was dismissed), and came to live in a house let by Joseph Johnson on George Street in Blackfriars around the time that the trial of Hastings begins. She wrote her *Vindication of the Rights of Woman* at the height of her ardor for the French cause. After its publication in 1792, she set off to live in revolutionary France, meeting Gilbert Imlay in 1793 and having his child the following year. She would not return to London until 1795, when the trial was drawing to a close. Everyone who was someone—whether of intellect, politics, art, royalty, or sensibility—was present at the impeachment: the company ranged from Sheridan to Reynolds to Siddons, to the Prince of Wales himself. It is not known for certain whether or not Wollstonecraft was present on those early days of the process in February of 1788; however, it is tempting to think that she and Godwin perhaps discussed the popular trial when they first met at Johnson's in 1791. Wollstonecraft's position in revolutionary France during the latter years of the trial, and her stances as a pregnant, outcast woman, no less, would have certainly granted her a sort of sardonic and perceptive distance to the entire fiasco. Perhaps this was a contributing factor to the retreat from political writing that she takes upon returning to London. While a case exists that her absence ftom England during the rest of the trial may have lessened its immediate impact upon her, it is also possible that her position would have made its initial melodrama, and its subsequently various conveyed renditions, all the more highly imaginative and provocative, if not increasingly ironic to a woman of Wollstonecraft's perceptive receptivity and shrewd eye for personal, as well as public, politics.

However, Wollstonecraft's initial proximity to the Hastings trial when it was at its most dramatic pitch, coupled with her reaction to Burke in her first *Vindication*, certainly must have primed her interest in the trial, and in the strategic opportunities for audience appeal that it offered. Her implicit dialogue with Hastings's trial takes multifarious forms. Burke maintained a keen interest in India for many years, but it was during the trial of Hastings, Brian Young argues, that Burke made himself an authority on Hinduism, almost to the point of becoming a self-appointed apologist for the "Mahometan" (95).[11] At first glance, Wollstonecraft's references to the Mohammedan seem merely misinformed and derogatory, implying a colonial dismissal of the true complexity of the Islam religion. Such references also seem to simply substitute one patriarchal form of the oppression of women (the British, or Protestant) with another (the Indian, or Islamic). However, her strategic alignment of women with the cultural "other" proves to be more loaded than it at first may seem. She is, in fact, playing Burke at his own game, using his own language and knowledge for her own cause. When she writes that women have been oppressed by the production of men—that the proliferation of conduct books by educated men has ironically kept women from being educated themselves—and that such a system "puts a natural scepter in a feeble hand," one cannot help but draw the parallels between the exploitation of India by both trade and government, and the exploitation of women by the politics of production and consumption (or genius and taste). Money, the demon on which Burke pins all of Hastings's evildoings, is also at the heart of how men control women in the sphere of literary immortality as well as in a pecuniary society still operating, for instance, in rules such as primogeniture.

Moreover, how can Wollstonecraft's emphasis on "scepter" be read without recalling Burke's famous replies between absolute authority and arbitrary power in his attack on Hastings, the latter of which he accuses Hastings of using to justify his acts of despotism? At the second day of impeachment, Saturday, February 16, 1788, Burke announces "We have no arbitrary power to give, because arbitrary power is a thing which neither any man can hold nor any man can give ... Those who give and those who receive arbitrary power are alike criminal; and there is no man but is bound to resist it to the best of his power, wherever it shall show its face to the world" (*WEB*, 9:455–58). In his argument that no man should rule over another as this usurps God's will and omnipotent position, Burke blames both the oppressors and those who would allow themselves to be oppressed. Wollstonecraft infuses her critique of gender power relations in the *Vindication* with a similar reasoning. Thus Burke's assertion becomes the premise of Wollstonecraft's critique of, and call to, women as well as men in her second *Vindication*. The adoption and application is unique; yet she also gleans attention and validity from Burke's own oratorical power and reputation—someone who was, according to Macaulay, "in amplitude of comprehension and richness of imagination superior to every orator, ancient or modern" ("Impeachment of Hastings," 150). As it is an obvious symbol of male potency, Wollstonecraft may also have been playing with her audience's intrigue and yet offence at the "lingam," or the "divine phallus" of the creator god Shiva (this, of course, gives an entirely different twist to the "divine right to rule"). In his *Historical Disquisition Concerning the Knowledge which the Ancients had of India*, published in 1791, William Robertson praises much of India's religious culture along with Hindu and Mohammedan laws and literature; but he is also critical of its superstitions and objected to the "sensuality" of many Eastern forms of worship (interestingly, although Robertson takes particular offence at the prostitutes who danced and sang in temples, it seems that he witnessed them often).

This dynamic of attraction and repulsion signifies the British audience's ambiguous fascination with, and yet repugnance at, such exotic religions. Wollstonecraft knows her audience, and I believe is playing it, like Burke, to its highest imaginative pitch for the sympathetic ends of her argument. In her dedication to the Bishop Talleyrand-Perigord, reason "loudly demands Justice for one half of the human race" (*VRW*, 5:67) This "Justice" is what Burke hangs his entire argument upon at Hastings's trial: "There is one thing, and one thing only, which defies all mutation: that which existed before the world, and will survive the fabric of the world itself—I mean justice ..." Just as Burke announces to the tribunal of lords that "[w]e commit safely the interests of India and humanity into your hands," so Wollstonecraft aligns her cause for women with the larger cause for humanity (*WEB*, 10:142). Often, by substituting "women" for "India" in Burke's speech, we arrive at the essence of Wollstonecraft's argument: she adopts such rhetoric and applies it to the politics of sex rather than to that of nations. As a result, she draws on the notion of India as submissive, raped "female," implying that this outrage has its counterpart or echo in the less seemingly "shocking" and yet equally horrendous condition of the oppressed women of England—a condition that remains neglected precisely because it is domestic and diurnal. Thus Burke's argument for the upholding of justice in India as having universal ramifications finds its gendered counterpart in Wollstonecraft's appropriated rhetoric.

Such evocations ultimately prove to be a subversive act against Burke, and all he so vividly represents, as Wollstonecraft makes a sympathetic identification between the plight of women in patriarchal Britain with that of the Indian people who are exploited under British trade and governmental rule. Considering Wollstonecraft's rhetoric from this point of view complicates further constructions of "woman" as "Other" in British Romanticism, in which the feminine becomes aligned with what is "foreign," thereby encouraging connections between the plight of the woman in patriarchal society and that society's reaction to other cultures."[12]

By the 1780s, with Britain's confidence in long-distance rule shaken by the situation in America, a general suspicion surely grew regarding the immense patronage of the East India Company being twisted to serve the political ends of the government. In addition, there was a growing humanitarian feeling which led to attacks upon the company for neglecting—or outraging—the basic rights and decencies of the Indian population in areas of British influence. By suggestively aligning women with the Indian population currently being exploited by the British, Wollstonecraft generates sympathy for her cause. Like Burke, Wollstonecraft has a keen ability to "read" her own audience. And like Burke, Wollstonecraft is a sharp marketer of her words. Not only is she writing quickly and in the heat of the moment herself—the *Vindications* representing a sort of "emotion recollected in alacrity"—but she is also highly aware of how to move, and even manipulate, her audience based on their sensibilities and the "theatricizing" of the current political milieu. As Macaulay would write of the trial's opening day on the 13th of February, 1788: "there never was a spectacle so well calculated to strike a highly cultivated, a reflecting, an imaginative mind" ("Impeachment of Hastings," 146). I say "theatricizing" rather than simply "dramatizing" because of the grandeur of spectacle that the former term more immediately suggests. After all, Macaulay's report of Hastings's trial smacks more of live theater (or more precisely, of pomp pageantry and mystery play) than of the dreary proceedings usually associated with the Shelleyan or Dickensian courts:

> The charges and the answers of Hastings were first read. The ceremony occupied two whole days, and was rendered less tedious than it would otherwise have been by the silver voice and just emphasis of Cowper, the clerk of the court, a near relation of the amiable poet. On the third day, Burke rose ... The energy and pathos of the great orator extorted expressions of unwonted admiration from the stern and hostile Chancellor, and, for a moment, seemed to pierce even the resolute heart of the defendant. The ladies in the galleries, unaccustomed to such displays of eloquence, excited by the solemnity of the occasion, and perhaps not unwilling to display their taste and sensibility, were in a state of uncontrollable emotion. Handkerchiefs were pulled out; smelling bottles were handed round; hysterical sobs and screams were heard: and Mrs. Sheridan was carried out in a fit." (150–51)

With its fainting women unable to cope and the Christ-like rendition of Burke, the scene is a Wollstonecraftian nightmare. And yet all these elements probably combined to make it fodder for her cause. As Burke claims on the fourth day, "We know, I say, and feel the force of money" (*WEB*, 10:450).

Through her use of comparisons with such "unorthodox" religious figures as the Mohammedan, Wollstonecraft appeals to a discourse of scandal that characterized the Romantics (not unlike P.B. Shelley writing "atheist" in a guest book whilst abroad), which she nevertheless appropriates to her own distinct ends. She appeals to her readership through both shock and intrigue—shock, that the domestic should be so outrageously compared to a foreign and monstrous form of religious and societal assumptions, and intrigue at the introduction of such "foreign" elements. Through the latter, Wollstonecraft particularly subverts Burke's claim of liberty and rights for all; for, what if what was deemed to be so monstrous happening "far and away," and which could captivate its audience with its gothic horrors, was actually also happening in the domestic sphere, albeit in a less "dramatic" yet equally insidious way? The language of her argument consequently raises a nagging question in her reader's mind: was it possible that what we have been shown to be happening far from home is in fact taking place—and is politically instutionalized as well as perpetuated socially—to one half of Britain's own race on a daily basis? Are not the souls of all people, male and female, at stake—not only in terms of their religious and spiritual constructions, but also in light of their human right to dignity, as well as their immortal social legacy? Does this not also apply to all those whom some system has "de-souled," and so rendered unthinking, inconsequential, brutish, edible—in all sorts of "consumerist" ways? Conversely, what if the subjection of women was not only a British issue, but also a universal weakness in the world's system? This would prove a particularly forceful topic within Romanticism, fascinated as it was by comparative religion. In her domestic wake-up call, Wollstonecraft also appeals to the British empiric desire, even ego, to act as a model of sophistication, a touchstone of decency, even as a cultural savior, to other countries more in need of being properly "civilized."

Inherent, then, in her association between the women of Britain and the "Mahometan" dismissal of their souls, is Wollstonecraft's (in the tradition of Condorcet) radical critique of her own nation: Britain, for all its "civilization" and obedience to a right "God," Wollstonecraft asserts, is based on an implicit and unspoken gendered "caste system" of its own. Women are rendered "untouchables" by their omission from intellectual pursuits and true training in the virtues. And thus, these ignoble—even animalistic—souls can only, whether knowingly or not, debase all they come in contact with: "For they [women] are now made so inferior by ignorance and low desires, as not to deserve to be ranked with them [educated men]; or, by the serpentine wrigglings of cunning they mount the tree of knowledge, and only acquire sufficient to lead men astray" (*VRW*, 5:173). Tellingly, the summer before her death, Mary Wollstonecraft would write to a friend: "I am not fond of vindications" (*MWL*, 413).

**Notes**

1  Mary Wollstonecraft is referring to John Milton's *Paradise Lost*, IV. 295–98. All citations from texts by Wollstonecraft are taken trom *The Works of Mary Wollstonecraft*, cited as *MWB* in the text.

2  Wollstonecraft makes a similar reference in the second paragraph of her intrduction. Janet Todd notes that the misunderstanding was largely based on confusion over the concept of the caste system. See *VRW* 5:88n.

3  See, for example, *The Mythology and Rites of the British Druids* and Robbins, *The Religions and Religious Ceremonies of All Nations*. For a general discussion of such misconceptions, as well as general knowledge of Eastern religions in England at the time , see Drew, *India and the Romantic Imagination*; Young, "'The Lust of Empire and Religious Hate'"; Collini, *History, Religion and Culture*; Marshall, *The British Discovery of Hinduism in the Eighteenth Century*. There was also a rise in such dictionaries and encyclopedias in the United States during this period, see, eg., Adams, *A Dictionary of All Religions*; Wright, *A Lecture on the Condition of Women*.

4  Though published in 1822, its individual essays date from the 1790s to 1814.

5  In her essay "Orientalism," Butler disagrees with Said's argument that the West created an alter ego by which to "control" the East that was "effeminate" and "weak." Rather, she sees the English Romantic poetry produced in discourse with the East as powerfully imaginative and "an intellectually ambitious strain of

Romanticism," (397–98).

6 Mrs. Elizabeth Inchbald, whom Godwin had courted and whom Wollstonecraft referred to as "Mrs. Perfection," wrote a play based on James Miller's translation of Voltaire's story of the Mohammed (1744); in her introductory notes, Inchbald not only gives a relatively derogatory version of Mahomet's character and life, but she also describes the volatile history of the dramatized story in Ireland. The play went on to be performed in England and in America. See Inchbald.

7 For connections between vampirism and Mahommedism, see Thorslev (9).

8 All references to Edmund Burke's speeches are taken from *The Works of the Right Honorable Edmund Burke* and will be cited "*WEB*" parenthetically with the volume number folowed by the page number.

9 It is interesting to note here that the translator Thomas Taylor, with whom Wollstonecraft lived briefly (and supposedly platonically) publishes a parody of Wollstonecraft entitled *A Vindication of the Rights of Brutes* in 1792; its central trope is metempsychosis. I examine their relationship based on a shared interest in soul theories further in a forthcoming article.

10 Mary Wollstonecraft to Everina Wollstonecraft, February 12, 1787 in *Collected Letters of Mary Wollstonecraft* (413). Subsequent references to Wollstonecraft's letters (*MWL*) are from this edition.

11 For Burke's speeches during the trial of Warren Hastings, see vols 5 and 6 of P. J. Marshall, ed. *Complete Writings of Edmund Burke*.

12 This topic has been heavily discussed since the rise in feminist and cultural studies; see, eg., Gamer, Kahane, and Sprengnether, *The (M)other Tongue*; Jardine, *Gynesis*; Chesler, *Women and Madness* (38); Jacobus, *Reading Woman*.

**Works Cited**

Adams, Hannah. *A Dictionary of All Religions and Reigious Denominations, Jewish, Heathen, Mahomentan, and Christian, Ancient and Modern*. New York and Boston, 1817.

Aikin, M. *Memoirs of Religious Imposters, from the Seventh to the Nineteenth Century*. London, 1822.

Blair, Hugh. *Lectures on Rhetoric and Belles Lettres*. 3 vols. Philadelphia: James Kay, 1844 facsimile edn. New York: Garland, 1970.

Burke, Edmund. Speeches during Warren Hastings trial. *Complete Works of Edmund Burke*. vols 5 and 6. Ed. P.J. Marshall.

Burke, Edmund. *The Works of the Right Honorable Edmund Burke*. 12 vols. Boston: Little, Brown and Company, 1899.

Butler, Marilyn. "Orientalism." In *The Romantic Period*. Ed. David B. Pirie. London: Penguin, 1994.

Chesler, Phyllis. *Women and Madness*. New York and London: Four Walls Eight Windows, 1997.

Collini, Stefan. *History, Religion and Culture: British Intellectual History 1750–1950*. Cambridge: Cambridge UP, 2000.

Daries, Edward. *The Mythology and Rites of the British Druids, Ascertained by*

*National Documents, and Compared with the General Traditions and Customs of Heathenism, as Illustrated by the most Eminent Antiquaries of our Age.* London, 1809.

Drew, John. *India and the Romantic Imagination.* Oxford: Oxford UP, 1987.

Elfenbein, Andrew. "Mary Wollstonecraft and the Sexuality of Genius." *The Cambridge Companion to Mary Wollstonecraft.* Cambridge: Cambridge UP, 2002. 228.

Garner, Shirley Nelson, Claire Kahane, and Madelon Sprengnether, Eds. *The (M)other Tongue: Essays in Feminist Psychoanalytic Interpretations.* Ithaca, NY: Cornell UP, 1985.

Inchbald, Elizabeth. *Mahomet, the Imposter; A Tragedy in Five Acts.* In *The British Theatre; or A Collection of Plays, which are Acted at the Theatres Royal, Drury Lane, Convent Garden, and Haymarket, with Biographical and Critical Remarks by Mrs. Inchbald.* London, 1808.

Jacobins, Mary. *Reading Woman: Essays in Feminist Criticism.* New York: Columbia UP, 1986.

Jardine, Alice A. *Gyersis: Configurations of Woman and Modernity.* Ithaca, NY: Cornell UP, 1982–83.

Macaulay, Thomas Babington. "Warren Hastings." *Macaulay: Prose and Poetry.* Ed. G.M Young. Cambridge: Harvard UP, 1967. 373–469.

———. "The Impeachment of Warren Hastings." *Selections from the Writings of Lord Macaulay.* Ed. Sir George Otto Trevelyan. London, New York and Bombay: Longmans, Green and Company, 1905. 149.

Marshall, P.J. *The British Discovery of Hinduism in the Eighteenth Century.* Cambridge: Cambridge UP, 1970.

Moon, Penderel. *Warren Hastings and British India.* New York: Macmillan, 1949.

Robbins, Thomas. *The Religions and Religious Ceremonies of All Nations, at the Present Day and in Two Parts.* Hartford, 1849.

Said, Edward. *Orientalism.* New York: Pantheon, 1978.

Schwab, Raymond. *Oriental Renaissance: Europe's Rediscovery of India and the East 1680–1880.* Trans. Gene Patterson-Black and Victor Reinking. Paris, 1950, 1984. New York: Columbia UP, 1987.

Thorslev, Peter. *The Byronic Hero.* Minneapolis: U of Minnesota Press.

Wolfson, Susan. "Gendering the Soul." *Romantic Women Writers: Voices and Countervoices.* Eds. Paula R. Feldman and Theresa M. Kelley. Hanover and London: UP of New England, 1995. 33-68.

Wollstonecraft, Mary. *Vindication of the Rights of Women. The Works of Mary Wollstonecraft.* 7 vols. Eds. Marilyn Butler and Janet Todd. London: Pickering and Chatto. New York: New York UP, 1989.

———. *The Works of Mary Wollstonecraft.* 7 vols. Eds. Marilyn Butler and Janet Todd. London: Pickering and Chatto. New York: New York UP, 1989.

Wright, Caleb. *A Lecutre on the Condition of Women, in Pagan and Mahometan Countries, by Caleb Wright, lecturer on the Manners, Habits and Superstitions of the Hindoos.* Troy, NY, 1845.

Young, Brian. "'The Lust of Empire and Religious Hate': Christianity, History, and India, 1790–1950." Ed. Stefan Collini. Cambridge UP, 2000. 95.

Chapter Eight

# Ithuriel's Spear and Detecting the Counterfeit: Edgeworth's Miltonic Allusions in *Belinda*

Jeffrey Cass

"I am like the needy knife grinder—I have no story to tell."
—Maria Edgeworth

## Maria Edgeworth, Fathers, and the Problem of Miltonic Influence

Gilbert and Gubar, the authors of *The Madwoman in the Attic*, use the above epigraph to frame their chapter on Jane Austen, in which they argue that Jane Austen follows Maria Edgeworth's example by "combin[ing] her implicitly rebellious vision with an explicitly decorous form" (153). Gilbert and Gubar suggest that the strategy for female writers who wish to criticize a burdensome patriarchy is to feign submission, to hide harsh judgments against its oppression within a bland, pleasing, and "decorous" narrative. For Gilbert and Gubar, Jane Austen succeeds in this covert operation while Maria Edgeworth generally fails, subsuming herself within the very discourse that imprisons her–doubly so, since she abandons the lurking social criticism of her early novels such as *Castle Rackrent* or *Belinda* for the task of assisting her father, Richard Lovell Edgeworth, in his writing projects. Maria Edgeworth has no "story to tell" of her own because she must relay her father's. The epigraph reveals that she has had to transform herself into a "literary lady," into a "creature of her father's imagination who was understandably anxious for and about her father's control" (148).

But Gilbert and Gubar are not merely concerned with the general effect of patriarchal discourse on nineteenth-century women writers or the specific father/daughter relationship evinced by the case of Maria Edgeworth and Richard Lovell Edgeworth. Their use of the phrase "creature of her father's imagination" in the preceding passage reinforces Gilbert and Gubar's Bloomian psychoanalytic readings about the influence of powerful literary fathers. And, for them, the most notable of these literary fathers, John Milton, reifies the monstrous "bogey" of the female imagination that "cuts women off from the spaciousness of possibility" (188). Women writers desiring to free themselves from the stranglehold of Miltonic influence must "covertly reappraise and repudiate the misogyny implicit in Milton's mythology ... Parodic, duplicitous, extraordinarily sophisticated, all this female writing is both revisionary and revolutionary, even when it is produced by writers we usually think of as models of angelic resignation" (80). Like the other "models of angelic resignation," Maria Edgeworth ought to have used the scene of writing to re-evaluate, revise, and then repudiate Milton, her dominant literary father. Since "she seems to have used her writing principally to gain the attention and approval of her [real] father" (147), Gilbert and Gubar announce, her modesty and reticence become true psychic impediments to her literary (and presumably her psychic) development. Rather than being the secret weapons of an elaborate "cover story" that permit an imaginative expansion, as they do, for example, for Jane Austen, modesty and reticence become tools of patriarchal compliance and complicity. In short, Maria Edgeworth becomes Milton's secret agent in propagating a patriarchal sexual politics.

With regard to real and literary fathers, and their problematic influence, Edgeworth critics tend to follow the Gilbert and Gubar theoretical line. Like Gilbert and Gubar, Jacqueline Pearson borrows from Harold Bloom, contending that Maria Edgeworth's "constant role as compliant, even hagiographical, junior partner, might well have created or fed both fear and desire to trespass on the preserve of the Father" (233). "Appropriating the work and patriarchal authority of her literal father as well as various literary parents," Pearson adds, "seems to have caused Edgeworth both pleasure and the anxious, guilty need to exorcize the act of appropriation in the novel itself" (233). Perhaps the most aggressive in affirming Gilbert and Gubar's conception of Milton and his influence on his literary daughters (such as Maria Edgeworth and Hannah More) is the oft-cited Edgeworth critic, Elizabeth Kowaleski-Wallace. She writes:

> Yet Gilbert and Gubar's examples work so well because these women writers can be shown to have reacted to Milton with emotions that seem, at least on some level, recognizable to us. Evidence can be produced to demonstrate that these women shared our own vexed feelings toward Milton. They are our sisters by virtue of their response to Milton; their righteous indignation in the face of disturbing images of the female principle is our indignation. (28)

Yet this reading of Milton's influence is not only a misreading of Maria Edgeworth (and many other women writers of the eighteenth and nineteenth centuries), it is also a misreading of Milton, for such a "vexed" version of Milton depends upon a false premise, namely, that Milton's patriarchal universe blames Eve for the Fall and postlapsarian punishment of the human race and then utterly absolves Adam for his sin. In this view, Milton transforms God the Father into Victimizer Almighty, creating Eve as innocent woman, who, unlike Adam, has been brought into existence without highly developed reasoning skills or profound knowledge, and then blaming her for loss of innocence and illicit acquisition of knowledge.

Yet even a brief reading of *Paradise Lost* concerning the Fall and its consequences suggests that Milton condemns Adam far more than he does Eve, for whilest Eve falls prey to the temptations of the serpent, she falls deceived. By contrast, Adam falls "undeceiv'd"—his crime, therefore, is far greater than Eve's. As such, Gilbert and Gubar follow a mistaken interpretation of *Paradise Lost*. They suggest that, "Adam's fall is fortunate because, among other reasons, from the woman's point of view his punishment seems almost like a reward ..." (197). Eve's perspective, however, ultimately reveals a woman directly attuned to God the Father, for it is she who receives the divinely inspired vision of man's restoration through Christ and not Adam. Through Eve, Eden is indeed lost, but through her the world is also restored. Gallantly and heroically, she accepts her penance (in the truest sense of that word) and proclaims the power of the woman to reclaim human loss ("... though all by mee is lost,/Such favor I unworthy am voutsaf't,/By mee the Promis'd Seed shall all restore," [12.621–623]). In *Gender and the Power of Relationship*, Kristin Pruitt bracingly offers this remark: "Eve's words proclaim a poetically just, divinely authored revision of the satanic script of loss through self-exaltation, for while 'Man's First Disobedience, and the Fruit/Of that Forbidden Tree ... /Brought Death into the World, and all our woe,/With *loss* of Eden (1.1–4), Eve's dreams, 'some *great good*/Presaging,' herald the creation of 'one greater Man' who has the power to '*Restore* us, and regain the blissful Seat" (1.4–5; emphasis Pruitt's). Finally, and perhaps most tellingly, Eve and Adam depart Paradise together—equal in their tribulation, equal in their eventual triumph, equal in the promise of "restoration" ("They hand in hand with wand'ring steps and slow,/Through Eden they took thir solitary way," [12.648–9]). As Joseph Wittreich concludes in *Feminist Milton*, Eve is "not only a partner but also a protagonist in the mending of creation and in the ensuing drama of history" (95).

Pearson and Kowaleski-Wallace's iterations of Gilbert's and Gubar's version of Milton's influence thus produce an almost unrecognizable Maria Edgeworth, one that has little to do with the themes of restoration or reclamation or with her important literary debts to Milton. John Shawcross suggests that "while an anxiety of influence may hang over" some of the writers who appropriate Milton's work, many more regard him "as source and inspiration and presence" (3,4). "The Milton that this influence delineates," Shawcross continues, "is an admired force to be enveloped or to be ever like a star apart, an observation better stating Wordsworth's position and others' following after the seventeenth-century giant than Milton's position within his own world" (4). Closer to the mark among Edgeworth critics in accurately describing her attitudes toward patriarchy is Audrey Bilger. In her book *Laughing Feminism*, Bilger indicts Gilbert and Gubar and their followers by taking issue with their unquestioned seriousness, "attribut[ing] signs of madness, debility, and disease in women's texts to the condition of women under patriarchy" (219). In this vein, Edgeworth comically represents the relationships of power within patriarchy and imagines the historical balance between men and women by exposing the arbitrariness of their social and cultural divisions. Patriarchy is not the irrevocable and insuperable tragedy that Gilbert and Gubar presuppose. In fact, Edgeworth may even borrow her parodic representations of patriarchy from *Paradise Lost*, as it is Satan who is the patriarchal despot, not God the Father. It is Satan who attempts to naturalize and apotheosize patriarchy, thereby forever dividing Adam and Eve from God the Father (and from each other). And it is Satan who parodies patriarchy by forgetting that he is the patriarchal head of his own incestuous family—Sin, his "daughter" and "darling" (2.870) and Death, his "Son and foe" (2.805). As Satan and Death prepare to do battle in Book II, Sin cries: "… And know'st for whom; / For him who sits above and laughs the while/At thee ordain'd his drudge …" (2.730–32).

## Ithuriel's Spear, Charm, and Detecting the Counterfeit

In Book IV of *Paradise Lost*, the angel Ithuriel makes his only appearance. He and his companion angel Zephon find Satan, in the form of a toad, "assaying by his Devilish art to reach/The Organs of [Eve's] Fancy, and with them forge/Illusions as he list, Phantasms and Dreams…" (4.801–03). Ithuriel, whose name means "discovery of God", touches Satan with his celestial spear and restores him to his true form, "As when a spark/Lights on a heap of nitrous Powder, laid/Fit for the Tun some Magazin to store/Against a rumor'd War, the smutty grain/With sudden Blaze diffus'd, inflames the Air …" (4.814–17). The angels then escort the great counterfeiter and fallen angel to Gabriel, with whom Satan angrily parleys about the reasons for his escape from hell, his intentions in invading the Garden of Eden, and his outsized pride about his angelic powers, which, as the unfallen angels sternly remind him, have greatly diminished. Gabriel commands Satan to look at the "celestial Sign" (4.1011), a golden celestial scale that has weighed against him and found him wanting. Satan recognizes his ongoing defeat and flees the presence of divine displeasure. With Ithuriel's spear, however, which has no biblical precedent, Milton certainly suggests that evil can transform and hide its true nature from an unsuspecting gaze, even an angelic one. As Satan approaches Eden, for example, he assumes the form of a "stripling cherub" whose feigned youthful beauty and grace successfully deceive Uriel ("Flame of God"). Sufficiently crafty to deceive Uriel about his true physical self, when Satan inquires about the "new happy Race of Men" that now serve God, Uriel blithely and unsuspectingly directs him to "Adam's abode" and the "lofty shades" of his marriage bower, where Eve resides and innocently awaits her own destruction (3.733–34); indeed, the deception of Uriel foreshadows the Fall of Eve. Unlike Ithuriel, however, Eve is not armed with a restorative spear, a weapon to penetrate and puncture the disguises of temptation and deception. The woman in *Paradise Lost* faces the "false dissembler" alone (3.682).

When Maria Edgeworth casts Ithuriel's spear into the narrative matrix of *Belinda*, a novel about the chicanery of men and the vulnerability of women, therefore, it is no casual allusion. Possession of Ithuriel's spear would disclose the truth of suitors' intentions, the true face of male desire, the actual scope of male privilege and power, which men, like Satan, can easily cloak and mask. In a witty but serious conversation about the danger of poetical analogies, Lady Anne Percival says, "Our affections ... arise from circumstances totally independent of our will" (239), with which Belinda readily agrees. But Belinda balks when Lady Anne further argues that a woman's affections, in addition to being "excited" by "the agreeable or useful qualities" that women "discover in things or in persons" (250), are equally impelled by "fancies," a proposition with which Belinda appears far less sanguine than Lady Anne. Edgeworth writes:

> Belinda was silent; but after a pause she said, "That it was certainly very dangerous, especially for women, to trust to fancy in bestowing their affections." "And yet," continued she, "it is a danger to which they are much exposed in society. Men have it in their power to assume the appearance of every thing that is amiable and estimable, and women have scarcely any opportunities of detecting the counterfeit. Without Ithuriel's spear how can they distinguish the good from the evil?" (240)

Lady Anne appeals to Belinda's "fancy" in order to persuade her of the appropriateness of her possible union with Mr. Vincent, the West Indian planter, and the justification of any "fancies" that Belinda may harbor for him. But Lady Anne's use of the word "discover," as well as Belinda's reticence at prematurely revealing to Mr. Vincent her feelings for him (precisely Jane Austen's point about Marianne Dashwood in *Sense and Sensibility*), underscore the problematic nature of a woman's public displays of affection for men and the damage to her reputation should the public take too much notice of such displays. The incurable flaw in Vincent's character, his penchant for billiards gaming, remains deeply hidden and, like Satan's trickery of Uriel, Vincent succeeds in masking his true nature from Belinda. This situation becomes further evidence that securing some version of Ithuriel's spear by women, so dependent on the goodwill of men, would ensure "opportunities of detecting the counterfeit," of unmasking unworthy intentions, sinister secrets, and damaging alliances of a deceiver. More simply, Belinda wishes to be able to distinguish "the good from the evil"; she recognizes that, like most women in her position, she is not fully equipped to defend herself against the deceitful social practices of both men and women. Even prudence, Belinda's most prominent active virtue, that which most resembles the Ithuriel's spear that she wishes for as her protective arsenal, does not prevent or penetrate Vincent's "counterfeit" attentions. Though more than mere poetical analogy, prudence merely retards the progress toward Miss Portman and Mr. Vincent's marriage, allowing his vicious secret to remain hidden. As is the case with the Lady in Milton's *A Masque*, prudence incompletely insulates a woman from danger. Belinda's prudence initially fails to detect Lady Delacour's dangerous whimsy, completely deflect her patron Selina Stanhope's unscrupulous teachings, thwart the Percivals' good (if occasionally misguided) intentions, or discern clearly Clarence Hervey's tortured conflict between social respectability and social status. Sometimes it is a matter of sheer luck that women like Belinda survive the crucible of patronage and still manage, in the end, to marry for love and money. From Edgeworth's perspective (and, perhaps to some, extent Milton's), Eve in the Garden was in the wrong place at the wrong time and, though "sufficient to have stood" (3.99) was nonetheless insufficiently armed against falling for a practiced and charming tempter. Indeed, Edgeworth diffuses throughout her narrative the problematics of charm, perhaps the most important motif in Milton's work with regard to virtue and temptation.

Just prior to Belinda's and Lady Anne's friendly debate, Belinda has a curious conversation with Mr. Vincent, who consistently refers to Lady Anne and her family as "charming," as well as to Belinda herself—"Charming Miss Portman!" (237). Because of this exchange, the normally prudent Belinda begins to see Mr. Vincent as something other than a polite gentleman and close friend of the Percivals.

> Miss Portman had been too often called "charming" to be much startled or delighted by the sound: the word would have passed by unnoticed, but there was something so impassioned in Mr. Vincent's manner, that she could no longer mistake it for common gallantry, and she was in evident confusion. Now for the first time the idea of Mr. Vincent as a lover came into her mind. (237)

Not solely acting out "common gallantry," Mr. Vincent attempts to "charm" Miss Portman, to "come into her mind" as Satan does Eve in her dream (2.28–93), by passionately adverting to her own charms. But Vincent instinctively recognizes, as does Satan, that only by isolating the object of his desire will he succeed in making himself irresistible, and he jealously contrives to remove Belinda from Lady Delacour's house before his rival, Clarence Hervey, can arrive and threaten his standing. Predictably, Belinda tries to comfort Vincent's obvious disappointment, though she does not truly know its source, by quoting *Paradise Lost*: "The mind is its own place," a direct lifting of Satan's speech to the rebel angels in Pandaemonium (1.254). Moreover, Vincent knows that, if Belinda does discover that he has dissembled about his past, she will not submit to his charms and will break off their engagement. What he does not know is that his rival, Hervey, will save him from his basest desire by revealing to Vincent that he himself has been duped, the object of Mrs. Luttridge's deceit at fixing the gaming table, and only Hervey's generosity, his desire to be a friend to both Belinda and her future husband, rescues Vincent from financial ruin. Yet even when Vincent confesses his indiscretions to Belinda, he does not do so honestly, hinting at his financial devastation in order to gauge her devotion and sincerity. He unethically manipulates Belinda's emotions and then flatteringly concludes, "'My generous, charming, adorable, Belinda! My fortune is not lost. All stratagems, you know, the poet says are allowable in love and war. This was only a stratagem to excite your compassion'" (442). Although Belinda is angry at this deception, she forgives his indiscretion at this point, but his unsteady character—his fight with Sir Philip Baddely, the irretrievable loss of the ready money through gambling for the purchase of an estate, the unwise transaction with a Jewish usurer to recover the ready money, Henry Percival's untimely discovery of this transaction and his subsequent refusal to tell Belinda that Vincent had unequivocally given up the "charms of play"—resurfaces, finally forcing the vigilant and honest Belinda to reject him as suitor.

The case of Mr. Vincent is instructive because the real basis for his relationship with Belinda stems from their mutual charm, and Edgeworth generally indicts "charm" in her novel as the source of deceit and temptation. For example, recounting the financial details of her marriage and fortuitous death of one of Lord Delacour's rich relatives, Lady Delacour recalls her exhaustion at being a "slave" to social expectation. She tells Belinda, "I was obliged to find things 'charming' every hour, which tired me to death; and every day it was the same dull round of hypocrisy and dissipation" (41). The scheming artificer, Selina Stanhope, advises Belinda in a letter to encourage Sir Philip Baddely's attentions to her, whatever her affections, for "[h] is proposal at this crisis for you ... is a charming thing" (201). In the same letter, Stanhope cryptically instructs Belinda to tell Lady Delacour that Stanhope has "a charming anecdote for her, about another friend ... who has gone over to the enemy" (201). Perhaps the most reprobate of women in *Belinda*, Harriet Freke, the female Satanic figure in the novel, wishes to win Belinda "over to her party" through flattery of her beauty. When she fails to move Belinda in this manner, she attempts to woo Belinda through "a high opinion of her understanding" (227), and Freke wittily suggests that she would rather be "a strong devil than a weak angel" (227). Quoting *Paradise Lost* 1.157, Belinda replies that it is Satan who says, "'Fallen spirit, to be weak is to be miserable'" (227). Rebuffed, Freke cross dresses as a man in order to take revenge upon Belinda for refusing her invitation to Harrowgate and become one of her socially connected allies. In effect, Freke hopes to uncover Lady Delacour's secrets (and, thereby, Belinda's complicity with Lady Delacour in maintaining those secrets), deceitfully publicize the knowledge, and thereafter sully Belinda's reputation for prudence and moral gravity. Edgeworth writes: "Charmed with this hope of a double triumph, the vindictive lady commenced her operations.... She swore that 'it was charming fun to equip herself at night in man's clothes, and to sally forth to reconnoitre the motions of the enemy'" (310).

Detecting counterfeit charm in *Belinda* explains Edgeworth's clever incorporation of Ithuriel's spear into the narrative, as well as her own consistent allusions to Satan's own charm in *Paradise Lost*. The issue of detecting counterfeit charm also explains the absolute necessity of seeing through and rejecting offered temptations. Early in the novel, in a chapter aptly entitled "Masks," Clarence Hervey, who will eventually fall in love and marry Belinda, engages in the gamesmanship of the masquerade ball. He intends to entertain the party with an impenetrable costume, "wager[ing] with a friend that he can successfully disguise himself, 'perform[ing] the part of the serpent, such as he is seen in Fuseli's well known picture'" (Cass, 15). As I have argued elsewhere, the key to understanding this scene lies in identifying Fuseli's "well known picture" as *Satan's First Address to Eve* (from the Second Milton Gallery portraits of 1800, a year before the publication date of the first edition of *Belinda*) and not, as Kathryn Kirkpatrick suggests, *Thor Battering the Serpent at Midgard*. The importance of this ekphrasis becomes clearer when Hervey "contrive[s] a set of phosphoric rays" (23) to emanate from the snake's eyes. Ironically, the phosphorus ignites the serpentine disguise and destroys it, not unlike the burning "heap of nitrous powder" caused by the touch of Ithuriel's spear. Hervey cannot ultimately perpetrate his fraud on his unsuspecting female audience, a masking "which he was certain would charm all the fair daughters of Eve" (23). Hervey refers directly to *Paradise Lost* 4.324, a passage that celebrates the loveliness of Eve, whom Satan revengefully charms out of her innocence. Eve's fall from grace sets up Adam's scene of temptation, in which, "fondly overcome with Female charm" (9.999), he also falls and promptly blames Eve. The relevance of Eve's fate to Belinda's situation becomes apparent in subsequent exchanges between Lady Delacour and Hervey. These exchanges justify her concern that her own prudence may be interpreted as simply another devious female charm, justifying Belinda's suspicion that women require Ithuriel's spear to "discover" and repel the temptations men contrive for women, as well as to unmask masculine motivations, intentions, and desires. During the masquerade ball, for example, unaware that Lady Delacour and Belinda have actually traded costumes, with Lady Delacour dressed as the comic muse and Belinda donning the mask of the tragic muse, Hervey scoffs at the possibility that he could be taken in by "Belinda Portman's composition of art and affectation" (26). As one of the Stanhope School, Belinda cannot hope to deceive him, especially since he understands the nature of her graduates and their plots to ensnare men. Though playful in her badinage, Lady Delacour repudiates his boasting wit by reminding him that without his own artful disguise, women can now see his true self, one open to public scrutiny and even disapprobation, a particularly ironic possibility since Belinda has yet to reveal to him her mask. Not coincidentally, Lady Delacour cites the same passage from *Paradise Lost* to which he had earlier alluded: "Though you have lost your serpent's form your own may please any of the fair daughters of Eve" (26). His "form" may indeed please the "fair daughters of Eve," but the real stripping of Hervey's disguise signifies a deeper unmasking—that is, the cruel consequences of his charming wit, a sad truth inadvertently revealed because of Lady Delacour's and Belinda's last-minute decision to put on each other's costumes, a deception revealed because of a deception perpetrated.

**Chastity and the Vulnerability of Virtue in *A Masque* and *Paradise Lost***

Even if not duplicitous, however, charm can still be dangerous. After relinquishing the social status that comes with the exercise of charm, Hervey understandably wishes to atone for his earlier indiscretions in charming all the fair daughters of Eve, and so he assists his protégé Virginia (formerly Rachel), abandoned by her father (so it would at first seem) and raised by her now dying grandmother (after the early and untimely death of Virginia's mother). Hervey discovers Virginia in a "terrestrial paradise" that sounds with the "humming of bees" (364). But the sound of bees does not necessarily confirm the promise of new life (as it does in Virgil's *Georgics*). Rather, the sound of bees can signal danger, the possibility of death, as it does in Milton's Pandaemonium, "As bees In Spring time, as the Sun with Taurus rides,/Pour forth thir populous youth about the Hive/In Clusters ... So thick the aery crowd/Swarm'd and were strait'n'd (*PL*, 1.768–771; 1.775–76). Hervey's Romantic interpretation of the scene—indeed his foolish desire to see innocent bees where he should see scheming serpents, his reliance on Rousseau's dubious educational insights—become a source of future danger for Virginia. By maintaining her innocence, by protecting her from the temptations of society, she becomes like Eve, susceptible to charm and rashly fond of her own momentous feelings of love, for, fatherless as she is, she mistakes Hervey's claims of paternal affection for Romantic feeling. Hervey tests her taste at one point by offering her a pair of diamond earrings and a moss rose bud. When she takes the rose bud, she exclaims,

"How sweet it smells!" (371). She then describes the diamonds as "pretty sparkling things" (371), not recognizing their monetary worth. Hervey, as Edgeworth drolly notes, "was charmed with her" (371). Her indifference to the diamonds, however, is not borne of worldly wisdom or considered reflection. As Edgeworth suggests, "[Virginia] did not consider them as ornaments that would confer distinction upon their possessor, because she was ignorant of the value affixed to them by society" (372).

Virginia's simplicity in taste, too, is dangerous for Hervey, for he takes pride in protecting Virginia's innocence from the temptations of social life. But Hervey mistakes innocence for isolation, a cloistered imagination for a guileless one, or, as Milton so artfully intimates in *A Masque*, virginity for chastity. Virginia, after all, is not necessarily chaste, merely without the opportunity to indulge in what Milton would call "mirth." Thus, Hervey not only misinterprets her character, he savors having rescued it: "All that was amiable or estimable in Virginia had a double charm, from the secret sense of his penetration in having discovered and appreciated the treasure" (372). On her part, Virginia, who from Edgeworth's perspective has read too many romance novels, falls in love with Hervey in a purely mediated way. Having no experiences of her own, she appropriates those of literary women. She says to Mrs. Ormond that she cannot see into her mind: "In the daytime I often think of those heroes, those charming heroes, that I read of in the books you have given me" (383). To his credit, when Hervey learns of the young woman's passion for him, and that he is entirely responsible for it, he intends to marry her, but when he discovers that her father may well be alive, that, he lives abroad in the West Indies as a planter, he leaves for Portsmouth hoping that by giving Virginia back to the real world, she may shift her feelings for him onto a more real and less Romantic object. Indeed, because the father is rich, she may "become an heiress to a considerable fortune" (395), as if status will immunize her from dangerous and charming young men. As Edgeworth wryly suggests,

> New views might then open to her imagination: the world, the fashionable world in all its glory, would be before her; her beauty and fortune would attract a variety of admirers.... If love arose merely from circumstances it would change; if it were only a disease of the imagination, induced by her seclusion from society, it might be cured by mixing with the world ... (395)

Once odious to Hervey's Rousseauistic pedagogy, the "fashionable" world becomes the antidote to Virginia's infatuation and, given his passion for Belinda, the *deus ex machina* for Hervey's marital dilemma. But the "fashionable world" in this passage is also, *mutatis mutandis*, the end of *Paradise Lost* when the archangel evicts Adam and Eve from Paradise and forces them to descend to the plain to begin the rest of their lives ("The World was all before them, where to choose/Thir place of rest, and Providence their Guide;/They hand in hand with wand'ring steps and slow,/Through Eden took thir solitary way" (*PL*, 12.646–649). Like Adam and Eve, before or after the Fall, Virginia has no devices for separating good suitors from bad suitors; Hervey does not (and cannot) arm her with an Ithuriel's spear to distinguish one from the other. Nor does he give Virginia the tools of practiced resistance and prudence that Belinda wields. Like Eve, Virginia faces the tempter alone. The real *deus ex machina* in Edgeworth's novel, saving Hervey regret and Belinda resignation, lies, conveniently enough, in Virginia's dreams and with a man of good intentions—Captain Sunderland. He becomes the late entrant in Edgeworth's pantheon of would-be and actual lovers and the one who, rather unwittingly, completes the pattern of Miltonic allusion and representation.

Appropriately enough, Sunderland hears of an unapproachable "young beauty," who happens to live near his mother in the New Forest. Although the widow Smith keeps a vigilant eye on Virginia, Sunderland takes out his "spyglass," and hiding himself from her view, sees Virginia "watering her roses and tending her bees" (475). Like Satan ghoulishly spying on fair Eve, Sunderland "found a lair where he concealed himself, day after day, and contemplated at leisure the budding charms of the fair wood nymph" (475). Although he falls in love with her, after learning of the girl's tragic history, Sunderland defers a declaration of his passion until his return from the West Indies, which happens to coincide with Virginia's maturity as a young woman at the end of *Belinda*. Yet Sunderland's intense voyeurism also suggests the dangers of charm, whether or not one is Satanic stalker or noble patron. Immediately following the separation scene in Book IX of *Paradise Lost*, Satan "spies" the isolated mother of mankind, "Eve separate ... veiled in a Cloud of Fragrance where she stood, Half spi'd, so thick the Roses bushing round/About her glow'd ..." (9.424; 425–6). Fortunately, without "the fierceness of the fierce intent" (9.462), Virginia retains her virginal innocence, for Sunderland is no Satan, and he does not wish to tempt her from the very innocence he holds dear. Yet his very presence in her garden once again denotes how vulnerable unarmed women are, their delightfulness inspiring passionate intensity in men that may or may not result in craven deception or theft of virtue. Although a woman may attempt to repel the seducer by invoking prudence or faith in the divine, she often still stands alone. She may not even perceive the danger.

In the end, *Paradise Lost* is not the only Miltonic intertext useful in interpreting *Belinda*. Indeed, *A Masque* becomes equally relevant, for Virginia's situation recalls the Lady's, inasmuch as the Lady's stentorian ripostes do not counter Comus's arguments. She remains firmly under his control. When Comus threatens the Lady, she intones: "Fool, do not boast,/Thou canst not touch the freedom of my mind/With all thy charms" (663–64). Further, when Comus urges her to indulge in sensuous pleasure, to exploit her beauty selfishly ("Beauty is nature's coin, must not be hoarded ... Beauty is nature's brag, and must be shown," [739, 745]), she coldly replies: "I had not thought to have unlockt my lips/In this unhallow'd air, but that this Juggler/Would think to charm my judgment, as mine eyes,/Obtruding false rules prankt in reason's garb" (756–59). And yet with his magical wand, which utterly transforms men and women into bestial pleasure-seekers, Comus (the "Juggler") has the power to "charm" the Lady, to pinion her body to his imperial Chair so that she cannot move or escape. Possession of the wand, like possession of Ithuriel's spear, exposes the tempter's hidden power, his secret authority, which is why the Attendant Spirit urges the Lady's brothers to wrest the wand from Comus's hands. When they fail to do so, when Comus retains possession of his wand, the brothers have no natural or earthly means by which to free the Lady from the bondage into which Comus has placed her. Moreover, the Lady (or the virgins who follow her) has no weapon with which to restore the charmer to his true form. With Comus at large, with the satanic charmer unaccounted for, the tempter still lurks in the forest, voyeuristically gauging the woman's vulnerabilities, the chinks in her chaste armor, and weighing the possibilities for his return.

Even though Comus retains his wand and thus remains a threat, the conclusion of *A Masque* celebrates the routing of Comus and his revelers. The Attendant Spirit triumphantly eulogizes virtue: "Mortals that would follow me,/Love virtue she alone is free./She can teach ye how to climb/Higher than the Sphery chime;/Or if Virtue feeble were,/Heav'n itself would stoop to her" (1018–23). Interestingly, Lady Delacour transforms the end of the novel into a cheery stage in which Clarence Hervey and Belinda Portman will marry, and Lady Delacour has reconciled with her family. Like the Attendant Spirit in *A Masque*, she announces a moral to the story, the drama of virtuous reformation, which the audience must have the "wit" to discover (428). The upbeat endings about the triumph of virtue, which both Milton and Edgeworth assert, camouflage their deeper concern about virtue's inadequacy, particularly its innate capacity to prevent damage to its integrity. Drawing her philosophical edge from Milton, Edgeworth illustrates that neither Belinda's prudence nor Virginia's innocence necessarily shields them (or any woman) from the charms that Satanic tempters exercise or the dangers that their own feminine charms excite. The dramatic resolutions of both *A Masque* and *Belinda* are beautiful illusions, for deception may overturn virtue. Ithuriel indeed possesses his spear, Comus avidly protects his wand, and the virtuous woman may or may not detect the counterfeit. Weaponless, she frequently stands unguarded and alone.

## Works Cited

Bilger, Audrey. *Laughing Feminism: Subversive Comedy in Frances Burney, Maria Edgeworth, and Jane Austen.* Detroit: Wayne State UP, 1998.
Cass, Jeffrey. "Fuseli's Milton Gallery: *Satan's First Address to Eve*" as a Source of Maria Edgeworth's *Belinda*. ANQ 14 (2) 2001: 15-23.
Edgeworth, Maria. *Belinda.* Ed. Kathryn Kirkpatrick. Oxford: Oxford UP, 1994.
Gilbert, Sandra M. and Susan Gubar. *The Madwoman in the Attic: The Woman Writer and the Nineteenth-Century Literary Imagination.* New Haven and London: Yale UP, 1979.
Kowaleski-Wallace, Elizabeth. *Their Fathers' Daughters: Hannah More, Maria Edgeworth, and Patriarchal Complicity.* Oxford: Oxford UP, 1991.
Milton, John. *The Complete Poetry and Major Prose of John Milton.* Ed. Merritt Y. Hughes. Indianapolis: Odyssey Press, 1957.
Pearson, Jacqueline. "'Arts of Appropriation': Language, Circulation, and Appropriation in the Work of Maria Edgeworth." *Yearbook of English Studies* 28, 1998: 212–34.
Pruitt, Kristin A. *Gender and the Power of Relationship: 'United as One Individual Soul' in 'Paradise Lost'.* Pittsburgh: Duquesne UP, 2003.
Shawcross, John. *John Milton and Influence: Presence in Literature. History and Culture.* Pittsburgh: Duquesne UP, 1991.
Wittreich, Joseph. *Feminist Milton.* Ithaca and London: Cornell UP, 1987.

Chapter Nine

# Parting Songs: Hemans, Landon, and Barrett Browning Rewrite Friederike Brun

Kari Lokke

Friederike Brun (1765–1835) is known to literary critics today primarily as the writer whose poetry was the source and inspiration for Wolfgang von Goethe's "Nähe des Geliebten," Samuel Taylor Coleridge's "Hymn Before Sunrise, in the Vale of Chamouni" and William Wordsworth's "The Seven Sisters." Indeed, she has the singular distinction of being perhaps the only writer whose work was "adapted" by each of these three central figures of European Romanticism. Of her extensive correspondence with her lover, the Swiss philosopher Karl Victor von Bonstetten, only *his* letters have been published. Yet Brun was a gifted and prolific author in her own right who produced three volumes of poetry, a number of widely read travelogues composed of letters and diaries, an autobiography, *Wahrheit aus Morgenträumen* (*Truth from Daydreams*, 1810) and a fascinating record of her daughter's development from infancy into a gifted singer, pantomimist, and *improvisatrice*: *Idas Aesthetische Entwicklung* (*Ida's Aesthetic Development*, 1824).

Of German origin, she moved to Denmark as a small child when her father was made pastor of a German congregation in Copenhagen. Married at a young age to an international banker, she traveled extensively throughout her life in Switzerland, France, Germany, and Italy and was an astute observer of cultural and political practices. She held a celebrated salon for the leading artists of early nineteenth-century Copenhagen; corresponded extensively with Caroline von Humboldt and J.C.L. Simonde de Sismondi; was a welcome visitor to Germaine de Staël's international coterie in Coppet, Switzerland; and entertained Italian, Danish, German, and British artists and writers, from Canova and Angelica Kauffman to Bertel Thorwaldsen and Wilhelm von Humboldt. Thus, Friederike Brun is a kind of emblem for the cosmopolitan nature of European Romanticism, as well as a symbol of women's crucial and hitherto largely ignored participation in the republican and internationalist spirit of that moment in European history.

This essay explores the ways in which the refrain of Brun's brief lyric poem, "Ich denke Dein" ("I think of you"), written in 1792 and published in 1795, was reworked throughout the nineteenth century by a number of important British women poets, among them Felicia Hemans, Letitia Landon and Elizabeth Barrett

Browning.¹ Interpreting these British rewritings of "Ich denke Dein" as direct reader addresses, I trace the legacy of Brun's original love poem from Hemans's "Parting Song" (1828), to Landon's "Night at Sea" (1838) and Barrett Browning's "L.E.L's Last Question" (1839). My aim is to register the ways in which Brun's command/plea "Think of me" resonates in a lively international conversation throughout the next fifty years of British poetry, as women poets constitute themselves as audiences for each other's work. By delineating the shifting terms of these dialogues, I hope to offer a glimpse into the historical vicissitudes of the nineteenth-century European woman poet's complex and vexed relation to her audiences as she moves from cosmopolitan *salonière* to voice of an imperial nation. Clearly, this enduring legacy of Brun's poems suggests that they were not the "German dry bones" that De Quincey termed them nor the mere "curiosity" to which Henry Nelson relegated them in his effort to defend his father against De Quincey's charges of plagiarism.²

In straightforward biographical terms, "Ich denke Dein" may have been written to and for Brun's lover Karl Viktor von Bonstetten whom she met for the first time in 1791.³ Angela Esterhammer points out that "the phrase 'Ich denke dein' begins appearing in correspondence between Brun and the landscape poet Friedrich Matthisson (who was her lifelong friend, and possibly her lover) soon after they met in 1791" ("Improvisation," 12). Thus, in any case, the poem clearly registers the pain caused by the separation(s) from a loved one that were necessitated by her peripatetic life as she moved from her husband and children in Copenhagen, to her travels in Switzerland, Germany, and France, to salon life in Rome and Staël's Coppet. And, significantly, from its origin, the phrase "Ich denke dein" is associated with dialogue among artists and intellectuals.

The power of the poem, erotic and verbal, has its source in the obsessive repetition of the phrase, "Ich denke dein," in various forms, combined with the striking verse form—iambic pentameter in the first and third lines followed by short dimeter in the second and fourth lines. As the poem develops, the speaker finds her beloved in all moods and seasons of nature, in all landscapes and moments of the day. Only in the poem's climactic stanza does this key phrase and the second rhyme disappear, as the power of language fulfills the speaker's desire virtually and the whole of nature is suddenly transfigured by the light emanating from the image of the beloved:

Schnell is der Wald, schnell sind die Blumenmatten
**Mit Glanz erfüllt.(23-24)**⁴
(Quickly the woods, quickly the flowering meadows are filled with brilliance/splendour.)

The mood, however, changes abruptly and radically as the seventh stanza shifts to the past tense "Gedacht ich dein!" ("I thought of you"; line 26), and to dim lamplight as the speaker recalls the pain of separation. This pain brings forth the imperative—"'Gedenke mein!'" ("Think of me"; line 28),—that will be echoed throughout the next century, usually in interrogative form, in the poetry of Brun's British counterparts. This plea gains significance, in Brun's poem, by its presentation in quotes as the commemoration of a troubled rather than a certain voice:

> Die bange Seele flehte nah 'am Scheiden:
> "Gedenke mein!" (27–28)
> (The anxious soul implored at the moment of parting: "Think of me!)

The poem concludes with the speaker's effort to transcend her pain through the poetic assertion of the beloved's presence, even beyond the grave, in her consciousness. Even Lethe, the river of oblivion, cannot erase his name from her memory:

> Und selbst in Lethe's Strom soll unvergessen
> Dein Name blühn! (31–32)
> (Even in Lethe's stream your name shall bloom unforgotten!)

Felicia Hemans's "A Parting Song" (1828), through the vehicle of its epigraph from "Corinne's Last Song" in Germaine de Staël's novel, announces itself as a direct address from the poet to her audience and, in a sense, effects a conflation of Staël and her friend Friederike Brun. "Oh! mes Amis, Rappelez vous quelquefois mes vers, mon âme y est empriente," ("Oh! My friends, remember my poems sometimes; my soul is imprinted on them.") exclaims the dying Corinne as she bids good-bye to her countrymen and bemoans the victimization and betrayal of the woman artist at the hands of passionate love.[5] These torments of Romantic love are significantly absent from the farewell of Hemans's dying poet who instead directs all her erotic energy into the plea that she be remembered by her audience, her "kind" or "sweet" friends as she calls them. As the final poem in Hemans's *Records of Woman*, then, "A Parting Song" offers a fitting conclusion to a volume that honors women's historical heroism and cultural accomplishment. She addresses not a single reader or lover but, as Benedict Anderson would call it, an "imagined community" of readers, a nation.

If we hold "A Parting Song" up to "Ich denke Dein," we see that Hemans places her dying poet in the position of the absent beloved evoked by Brun's poem, as Brun's passionate intensity is transposed into a gentle and sentimental melancholy. And it is the speaker who imagines her own presence/memory diffused throughout nature's seasons and moods as she queries repeatedly at the opening of each of the poem's four stanzas, "When will ye think of me, my friends? / When will ye think of me?" (lines 1–2). Hemans answers her persona's question for the reader in the main body of each stanza through the evocation of perceptual and emotive responses to the passing of time as recorded in nature's processes. Here the poet seeks to direct and control her own reception. References to the "deep'ning hush" (line 5) of evening, the gathering of nature's blooms where her "footsteps no more may tread" (line 13), "the sound of some olden melody" (line 18), "the voice of a mountain stream" (line 19), and "the charm of a poet's dream" (line 20) explicitly register both the passing of the female poet and her afterlife in the memory and consciousness of the reader. Indeed the speaker's own answer to her repeated question is emphatic: "Thus ever think of me!" (line 23), meaning, I believe, somewhat modestly, "if you think of me, think of me in this way" and, much more ambitiously, "think of me always, for all time into eternity." Finally, the anxious plea of Brun's parting lover is replaced with the powerful prayer and invocation of poetic fiat that concludes each stanza: "So let it be!" (line 28).

As we move from Brun to Hemans via Staël's Corinne, we witness a growing sense on the speaker's part of her public and lasting significance as a poet. The individual love affair is replaced by the love affair between poet and audience and the concern for the place in the beloved's heart by the self-conscious concern for poetic legacy. Yet if we return to Brun's poem and read it intertextually in the light of Hemans's preoccupations, "Ich denke Dein" reveals itself as a more self-reflexive work than is perhaps obvious on first reading. Indeed, Brian Keith-Smith suggests that Brun was haunted by a lifelong anxiety about the lasting value of her poetry and a concern that her work was overshadowed by the renown of her now canonical male contemporaries and by her daughter's success as a performer (145). We note, for example, in stanza four, "Philomela's Klage," ("Philomela's plaint"; line 15) as a reference to the transformation of silenced female suffering into song. And in stanza five, the "bunten Blätterkranze" ("colorful wreath of leaves"; line 17) brings to mind the poet's crown of laurels just as the "trüben Lampenschein" ("dim lamplight"; line 25) might evoke the poet's often painful effort to capture the splendor of past memories in the faded light of present efforts to put words to paper. The final stanza presents the image of the speaker's grave surrounded by swaying cypresses, inviting the reader to join their symbolic mourning of her future demise. Perhaps most strikingly, in the final stanza, it is the *name*, not the memory or the image of the beloved, that the poem claims to preserve from oblivion. Why this emphasis upon the name? One can only speculate. Still it is worth asking whether Brun is not ultimately conflating lover and beloved, so that in preserving the beloved's name from the oblivion of Lethe, she is perhaps, more importantly, preserving her own.

Up to this point in my analysis, I have been proceeding as if under the assumption that Hemans had read Brun's poem. Although this seems likely, given the currency of Brun's poetry in the Wordsworth circle as well as Heman's vast knowledge of German literature, there is no proof that she did.[6] I had in fact originally thought it equally likely that her "Parting Song" had been inspired by Goethe's adaptation of Brun in "Nähe des Geliebten"—that is until I read that poem and realized that the line which future female poets, starting with Hemans, all take from Brun—the plea to the reader to think of them—is not to be found in Goethe. Instead, Goethe asserts at the beginning of each stanza, "I think of you," "I see you," "I hear you" until, in the final verse, the beloved appears: "Du bist mir nah!" ("You are near to me!"; line 14).[7] It is certainly tempting to conclude that the Olympian Goethe either took the reader's/lover's response for granted or did not really care about it. What exactly the absence of dialogue with, or query/command to, the reader means one can of course never know, although it certainly is clear that the call to reciprocity and mutual consideration by reader and speaker so prevalent in the poetry of Brun and her female successors is completely absent in Goethe's poem. Thus, we find in Goethe's adaptation a lack of emphasis upon intersubjective response similar to that which Esterhammer finds in her comparison of Coleridge's Chamonix hymn to Brun's original; as Esterhammer puts it in regard to Coleridge, "the poet is now left talking to himself" ("Voice Not Heard" 235).

The contrasting call to reciprocity finds a particularly rich and sophisticated expression in Letitia Landon's "Night at Sea," written in 1838 while Landon was sailing to her newly married life in an African slave trading post, and published posthumously in 1839. Eleven of the poem's twelve stanzas conclude with the following refrain or some slight variation on it:

> My friends, my absent friends!
> Do you think of me, as I think of you?(9–10)[8]

Thus Landon makes explicit what Hemans's "Parting Song" implied—the poet imagines her audience as she creates, that they are never far from her thoughts. Indeed, in her essay "On the Character of Mrs. Hemans's Writings" (1835), Landon had written eloquently on what she termed "the intimate relation that subsists between the poet and public," the bonds—emotional, economic, and erotic—that link poet and audience, thus making explicit the key role this relationship played in her own poetic practice as well as in that of her much admired contemporary.

> [T]hose who would shrink from avowing what and how much they feel to even the most trusted friend, yet rely upon and crave the sympathy of the many.... The ill-fated and yet gifted being, steeped to the lips in poverty—that bitterest closer of the human heart—surrounded by the cold and careless—shrinking from his immediate circle, who neglect and misunderstand him, has faith in the far away. Suffering discourses eloquent music, and it believes that such music will find an echo and reply where the music only is known, and the maker loved for its sake. (184)

Landon's essay records the loss of this "faith in the far away," this trust in the public, as she concludes by quoting Hemans's "Chamois Hunter's Love," reading it not as a poem about an abandoned woman, but as the lament of the woman poet, trapped by her desire for approval and sympathy from her readers: "It is my youth—it is my bloom—it is my glad free heart/I cast away for thee..." (184). In the end, Landon comments bitterly on the objectification and commodification of the woman poet by a material and psychic economy that brings about her ruin: "Nothing takes more complete possession of its follower than literature. But never can success repay its cost.... If this be true even of one sex, how much more true of the other" (184).

Three years later, on her way to an African outpost of the British empire, Landon seems to have rethought the relation between author and public radically, so that she now emphasizes the poet's debt to her audience rather than merely her disillusionment with it.

> Till the lone vigil that I now am keeping,
> I did not know how much you were beloved.
> How many acts of kindness little heeded,
> Kind looks, kind words, rise half reproachful now!
> Hurried and anxious, my vexed life has speeded,
> And memory wears a soft accusing brow. (13–18)

In a pointed rewriting of Wordsworth's "Tintern Abbey," "Night at Sea" memorializes not the poet's "little, nameless, unremembered acts/Of kindness and of love," but rather those of the poet's absent and dearly missed friends. And memory is not Wordsworth's "dwelling place/For all sweet sounds and harmonies," his picture of Dorothy's consciousness in years to come and his effort to define his legacy and direct his reception. Rather, it reminds the poet of her own perhaps unpaid debt, her unfulfilled responsibilities to her friends, her audience.

The "lone vigil" kept by the speaker is a night watch threatened by the darkness of "dim star[s]" (line 6), "dark wave[s]" (line 11), and "shadowy sails" (line 22) that evoke the "dark parting" (line 38) from absent loved ones. Their absence teaches not only "the value of all old familiar things" (line 36), as Landon writes, but also lays bare the violence and danger she fears in the world beyond her familiar native land. Landon was undoubtedly influenced here by the tragic fate of her fellow poet Maria Jane Jewsbury who composed her *Oceanides* (1833) on her voyage to India and died of cholera within a year of her arrival there. Landon, in "Night at Sea," is clearly echoing *Oceanides*.—VIII, "A New Year's Day Song," in which Jewsbury contrasts the cozy holiday cheer of her native, wintry England to the languid tropical heat of her ocean voyage and queries, "Do they think of us to-day?—" (line 33) and "Do they drink 'The dear and far,' / With a fond and silent prayer?—" (lines 39–40).[9]

At the heart of "Night at Sea" are the realities of British imperialism which Landon, in proto-Nietzschean fashion, without moral or political judgment, presents as both ominous and fascinating, an embodiment of a ubiquitous will to power and domination:

> [O]'er the waters is [man's] rule transmitted
> By that great knowledge whence has power its birth.
> How oft on some strange loveliness while gazing
> Have I wished for you—beautiful as new,
> The purple waves like some wild army raising
> Their snowy banners as the ship cuts through. (43–48)

Just as the ocean's force mirrors human militarism in Landon's eyes, so, perhaps influenced by horrific slave ship accounts, she imagines the ocean itself as an abyss of conflict and violence from which no escape is possible:

> No life is in the air, but in the waters
> Are creatures, huge and terrible and strong,
> The sword-fish and the shark pursue their slaughters,
> War universal reigns these depths along. (61–64)

In the previous stanza, these murderous "depths" are compared to the cruel world from which genius, an Icarus both gorgeous and grotesque, seeks to rise up and free itself, only to be destroyed by the light of knowledge, fame and publicity:

> Bearing upon its wing the hues of morning,
> Up springs the flying fish, like life's false joy,
> Which of sunshine asks that frail adorning
> Whose very light is fated to destroy.
> Ah, so doth genius on its rainbow pinion,
> Spring from the depths of an unkindly world;
> So spring sweet fancies from the heart's dominion.—

Too soon in death the scorched up wing is furled. (51–58)

The bright light of sunshine, then, is not the element that suits the anomalous figure of the female poet. And if Brun's poem moved from the brilliant light of the beloved's presence to the dim lamplight of composition, so Landon's female poet is identified with the Queen of the Night and the gentle power of moonlight "Whitening the dusky sails" (line 72), and "shedding / The softest influence that o'er night prevails" (lines 73–74). In Landon's poem, then, we see the elaboration of Brun's cryptic allusions to the light of poetic memory in an imperial context that allows the female poet room to expand her faculties even as it genders them much more explicitly. The cheerfulness and "glad endeavor" (line 83) of sunlight are, however, foreign to her as she is haunted by "passionate thoughts too fond, too deep" (line 76) of friends left behind.

> Sunshine and hope are comrades, and their weather
> Calls into life the energies of the earth;
> But memory and moonlight go together,
> Reflected in the light that either brings. (85–88)

The concluding stanzas of "Night at Sea" constitute a meditation on the relation of memory and vision, despair and hope, absence and presence, death and life, poet and audience as the speaker seeks to balance, if not reconcile, these antinomies under the influence of the luminous moonlight that shimmers glowworm-like upon the sea:

> All that the spirit keeps of thought and feeling,
> Takes visionary hues from such an hour;
> But while some fantasy is o'er me stealing,
> I start, remembrance has a keener power.
> My friends, my absent friends,
> From the fair dream I start to think of you! (105–10)

Thus, memories of her friends and readers block the realization of her visionary fantasies and "fair dream[s]" (line 110) as Landon's persona contemplates the death, both physical and spiritual, of her female genius. Poet and public seem locked in a dance of death; no Wordsworthian transcendence through memory seems possible. Yet ultimately the poem ends on a note of hope, not despair, as the moonlight traces out a shoreline ahead on the horizon and the "eager ship" (line 119) steers toward a much-anticipated landing. This assurance of an imminent landing concludes the poem with "the energies of earth" (line 86) that Landon had earlier associated with a call to life, suggesting even that, if she had lived, she might have found, in her African world, new and less destructive ways of envisioning her relation to her British public.

This task was instead taken over by Elizabeth Barrett Browning, among many others, whose "L.E.L.'s Last Question" (1839) once again takes up the refrain, "Do you think of me, as I think of you?"—this time as emblematic of Landon's role as British national poetess who "poured many a year / Love's oracles for England" (lines 29–30).[10] In the early stanzas Browning seems to be scolding Landon, whom she demeaningly terms "the craver of a little love" for her self-absorption and ineffectuality:

> And little in this world the loving do,
> But sit (among the rocks?) and listen for
> The echo of their own love evermore—. (11–13)

Such female meekness and narcissism hardly promises great poetry.

Yet the poem concludes by transforming Landon's plea into a universal emblem of human spiritual solitude, thus turning the introductory deprecation on its head:

> O friends, O kindred, O dear brotherhood
> Of the whole world—what are we that we should
> For covenants of long affection sue?—
> Why press so near each other, when the touch
> Is barred by graves? Not much and yet too much,
> This "Think upon me as I think of you." (51–56)

And with missionary zeal, Browning transforms Landon from a national "poetess" to a poet of universal human suffering, a Christ figure with a redemptive message for all:

> Above the unshaken stars that see us die,
> A vocal pathos rolls—and He who drew
> All life from dust, and *for* all, tasted death,
> By death, and life, and love appealing, saith,
> *Do you think of me as I think of you?* (59–63)

It is ironic that Brun's refrain should be put to such ideological uses, given her own strong anti-nationalist, anti-imperialist feelings based on her horror at the British bombarding of French-occupied Copenhagen in 1807. Furthermore, Browning's Christian orthodoxy seems a violation of both the spirit and the tone of Landon's work. We should remember, however, that in "L.E.L's Last Question," Browning's Christ in fact repeats exactly the female poet's query, which in a sense has authority and primacy in the poem, thus suggesting the sacredness of her suffering and underlining the possibility that her endless questioning is not, after all, in vain.[11] We should also remember that, even if Friederike Brun's name itself does not live on and flower in the poetry of her female successors, her art certainly does.

## Notes

1  Brun herself significantly rewrote "Ich denke Dein" several times. See Keith Smith (150). According to Esterhammer in "The Improvisation of Romanticism," Brun responded to the immediate success of the poem by publishing five different versions of the poem in the next fifteen years (12–13).

2  As quoted in Esterhammer, "Coleridge's 'Hymn before Sun-rise' and the Voice Not Heard," (227–28).

3  Povlsen asserts that Bonstetten was Brun's platonic lover and points to the fact that, of her correspondence, "[O]nly the crucial years between 1806 and 1810, when she lived in Rome and was in doubt about whether to leave her husband or not, whether Bonstetten really loved her or not, are unaccounted for" (109). Matthisson edited the correspondence between Bonstetten and Brun.

4  Matthisson's first edition of Brun's *Gedichte*, (44–45), is the source of quotations from "Ich denke Dein." Translations are mine.

5  Quotations of "A Parting Song" are from Leighton and Reynolds, (19–20).

6  Dorothy Wordsworth writes in her August 16 and 17, 1800 entry to the *Grasmere Journals* that William read his "Seven Sisters or The Solitude of Binnorie," an adaptation of Brun's "Die sieben Hügel," to Coleridge and her.

7  Quotations from and translations of Goethe's "Nähe des Geliebten" are from Goethe's *Selected Poems* ed. Middleton.

8  Quotations from "Night at Sea" and "On the Character of Mrs. Hemans's Writings" are from Landon, *Selected Writings*, ed. McGann and Riess, (205–08 and 173–86).

9  Quotations from *The Oceanides* are from Judith Pascoe's *Romantic Circles* (electronic edition). Pascoe notes that Jewsbury was close friends with Hemans and corresponded with Landon and that both poets admired her writings. Pascoe also asserts that Jewsbury clearly saw herself as part of "a coterie of talented women writers" that included Hemans and Landon.

10  Quotations from "L.E.L's Last Question" are from Ashfield, (284–85).

11  At the same time, Barrett Browning also offers here a clear challenge to the deprecation of women's spiritual and poetic capabilities as expressed by Romney in her later *Aurora Leigh* (45):

> 'Women as you are,
> Mere women, personal and passionate,
> You give us doating mothers, and perfect wives,
> Sublime Madonnas, and enduring saints!
> We get no Christ from you,—and verily

We shall not get a poet, in my mind.' (220–25)

**Works Cited**

Ashfield, Andrew, ed. *Romantic Women Poets, 1770–1838*. Manchester: Manchester UP, 1994.
Browning, Elizabeth Barrett. *Aurora Leigh*. Ed. Magaret Reynolds. New York: Norton, 1996.
Brun, Friederike. *Gedichte*. Ed. Friedrich Matthisson. Zürich: Orell, Gessner, Füssli, and Co., 1795.
Esterhammer, Angela. "Coleridge's 'Hymn before Sun-rise' and the Voice not Heard." *Samuel Taylor Coleridge and the Sciences of Life*. Ed. Nicholas Roe. Oxford: Oxford UP, 2001. 224–45.
———. "The Improvisation of Romanticism." Unpublished essay. Goethe, Johann Wolfgang von. *Selected Poems*. Ed. Christopher Middleton. Boston: Suhrkamp/Insel, 1983.
Jewsbury, Maria Jane. *The Oceanides*. Ed. Judith Pascoe. *Romantic Circles*.
Keith-Smith, Brian. "Friederike Brun, (1765–1835): In Tears There Is Joy." *Sappho in the Shadows: Essays on the Work of German Women Poets in the Age of Goethe (1749–1832)*. Ed. Anthony J. Harper and Margaret C. Ives. Bern: Peter Lang, 2000. 145–88.
Landon, Letitia Elizabeth. *Letitia Elizabeth Landon: Selected Writings*. Eds. Jerome McGann and Daniel Reiss. Peterborough: Broadview, 1997.
Leighton, Angela and Margaret Reynolds, eds. *Victorian Women Poets*. Oxford: Blackwell, 1995.
Lootens, Tricia. "Receiving the Legend, Rethinking the Writer: Letitia Landon and the Poetess Tradition." *Romanticism and Women Poets: Opening the Doors of Reception*. Eds. Harriet Kramer Linkin and Stephen Behrendt. Lexington: University of Kentucky Press, 1999. 242–59.
Matthisson, Friedrich, ed. *Briefe von Karl Viktor bon Bonstetten an Friederike Brun*. Frankfurt: Schäfer, 1829.
Povlsen, Karen Klitgaard. "Between Body and Text." *NORA: Nordic Journal of Women's Studies* 2 (1994): 107–119.

## Chapter Ten

# The Discourse of Religious *Bildung* in Anne Brontë's *Agnes Grey*

### Larry H. Peer

Anne Brontë's *Agnes Grey* has been overlooked or misjudged by even the most adamant Brontë enthusiasts. Apart from George Moore's surprising claim that it was the most perfect prose narrative in English literature, it has been treated on the whole, as Tom Winnifrith so aptly puts it, "with condescending indifference" (66). Among the few considerations *Agnes Grey* has received, it has been judged to consist of three principal purposes: "a pedagogic one, a protest against tyranny, and an attempt to reconcile the passionate yearning heart with life's realities" (Scott, 9). Some have, in identifying it with the original *Passages in the Life of an Individual*, dismissed it merely as a running diary of Anne's experiences as a governess, while others, in agreeing with the contemporary reviewers of the work, have found it a "somewhat course imitation of one of (Jane) Austen's charming stories ... [that] leaves no painful impressions on the mind ..." (see Winnifreth, 73). Many have agreed with Saintsbury that her work is "a pale reflection of her elders" (243), thus discouraging in-depth analyses of Anne Brontë's work in which "gentle Anne" would not be seen as a mere extension of her older siblings.

Perhaps a new appreciation of Anne Brontë as a novelist generally, and of *Agnes Grey* as a novel specifically, might be achieved if the work were to be approached in two previously ignored ways: first, it must be understood as a Romantic work, where the novel is not a mere retelling of Anne's experiences, but a self-projection of Anne the novelist into Agnes the character (see Peer), and just as importantly, where the work is seen as an organic whole, "eine progressive Universalpoesie", as Friedrich Schlegel put it in his well-known one-hundred-and-sixteenth *Athenäumsfragment*. Secondly, and this approach is a logical extension of the first, *Agnes Grey* must be viewed as a *Bildungsroman*, a suggestion or hint found in Winnifrith, Gerin, and Nash, but has never been explored in any detail. These two approaches necessarily implicate each other, since, as Marianne Osborne asserts, the *Bildungsroman* may be seen as "an affirmative form of Romantic fiction ..." where

> The organic and potentially harmonic natural world which lives and evolves through the hero or heroine in the *Bildungsroman* is an index of Romantic

faith in man's ability, himself, to grow in harmony and into wholeness with his environment. (33)

Put another way, the potential of showing dynamic characterization is married to the external structure of the genre, wherein the end of the novel does not come to a certain close, but allows for additional growth and *Werden*, additionally intertwining the *Bildungsroman* with the organicity of Romanticism and its valorization of the fragmented. At this stage in my revisionary reading of the novel, I wish to explore *Agnes Grey* as a particular kind of *Bildungsroman*, during which clues to its position in the Romantic movement will hopefully become apparent as well.

The *Bildungsroman* is central to Romantic genology. As is well-known in the field of comparative genre studies, the early *Bildungsroman*, wherein the hero merely sets out to be educated by the world, in order eventually to integrate himself into society as a useful and productive member, has at least two aesthetic limitations. First of all, thinking of the genre in terms of its external structural pattern alone ignores the central significance of attitude and tone, of "inner" structure, as Hegel observed (220). Secondly, limiting the understanding of genre to mere plot line collapses the idea of literary form to generalized literary thematics. As Martin Swales suggests:

> What, for me, separates the minor texts from the major ones is precisely the fact that the great works meet and explore the thematic possibilities of adolescent flux and change with a differentiation and generosity that is lacking in the minor works (6).

That is, this genre's openness to thematic differentiation expands the whole notion of plot, in fact, the whole notion of narratological complexity and possibility, which possibility links the study of the genre with hermeneutic theory, specifically in how these possibilities can be explained in terms of an oscillation between genre expectations and the individual text.

It is interesting to view a majority of English language scholarship in this regard. For example, Jerome Buckley, in his *Season of Youth: The Bildungsroman from Dickens to Golding*, lists *David Copperfield* and *Great Expectations*, and Thacckery's *Pendennis* (1849), as the first true *Bildungsroman* in English fiction. His analysis of the works that he chooses ignores the "inwardness of spirit" which most German theorists locate at the core of *Bildungsromane*. A clue to the differences between these two traditions is given by Buckley himself when he mentions that, while writing about the development of the *Bildungsroman* in England, he was constantly "struck by the awkwardness of the German term as applied to English literature", and that he has therefore applied "several possible synonyms: the novel of youth, the novel of education, etc." (vii). Buckley mentions several key characteristics of the English *Bildungsroman*, such as the move from provinciality to a large city, the role of wealth and money, and the necessity of an orphaned hero (or, at least, one who has an antagonistic relationship with his father). Although the element of "soul-searching" is also mentioned, it is the social environment of the hero, rather than his inward *Bildung* that is emphasized. Despite the fact that there are common elements among the two traditions, such as the basic plot of a hero who embarks on a journey in order to become educated in some way, the underlying main thrusts are quite different. This is why, I would argue, there is an inappropriateness in applying the term *Bildungsroman* to the "Victorian" novels mentioned above.

This distinction is key because *Agnes Grey* does not fit into the paradigm constructed by English-language scholarship. *Agnes Grey* is a *Bildungsroman* that carries this term without awkwardness. As Scott observes, it is the inward reflections and ponderings of Agnes that determine which exterior scenes will be described:

> We move without effort from the young appointee's inward musings to the exterior scene, first in its totality and then particulars—as her new place of work swings into view; then back again to the interior ponderings which have now (at the crisis of the journey as it were) become self-examination. (15)

It is apparent that, although the English tradition of the *Bildungsroman* does not very well fit into continental genological patterns, *Agnes Grey* has no difficulties, as it follows in the tradition of the German *Bildungsroman*. I would argue that the late nineteenth-century works consistently cited in English language scholarship are *not* the first true *Bildungsromane* created in England, but that *Agnes Grey* is.

The second problem one encounters in establishing a *Bildungsroman* of expectation as applied to *Agnes Grey* is the fact that the hero of this work is not a hero, but, in fact, a heroine. When one speaks of *Bildung*, one also thinks of a *Bildungsreise*, wherein the hero embarks upon some sort of a journey away from his parental home. There are no limitations at all imposed upon him, since a young man many pursue whatever life he desires. When one thinks of a heroine in the England of Anne Brontë, however, there are several limits placed upon the *Bildungsreise*. A woman in the position of Agnes has two options that will take her away from her home: she can get married, or she can become a governess. Agnes chooses the life of a governess, so that she can fulfill her "secret wish to see a little more of the world" (*Agnes Grey*, 2). The greatest advantage to this situation is that, because of the necessity to remain stationary for the most part, her *Bildung* necessarily turns inward, the infrequent journeyings from house to house merely marking for the reader the successive stages of her inner development. This allows for that posited by David Miles, of the hero as "confessor" rather than as "picaro" (989). And Marianne Osborne explains this very well:

> For the woman, the chances of a satisfactory reconciliation between the will and the form that life finally takes, seem even more tenuous because of the greater number of conditions set upon her by nature and by society. Though she may be incapable of "heroic action" ... within the *Bildungsroman* she can achieve an inward heroism at least as great as the man's, for her struggle is at least as intense as the man's. (54)

Thus, are two basic problems with the Romantic *Bildungsroman* resolved; namely, the *Bildung* as inward journey as the possibility of a female hero.

But it is what Anne does with the possibilities inherent in this genre that makes *Agnes Grey* so important. I suggest that the source of Agnes's *Bildung* is not only experience, but her specific means of dealing with experience, her religious *Bildung*. I do not mean that the purpose of this novel is a didactic one; I mean that it is Agnes's realization of what the faith she has been brought up with truly means, beyond the theoretical lessons she has learned about overcoming the world and being a good Christian, that constitutes her real *Bildung*. This *Bildung* cannot be achieved, though, without the Miss Murrays and Mr. Hatfields that she must first encounter along the way. In addition, the protagonist's religious *Bildung* is inseparable from, and often manifested in, nature outside her. Of course, this corresponds to the Romantic idea of the relationship of natural imagery to the meditative mind. Thus, in the world of *Agnes Grey*, the reader is in touch with both the empirical world and a working Romantic mind (see Osborne, 25).

There are, of course, other types of events that mature Agnes, yet her entire *Bildung* seems to revolve around her religious *Bildung* (partially suggested by Chitham, 19 ff.) and, as a consequence, her feeling of being at one with nature. In the course of the novel she not only learns what it means to put her faith into practice, but she also is able to recognize the true meaning and purpose of religion. This occupies the site of Romantic ideas of inward religion, and it also makes the link to nature more understandable. The following comment by Thomas Mann about the inwardness of core *Bildung* is relevant here:

> The inwardness, the "Bildung"... implies introspectiveness; an individualistic cultural conscience; consideration for the careful tending, the shaping, deepening and perfecting of one's own personality or, in religious terms, for the salvation and justification of one's own life; subjectivism in the things of the mind, therefore, a type of culture that might be called pietistic, given to autobiographical confession and deeply personal ... (cited in Swales, 159).

François Jost mentions that:

> ... the hero of the *Bildungsroman*, rather than following a program of studies like the hero of the *Erziehungsroman*, pursues a goal that he himself has per-

haps only vaguely formulated, a goal to which he has entirely dedicated himself; the struggle for attaining that goal forms and perfects him, although he remains in his natural milieu, in his professional and social environment. (137)

In other words, the heroine follows that type of *Bildung* which will best form and shape her character, even though she is not always aware of it. Indeed, at the start of the novel, Agnes is not aware of why she must leave her parental home; she only realizes that she has not yet been sufficiently exposed to "life":

> ... father, mother, and sister, all combined to spoil me—not by foolish indulgence, to render me fractious and ungovernable, but by ceaseless kindness, to make me too helpless and dependent—too unfit for buffeting with the cares and turmoils of life. Mary and I were brought up in the strictest seclusion. (*Agnes Grey*, 1)

The sheltering that Agnes has received has put her in a position where she is incapable of being tried, incapable of testing what she has learned to be true. After informing her mother of her intentions to become a governess, the following exchange takes place:

> "But, my love, you have not learned to take care of *yourself* yet: and young children require more judgement and experience than older ones."
> "But, mamma, I am above eighteen, and quite able to take care of myself, and others too. You do not know the wisdom and prudence I possess, *because I have not been tried.*" (8)

Although Agnes's outward reason for becoming a governess is to earn money for her debt-ridden-family, by this point it has already been made clear that it is her secret desire to go into the world that is her key motivation. Yet, she does not seem to be aware of exactly how her character will be shaped, or why she needs to be tried. It is often while she and her sister are wandering on the "heath-clad hills" that her inward fire of a longing to progress in some other way is kindled:

> What happy hours Mary and I have passes, while sitting at our work by the fire, or wandering on the heath-clad hills, or idling under the weeping birch (the only considerable tree in the garden), talking of future happiness to ourselves and our parents, of what we should do, and see, and possess; ... (4)

It is significant that much of her desire to commence with her *Bildungsreise* is inspired by the nature that surrounds her, it being, after all, the perfect metaphor for dynamic progression. It is in terms of nature that Agnes describes what she feels she will be able to do with the children that will be entrusted to her:

> How delightful it would be to be a governess! To go out into the world; to enter upon a new life; to act for myself; to exercise my unused faculties; to try my unknown powers; to earn my own maintenance, and something to comfort and help my father, mother and sister ...
> Whatever others said, I felt I was fully competent to the task: the clear remembrance of my own thoughts in early childhood would be a surer guide than the instructions of the most mature advisor. I had but to turn from my little pupils to myself at their age, and I should know, at once, how to win their confidence and affections: how to waken the contrition of the erring; how to embolden the timid, and console the afflicted; how to make Virtue practicable, Instruction desirable, and Religion lovely and comprehensible.
> —Delightful task!
> To teach the young idea how to shoot!
> To train the tender plants, and watch their buds unfolding day by day! (9)

Although it is a worthy goal, Agnes does not realize at the point that her plan of attack will not work. This statement seems to apply better to her own development, as it is her "buds" that will unfold day by day, and since it is to her that "Virtue will become practicable and Religion lovely and comprehensible."

It is with these high aspirations that this young heroine leaves her secluded little parsonage to accept her first position as governess. Along her *Bildungsreise*, Agnes will pass through three different stages of *Bildung*, each of which has a unique and significant importance in contributing to her character development. It is during the first stage, while she is employed with the Bloomfield family, that she is mainly prepared for the next stage. Although she must learn patience and perseverance, and while the cruelty of her first pupils brings out the gentle mildness in her character, the main purpose of this ordeal is to bring down her high aspirations and give her a taste of how trials must be overcome in life. She certainly does have her share of trials while at Wellwood, all of which teach her that her original goals of "being able to act for herself", of "exercising her unused faculties", of "gaining the confidence and affection of her pupils", and of "teaching their young ideas how to shoot" would not be realized. Through all of her afflictions, which not only include the children's tormenting, but the lack of privacy and power to act according to her own will, she is only able to turn to one solace, her faith in God:

> I knew the difficulties I had to contend with were great; but I knew (at least I believed) unremitting patience and perseverance could overcome them; and night and morning I implored Divine assistance to this end. But either the children were so incorrigible, the parents so unreasonable, or myself so mistaken in my views, or so unable to carry them out, that my best intentions and most strenuous efforts seemed productive of no better result than sport to the chil-

dren, dissatisfaction to their parents, and torment to myself. (25)

At this point Agnes is trying to come to terms with the fact that not every family is like the family she grew up in, and she is questioning why these children cannot be gently steered by the moral example she provides. Here she has the faith to turn to her Maker, yet she cannot understand why she must experience these trials. After her optimistic hopes of chapter one, she has now been plunged into an abyss of despair; she does not know, though, that she, herself, if anyone, is being educated. We see the blatant contrast of her inner development of faith to the seemingly pious grandmother, who lectures to Agnes on what piety encompasses:

> "But there's one remedy for all, my dear, and that's resignation" (a toss of the head) "resignation to the will of heaven!" (an uplifting of the hands and eyes ... "but I'm one of the pious ones, Miss Grey!" (a very significant nod and toss). "And, thank heaven, I always was" (another nod), "and glory in it!" (an emphatic clasping of the hands and shaking of the head). And with several texts of scripture, misquoted or misapplied, and religious exclamations so redolent of the ludicrous in the style and delivery and manner of bringing in it, if not in the expressions themselves, that I decline repeating them, she withdrew ... (35)

Mrs. Bloomfield the elder is much like Mr. Hatfield of the later chapters. Both of these characters exemplify the type of outward "non-Romantic" religiosity Agnes learns about and rejects in the course of her development. At this point she realizes that Mrs. Bloomfield's convictions of "resignation" and "always having been pious" (a non-Romantic idea in and of itself, since humans are imperfect and always progressing), are not true Religion, yet she has not yet completely come to terms with what true Religion is. She does not really understand this until she learns a very significant lesson from Mr. Weston through Nancy Brown much later in her development.

It is significant that the Bloomfields' garden and the vegetation therein are described very much in terms of the neo-classical French garden. It is when Agnes later moves on to take up her position with the Murrays that she reflects back on the "tastefully" laid-out garden of the Bloomfields, with its "smooth-shaven lawn and young trees guarded by palings"; Agnes seems to prefer the more natural garden of the Murrays. It is for this reason that she does not feel comfortable in her natural surroundings while at Wellwood. The garden there is human—controlled by man, a fact she learns within the first few hours of her arrival there:

> There were two round beds, stocked with a variety of plants. In one there was a pretty little rose tree. I paused to admire its lovely blossoms.

> "Oh, never mind that!" said he contemptuously. "That's only *Mary Ann's* garden; look THIS is mine." After I had observed every flower, and listened to a disquisition on every plant, I was permitted to depart; but first, with great pomp, he plucked a polyanthus and presented it to me, as one conferring a prodigious favour. (17–18)

The purpose of all this is to reaffirm to us and to Agnes the great change that has taken place within the heroine. She is now able to equate happiness with wisdom and goodness. Her character is the source of her happiness, despite the fact that her secret wish appears to have no hope in sight. She returns to her home completely at peace with herself.

That Anne was at peace with her own religiosity seems clear from her poems and letters. Her major biographers (Gerin and Stanford) have found evidence that her search for the divine began in infancy and became a passionate dedication. Her family knew her heart to be religiously "avid, eager, and sensitive" (Chitham, 19), and her fictional self-projection manifests the exact notion of religion as comprehending the core of moral knowledge and action that we find in Anne's personal experience. As Anne writes, and as Agnes learns,

> But most throughout the moral world
> I saw his glory shine;
> I saw his wisdom infinite,
> His mercy all divine ...
> And while I wondered and adored
> His wisdom so divine,
> I did not tremble at his power,
> I felt that God was mine. (Chitham, 82–3)

**Works Cited**

Brontë, Anne. *Agnes Grey*. London: Thomas Cautley Newby, 1847.
Buckley, Jerome Hamilton. *Season of Youth: The Bildungsroman from Dickens to Golding*.Cambridge: Harvard UP, 1974.
Chitham, Edward. *The Poems of Anne Brontë: A New Text and Commentary*. Totowa: Rowman and Littlefield, 1979.
Gerin, Winifred. *Anne Brontë: A Biography*. London: Allen Lane, 1976.
Jost,François. *Introduction to Comparative Literature*. New York: Bobbs-Merrill, 1974.
Kohn, Lothar. *Entwicklungs- und Bildungsroman: Ein Forschungbericht*. Stuttgart: Metzlar, 1969.
Miles, David H. "The Picaro's Journey to the Confessional." *PMLA* 89 (1974): 980–92.

Nash, Julie and Barbara A. Suess, eds. *New Approaches to the Literary Art of Anne Brontë*: Aldershot: Ashgate, 2001.
Osborne, Marianne. "The Hero and Heroine in the British Bildungsroman: *David Copperfield* and *A Portrait of the Artist as a Young Man* and *The Rainbow*." Tulane University dissertation, 1971.
Pascal, Roy. *The German Novel*. Toronto: University of Toronto Press, 1956.
Peer, Larry H. *Beyond Haworth: Essays on the Brontës in European Literature*. Provo: Brigham Young UP, 1985.
Saintsbury, George. *The English Novel*. London: J.M. Dent and Sons, 1913.
Scott, P.J.M. *Anne Brontë: A New Critical Assessment*. London: Vision, 1983.
Stanford, Derek and Ada Harrison. *Anne Brontë: Her Life and Work*. New York: John Day, 1959.
Swales, Martin. *The German Bildungsroman from Wieland to Hesse*. Princeton, NJ: Princeton UP, 1978.
Swales, Martin. "Unverwirklichte Totalität: Bemerkungen zum deutschen Bildungsroman." *Der deutsche Roman unde seine historischen und politischen Bedingungen*. Ed. Wolfgang Paulsen. Bern: Francke Verlag, 1977. 90–106.
Tennyson, G. "The Bildungsroman in Nineteenth Century Literature." *Medieval Epic to the "Epic Theatre" of Brecht*. Ed. Richard Spalek. 135–46.
Winnifrith, Tom. *The Brontës*. New York: Macmillan, 1977.

# Part 3
# Varieties of Revisionist Discourse in Romanticism

Chapter Eleven

# Readerly Agency and the Discourse of History in *The Antiquary*

## Bonnie J. Gunzenhauser

In 1823 Walter Scott masterminded an effort to establish an Edinburgh antiquarian society known as the Bannatyne Club. The Club's specific purpose, Scott writes to a prospective member, is "to rescue from the chance of destruction, the documents most essential to the history and literature of Scotland" (VIII.19–20). But its more general purpose, he explains in his *Journal*, is to counteract "the usual habit of antiquaries" by overlooking "things that are merely curious" in favor of focusing on "what is useful" (170). What, precisely, does Scott see as "useful" in the Club's practice of publishing documents from the Scottish past? Scott himself provides one answer to this question in an 1822 letter to his son, in which he speculates on the singularly important role history plays in shaping the course of human progress:

> Our ancestors lodged in caves and wigwams where we construct palaces for the rich and comfortable dwellings for the poor. And why is this but because our eye is enabled to look back upon the past and to improve on our ancestors' improvements and to avoid their errors[?] This can only be done by studying history and comparing it with passing events. (VII.734)

The claim is particularly striking since several of Scott's contemporaries want to deny him this kind of panoptic view. Hazlitt, for instance, insists that Scott "is just half what the human intellect is capable of being ... he knows all that it *has been*; all that *is to be* is nothing to him" (IV.241). But in the letter Scott clearly insists on history as a progressive force, something with a forward-looking pedagogical capacity: "studying history" allows the members of any given society "to improve on ... improvements" in order to build a better future. According to Scott's claim, history stands as a key force of social regulation; a full historical record provides individuals with the tools they require not simply to "avoid errors" but to become agents of individual and collective "improvement."

While Scott presumes, both here and in his *Journal*, that antiquaries and historians are motivated primarily by an altruistic desire for general "improvement," early nineteenth-century historical practice does not necessarily bear this out. The years leading up to Scott's novelistic career—a career that spanned nearly twenty years, from *Waverley*'s publication in 1814 to Scott's death in 1833—saw significant changes in the practice of history. The situation Hayden White describes in eighteenth-century England, when "historical studies had no discipline proper to itself alone ... [and] was for the most part an activity of amateurs," was, by the early nineteenth century, gradually but irreversibly shifting. Despite some ongoing boundary disputes—the lines between "professional" and "amateur" historians remained somewhat blurred, and philosophical and antiquarian modes of practicing history competed for primacy—it is still the case that, by the early nineteenth century, a "properly disciplined study of history" had begun to emerge (60).[1] As history became "disciplined" in the early nineteenth century, White notes, it also became institutionalized, and two key consequences ensued. First, the practice of history was increasingly consolidated in the hands of relatively few professional historians; and, second, these historians in turn became increasingly interested in creating historical narratives that supported and justified their particular institutional positions. In other words, White argues, most historians were indebted to, or motivated by, hegemonic political interests, which meant that the emergence of history as a discipline helped to further "consolidat[e] ... the bourgeois nation-state" (61). In this relatively new early nineteenth-century situation, White suggests, professional historians did much to make history into a tool to further special interests and little to preserve history as a vital regulatory force with an integrity of its own.

Recent readers of Scott's historical novels have tended to implicate him in this more circumscribed practice of history. Robert Crawford, for instance, argues that Scott uses his historical novels primarily to advance Scottish national interests, while Ian Duncan and Kathryn Sutherland claim that, in his novels, Scott uses history chiefly to further his own economic ends. Overlooking the Scott of the Bannatyne Club, who describes history as a crucial social link between past, present, and future, Duncan points to Scott's romance form as proof that Scott sees history as an appropriable "object." The genre emphasizes, as Duncan puts it, "exclusion from historical process," and therefore allows Scott to construct a world in which "to be a British subject is to have transcended historical process in order to occupy a generic idyll of private life" (15, 58). Duncan concludes that Scott's readers, influenced by this view, come to see little relation between their daily lives and the practice of history, and that these readers thus readily concede the practice of history to a few "representative citizens" (18)—among whom Duncan numbers Scott.

But does Scott fit so neatly into the company of professional historians ready to adapt their narratives to the needs of the moment? Let us consider Scott's 1816 novel *The Antiquary* as an historiographical commentary in which Scott operates according to a more split agenda. The novel, which Scott identified as his personal favorite, has a fundamentally descriptive purpose: Scott explains that he writes it largely to illustrate "the manners ... passions ... and language" of a small Scottish community in the 1790s (5). Critics have often read the novel, which tells the story of a middle-aged gentleman watching his community to find a lost heir and prepare for a French invasion that never comes, as a gently mocking self-portrait on Scott's part, identifying Scott exclusively with the titular protagonist Jonathan Oldbuck.[2] But I think we might better identify Scott with each of the novel's two central characters—Oldbuck and the repository of local lore, the old beggar Edie Ochiltree—because the two, taken together, neatly externalize a key conflict that plagues Scott throughout his career as an author and historian: namely, can one look to history as the basis of a profitable professional career yet simultaneously rely on history as a dynamic force of social and civic "improvement"? Oldbuck, whose claims to professional, disinterested historical inquiry only very thinly veil a web of more self-interested motivations, stands in for the authorial Scott—a figure who is, in Duncan's words, committed to effecting "the appropriation, and reinvention, of a common cultural heritage as individual literary property" (58). Ochiltree, on the other hand, replaces Oldbuck's ostensibly "professional," but clearly self-interested, history with narratives that account for the full range of available historical evidence. He thus preserves far more effectively than Oldbuck the full historical record on which Scott predicates history's pedagogical, "improving" function. We might read Ochiltree, then, as an illustration that when historians like Oldbuck (and perhaps by extension, Scott's author-of-*Waverley* self) allow specialized agendas (political, personal, or both) to shape the historical narratives they produce, they limit and therefore compromise the completeness and accuracy of the available historical record—actions which in turn limit and compromise the "improving" function of historical discourse. The Oldbuck—Ochiltree character pairing merits further attention not only because it helps sort out Scott's historiographical critique, but also because, finally, it points us toward Scott's solution for the limitations imposed by the emergent discipline of professional history. Through the figure of Ochiltree, Scott begins to show his readers how to practice history for themselves—a lesson that he returns to throughout his oeuvre in order, finally, to establish a grass-roots historicizing network that ensures history's ability to realize its full civic "improving" function.

Ochiltree challenges Oldbuck's singular and ultimately self-interested historical narratives from their very first scene together. Early in the novel, Oldbuck attempts to impress the young outsider, Lovel, that Oldbuck's community of Fairport is home to a site of great "national concern" (29); specifically, the battlefield on which the Roman general Agricola met and defeated the Caledonian forces in the first century. Oldbuck is correct to identify the battlefield site as a question of national concern; it was a matter of much debate among Scottish historians, who saw the battle as a watershed in Scottish national history and identity formation, and who sought to recover the battle site as a physical location upon which to project a Scottish patriotism. But Oldbuck quickly demonstrates that he invokes the rhetoric of "national concern" only to cover the fact that his concerns in the matter are very personal indeed. That the site is "the property of the obscure and humble individual who now speaks" to Lovel is clearly what's important to Oldbuck, given both the "sly pride" with which he utters the claim (29) and the fact that he determinedly reads the physical evidence of the site in ways that satisfy not a national need for patriotism, but a personal need for recognition. He first explains that the landscape's various features align perfectly with those Tacitus describes in the only contemporary account of the battle. "It was near to the Grampian Mountains; lo! Yonder they are," Oldbuck notes. "It was *in conspectus class is*—in sight of the Roman fleet; and would any admiral, Roman or British, wish a fairer bay to ride in than that on your right hand? (29). With these observations, Oldbuck claims a special status for himself, exclaiming, "It is astonishing how blind ... professed antiquaries sometimes are; Sir Robert Sibbalk, Saunders, Gordon, Doctor Stukely, why, [these corresponding features] escaped all of them" (29). His unique ability to read the landscape, Oldbuck imples, establishes him not simply as a "professed" antiquary, but as a real one. He cements his self-proclaimed status as master interpreter by turning his attention to the site's linguistic evidence, playing what he clearly sees as his trump card by offering his translation of a presumed Latin inscription found on a stone in what Oldbuck identifies as "the central point, the *praetorium*, doubtless, of the camp" (30). This stone, Oldbuck explains, "bears a sacrificing vessel, and the letters A.D.L.L., which may stand, without much violence, for *Agricola Dicavit Libens Lubens*, or 'Agricola dedicated this willingly'" (30). Oldbuck's editorializing—"without much violence"—already bears witness that he may protest too much, and when Edie Ochiltree responds to Oldbuck's claims, his revisionary readings not only challenge Oldbuck's but effectively dismantle them by reviving the historical voices which Oldbuck so assiduously represses.

Ochiltree replaces the tortuous and esoteric antiquarian interpretations on which Oldbuck has relied with information drawn from local communal culture. He identifies the site not as a matter of grave national concern, but simply as the location of a wedding held twenty years earlier. He first rereads the landscape, explaining that its more particular features—what Oldbuck had taken for a fort and a *praetorium*, respectively—are simply a "lang dyke" built for drainage and a shelter that he and some others built for "auld Aiken Drum's bridal" (32). Ochiltree advances, as definitive proof of his claim, the same inscription on which Oldbuck rests *his* own case. Ochiltree says:

If ye dig up the bourock [the central heap of stones that Oldbuck identifies as the *praetorium*], ye'll find, if ye hae not fund it already, a stone that one o' the masons cut a ladle on to have a joke at the bridegroom, and he put four letters on't; that's A.D.L.L.— "Aiken Drum's Lang Ladle"; for Aiken was one o' the broth-drinkers' o' Fife. (32)

With this explanation, the initials that Oldbuck readily interprets as conclusive proof in this matter of "national concern" are revealed to be nothing more than a cryptic private joke, and the site on which he locates "the scene of so celebrated an event" as the historic battle becomes nothing more than a "barren spot" on which some local peasants were wed. Ochiltree adds insult to injury when he observes that this revisionary account makes Oldbuck's proprietary claim to it a matter not for pride, but for pity. "They tell me your honour has given Johnnie Howie acre of acre of [good land] for this heathery knowe!," Ochiltree exclaims. "Now, if he has really imposed [this] on ye for an ancient wark," he counsels, "it's my real opinion the bargain will never hauld gude, if you would just say that he beguiled ye" (33). Oldbuck, who had earlier cited the acquisition as a mark of his own shrewdness, is left speechless.

This scene neatly crystallizes both the relative positions of Oldbuck and Ochiltree and, more broadly, the competing practices that characterize Scott's own approach to history. In Oldbuck, Scott illustrates how historians driven by special interests tend to privilege those interests and thus generate flawed (if not altogether untenable) historical narratives. In Ochiltree, on the other hand, Scott models the kind of historiography he advocates in the Bannatyne Club project: lacking any special interest in the case, Ochiltree brings a broad range of past experiences to bear and makes an accurate interpretation of the historical evidence at hand. But one similar key remains: both men are, in their own way, antiquarians. Oldbuck and Ochiltree both specialize in interpreting the discrete material details of their community to produce their historical accounts, and Ina Ferris suggests that their status as antiquarians precludes either from serving as a model for Scott's own position. While Ferris would agree that *The Antiquary* is an historiographical critique—indeed, she suggests that *The Antiquary* participates in "a contention internal to the genre of history itself, one in which what was at stake was the public form of modern historical reason" (275)—she argues that what Scott critiques, finally, is the antiquarian practice of history. While Scott the man—owner of Abbotsford and lover of all forms of Scottish antiquarian curiosities—may have appreciated the discrete material details of antiquarian inquiry, Ferris suggests that antiquarianism's focus on the local and the material ultimately works against Scott's larger novelistic project of creating a coherent narrative out of the Scottish past. Since the value of antiquarian detail lies precisely in its status as "curiosity" or anomaly, so called largely because it does not fit into standard narratives, Ferris argues that Scott finally "aligns himself and his fictional project with historian's history" (278)—that is, with the production of neatly polished, fully-formed narrative prose that realizes "the communicative power of history" (278).³

But Ferris's account does not consider just how fully Scott-the-author eschews the authoritative voice that underlies most "historian's history." Rather than positioning himself as a figure who speaks singular truth about the past, Scott repeatedly undermines his own authority, both by focusing on his economic motivations and by calling into question the validity of any singular voice. Consider, for instance, the Introductory Epistle to Scott's 1822 novel *The Fortunes of Nigel*, in which Scott subjects his pseudonymous self, the Author of *Waverley*, to this question from a later pseudonymous creation, Captain Clutterbuck: "Are you aware that an unworthy motive may be assigned for this rapid succession of publication? You will be supposed to work merely for the lucre of gain" (xxv). The Author of *Waverley* is untroubled by this suggestion, calmly asserting that "his works constitute as effectual a part of the public wealth as that which is created by any other manufacture" (xxvi), and Scott in fact echoes these descriptions of the author as a cog in the capitalist wheel throughout his metacommentaries and correspondence. It is worth noting, though, that there are very few instances in which he implicates his readers in this kind of commercial rhetoric. While Scott-the-writer is a good diligent producer, he almost never figures his readers as simple consumers. Instead, his narratives and metanarratives typically invoke a rhetoric of literary partnership in which author and reader are fellow travelers through the historical terrain and in which readers, finally, bear the lion's share of the interpretive burden. Little has been made of this rhetoric of readerly partnership in Scott's works, but this rhetoric merits some attention because in it lies part of the solution to the historiographical dilemma that Scott maps onto the characters of Oldbuck and Ochiltree in *The Antiquary*—and onto himself during the course of his novelistic career.

It is not difficult to claim that Scott is a writer who seeks to activate his readers' interpretive energies. From the outset of his novel-writing career Scott made it difficult for readers simply to identify with his singular authorial voice. The 1814 *Waverley* presents an omniscient narrator who undercuts his own authority with the strategically misplaced "Postscript, which should have been a Preface" and with his conflicting statements of purpose; while the narrator claims initially that the novel focuses on "men [rather] than manners" (35), he concludes by observing that the novel attempts primarily to "preserv[e] some idea of the ancient manners of Scotland" (492). And in the 1824 *Redgauntlet*, Scott eschews a consistent narrative voice altogether, combining epistolary novel, journal, and narrative precisely because he sees readerly interests, rather than writerly integrity, as paramount:

> A genuine correspondence ... can seldom be found to contain all in which it is necessary to instruct the reader for his full comprehension of the story.... The course of story-telling which we have for the present adopted, resembles the original discipline of the dragoons, who were trained to serve either on foot or horseback, as the emergencies of the situation required. (141)

When Scott thus makes the author into a chameleon willing to do whatever is necessary to "instruct the reader" or to ensure the reader's "full comprehension," he is echoing strategies he uses throughout the *Waverley* novels. These strategies, taken together, do much to achieve the goal Scott sets forth in the preface to *The Fortunes of Nigel*: the author's presence, Scott claims there, should be "as little thought on as the snow of last Christmas" (xxi). Scott may privilege readerly interpretation over writerly authority, but to suggest that Scott wants his readers to engage in the practice of history for themselves is to make a qualitatively different kind of claim. We can begin to understand Scott's call for this kind of readerly activism, though, by looking at one of his own readerly roles—namely, his stint as a reviewer for the *Edinburgh Review*. In this capacity, Scott wrote a review of the *1805 Report of the Highland Society Upon Ossian*—the report that declared James Macpherson's so-called discovery of ancient Scottish poetry to be a forgery—in which he concluded that Scotland might have been saved the embarrassment and potential danger of these false historical claims had readers (individually and collectively) been equipped or accustomed to judge historical evidence for themselves. "Nothing is more easy than to smoke into antiquity the mere language of a poem" (453), Scott observes, and he invokes Humean empiricism to explain how readers might avoid being duped in the future:

> Get positive testimony from many different hands.... The testimony must be as particular as it is positive. It will not be sufficient that [someone] say or write to you that he has heard such poems: nobody questions that there are traditional poems in that part of the country.... let [those who make such claims] write back to you, and inform you that they heard such a one (naming him), living in such a place, rehearse the original of such a passage, which appeared exact and faithful.... Nothing less will serve the purpose. (434)

This detailed historiographical tutorial effectively schools readers in the practice of history that Scott goes on to embody in *The Antiquary*'s Edie Ochiltree. Even in 1805 Scott is insisting that specific, verifiable details from local culture (the very sort of information on which Ochiltree relies) provide the surest way to authenticate the historical record. If readers make the effort to compile multiple, verifiable historical details, Scott suggests here, they will effectively be engaging in the practice of history for themselves. Such engagement is crucial, according to Scott, because it prevents history from falling prey to special interests like Macpherson's and provides the authentic historical narratives central, in Scott's view, to history's "improving" function.

But we might well ask how—or whether—the historiographical lesson that Scott offers in the Ossian review is reinforced in his novelistic writings. I have suggested above that Oldbuck's consistent wrong-headedness reinforces it strongly, but Scott offers other reinforcements throughout his novels, and we might consider one particularly important reinforcement by way of conclusion—his use of dialect.

Katie Trumpener suggests that before Scott, authors who employed dialect quite clearly did so as a form of "celebratory nationalist politics" (703). Scott explains, however, that he uses dialect chiefly to stimulate readerly sympathy—to create identification between his contemporary readers and his historical characters. "In listening to [dialect]," Scott writes in a review, "we not only do not experience even the slightest feeling of disgust or aversion, but our bosoms are responsive to every sentiment of sublimity, or awe, or terror" (*Quarterly*, 469–70). Through dialect, then, Scott encourages readers to see historical language as a living link between past and present. This living link does not merely create a sense of goodwill about the past, but provides readers with direct access to a diverse set of historical voices. By emphasizing this diverse set of voices—something Scott does especially pointedly in *The Antiquary*, whose expressed aim is to profile the "manners and the language" of a Scottish community in the 1790s—Scott's novels take on the characteristics of what Susan Stewart calls a "distressed genre": a genre that both "defer[s] to and creat[es] a sense of anterior authority" as part of a "gesture against the limitations of the self and the self's limited access to history" (92). Such genres typically include, according to Stewart, only oral forms (such as the ballad and the epic) that function as artifacts of collective experience. But Scott couples the dialect's "anterior authority" of past communal experience with an authorial mode that renounces controlling authority, thus allowing his readers relatively unmediated access to the historical experiences he represents. In other words, Scott provides his readers with the raw materials they need to make sense of history for themselves.

So, while Scott-the-author may use history much as Oldbuck does—to further his own personal interests—Scott-of-the-Bannatyne Club provides readers with the tools they need to piece together other kinds of historical discourse that he models in Ochiltree. This splintered authority allows Scott to establish what Stewart describes as perhaps the most central feature of the distressed genre: namely, an "antipersonal dimension." This anti-personal dimension allows Scott, finally, to transfer authority away from his singular authorial self and onto the collective body of his readers, thus providing them with the range of historical perspectives needed to preserve the discourse of history as a force that allows society to, as Scott himself put it, "look back upon the past and to improve on our ancestors' improvements and to avoid their errors."

**Notes**

1   Clifford Siskin writes about the persistent renegotiations of what counted as "professional" in the period. See *The Work of Writing*. Ina Ferris also discusses the professional/amateur boundary in her article; see p. 274 especially. The emerging institutional discipline of history was not without internal conflicts: philosophical historians sought to make grand claims about sweeping stages of historical experience, while antiquarians interrogated material culture on a much more local scale. But despite these methodological conflicts, both modes of historical practice effectively distanced the past from the present by objectifying the past, by claiming that "history" is defined partly by its otherness from the present moment. See Forbes, "The Rationalism of Sir Walter Scott"; Gamer, "Scott, Antiquarianism, and the Gothic."
2   See, for instance, Robert Crawford's claim that "The Antiquary [Oldbuck] represents a degree of self-mockery on the part of his creator" (113).
3   It is interesting that many discussions of antiquarians focus on the antiquarian love of "the curiosity" as a way of dismissing antiquarians' allegedly "trivial" concerns with the material details of history given Barbara Benedict's persuasive claims about the potential social disruption attached to curiosity. To be sure, Benedict is focusing on curiosity as an intellectual faculty rather than a material object, but it nonetheless seems significant that even one hundred years before Scott's novelistic project, "curiosity itself, rather than any invention, seemed the instrument for a progress that would launch unorthodox ideas and new people into power" (28).

**Works Cited**

Benedict, barbara. *Curiosity: A Cultural History of Early Modern Inquiry*. Chicago: University of Chicago Press, 2002.
Crawford, Robert. *Devolving English Literature*. Oxford: Clarendon Press, 1992.
Duncan, Ian. *Modern Romance and Transformations of the Novel: The Gothic, Scott, Dickens*. Cambridge: Cambridge UP, 1992.
Ferris, Ina. "Pedantry and the Question of Enlightenment History: The Figure of the Antiquary in Scott." *European Romantic Review* 13.3 (2002): 273-284.
Forbes, Duncan. "The Ratimalism of Sir Walter Scott." *Cambridge Journal* 7 (1953): 20–35.
Gamer, Michael. "Scott, Antiquarianism, and the Gothic." *Studies in Romanticism*. 32 (1993): 523–49.
Hazlitt, William. "Sir Walter Scott," in *The Spirit of the Age*. In *The Collected*

*Works of william Hazlitt.* 12 vols. Eds. A.R. Waller and Arnold Glover. London: J.M. Dent, 1902.
Scott, Sir Walter. *The Antiquary.* (1816). London: A. & C. Black, Ltd, 1935.
———. *The Fortunes of Nigel.* (1822). London: A.& C. Black, Ltd, 1932.
———. *The Journal of Sir Walter Scott.* Ed. W.E.K. Anderson. Oxford: Clarendon Press, 1972.
———. *The Letters of Sir Walter Scott.* 12 vols. Ed. H.J.C. Grierson. Oxford UP, 1932–1937.
———. "Review of *The Report of the Committee of the Highland Society Upon Ossian* and Laing's edition of *The Poems of Ossian.*" *Edinburgh Review* 6 (1805): 420–62.
———. "Review of *Tales of My Landlord, First Series.*" *Quarterly Review* 16 (1817): 430–80.
Siskin, Clifford. *The Work of Writing: Literature and Social Change in Britain, 1700–1830.* Baltimore, MD: Hongs Hopkins UP.
Stewart, Susan. *Crimes of Writing: Problems in the Containment of Representation.* Durham, NC: Duke UP, 1994.
Sutherland, Kathryn. "Fictional Economies: Adam Smith, Walter Scott, and the Nineteenth-Century Novel." *ELH* 54.1 (1987): 97–127.
Trumpener, Katie. "National Character, Nationalist Plots: National Tale and Historical Novel in the Age of *Waverly*, 1806-1830." *ELH* 60.3 (1993): 685–731.
White, Hayden. *The Content of the Form: Narrative Discourse and Historical Representation.* Baltimore: Johns Hopkins UP, 1987.

Chapter Twelve

# Reading Beyond Body, Cane, and Crosier: Talleyrand as Romantic Discourse

Rodney Farnsworth

Great individuals, particularly those with a colorful flair, have a way of becoming a whole composite of signs created by themselves or others—friendly, hostile, or merely inventive. Often the person gets lost in a plethora of metonymies: high forehead, red hair, and a very pale hand on a scepter—virginity and monarchy; a hand behind the lapel—militarism and megalomania; the sunflower in the buttonhole—witty epigrams and Queerness; a white bandage over an ear—serpentine brushstrokes and mad genius. To all this, add a sea of words—telling of triumph, defeat, scandal, or eccentricity—that surrounds the visual rhetoric of the figure of fame. A mountain of speeches, newspapers, letters, memoirs, or works of literature—a veritable discourse system has arisen around one human being, whose complexities have become a heap of contradictions. Later, the histories and biographies follow—thus adding yet more contradictions. And of no one is this truer than of Charles-Maurice de Talleyrand-Périgord. When read by his contemporaries and by many of their intellectual heirs, his human destiny seems subjected totally to the signifier; the body of the Other, the socially coded "monster." From that generative core, much Talleyrand discourse has flowed.

Writers contemporaneous with Talleyrand inevitably read his actions—both as a diplomat and as a human being—through the Romantic metaphors of the body: the lame body of the *ci-devant* bishop of Autun. The crosier and the cane seem to form the gravamens that motivate the negative and predominant voices in the Talleyrand discourse. The cane is a metonymy, not only for Talleyrand's limp, but also for his class: as Thorstein Veblen expressed it later in the same century, the "walking-stick serves the purpose of advertisement that the bearer's hands are employed otherwise than in useful effort" (176). The limp, however, forms the determinative signifier: a whole Romantic discursive system about Talleyrand was conceived and composed through the configuration of him as the "monstrous" Other. Many key French writers on history[1] of the early twentieth century read him in light of the often-Satanic metaphors. Writers on history—such as Maurice Paléologue, Georges Lacour-Gayet, and Emile Dard—use the transfigured Talleyrand as a stage Machiavelli, on whom to pin as many of the mistakes and crimes of Napoleon as they can, and they, above all, picture him as the great betrayer of their imperial hero. Although Paléologue's book is entitled *Romanticism and Diplomat*, this diplomat and scholar never really grapples with how the real Talleyrand is Romantic, but rather, how contemporaneous writers wrote him into a Romantic legend. Other writers of history—like Joseph McCabe, Jules Cambon, Crane Brinton, and J.F. Bernard—have conveyed a more moderate picture; however, in doing so, several have purged him of any hint of Romanticism, picturing him as a person of the Enlightenment. For example, according to Cambon, Talleyrand "was and always remained a creature of the eighteenth century" (Cambon, 49).[2] I seek to show, through readings of *four* segments of the Talleyrand discourse system, that he had a Romantic vision beyond body, cane, and crosier.

# I

Talleyrand's aristocratic parents set in motion events that led toward three key physical–mental challenges. First, through his parents he became a member of a class that, especially in France, was soon to be very much in harm's way. Second, his parents followed the ways of their class and put him out to live with a wet nurse, who set the infant on a table or chest and then carelessly allowed him to fall off. Ignored, the injury became permanent: Talleyrand had a limp all his life. Third, feeling that he could not fulfill even the outward figure of a noble de l'épée with his limp, his parents made the adolescent Talleyrand sign away his title as count to a younger brother and enter the priesthood against his will. As Versailles courtiers, his parents had enough prestige with the king eventually to secure Talleyrand a bishopric. A special device made his limp less noticeable and a fashionable cane made it less apparent, without hiding it entirely. The French Revolution allowed him the freedom to give up the bishopric of Autun and outwardly to appear secular; however, not all his considerable powers of persuasion, nor Napoleon's power, could make him any less of a bishop in the eyes of the pope, devout Catholics, or even anti-Catholic Anglicans. Worse still, in the eyes of his sentimental age, he conducted himself with an air and grace redolent of the ancien régime, rather than petitioning pity. He always would be a bishop who limped and—most unforgivable of all—enjoyed great success in all his worldly endeavors from the bedroom to the conference room.[3] Surpassing success is the supreme crime of the Other. Certain Romantics, armed with a whole arsenal of newly invented or recently unearthed archetypes, were able to transform the aristocratic, limping ci-devant bishop into one of the greatest, if, underappreciated, figures of Romantic legend.

Coleridge wrote a neglected "Metrical Epistle" published in the *Morning Post* on January 10, 1800, "Talleyrand to Lord Grenville"—in short, an imaginary letter from the French foreign minister to the British one, based on an earlier forged letter printed in the English papers and alleged to be from Talleyrand (*Poems*, 340–44).[4] Coleridge has considerable fun with the diplomat's mix of aristocrat with Revolutionary. The poet's "Talleyrand" writes that "he looks down upon" the mob (1.14). Coleridge is wrong to present Talleyrand as a snob: Talleyrand's friendships always transcended class, even before 1789 (see Brinton, 44–60, especially 46). Coleridge accuses Talleyrand of being hungry for bribes (see 11.17–20): this satirical harping on weakness for bribery is a standard feature of the discourse surrounding Talleyrand; other coeval diplomats accepted bribes but with relative impunity.

Coleridge then leads from an attack on Talleyrand's apostasy as a Catholic priest and bishop to the subject of bribes—a key point of talk and writings about the diplomat:

> My Lord! through the vulgar in wonder be lost at
> My transfigurations and name me *Apostate*,
> Such a meaningless nickname, which never incens' d me,
> *Cannot* prejudice you or your Cousin against me:
> I'm Ex-bishop. What then? Burke himself would agree
> That I left not the Church—'twas the Church that left me.
> My titles prelatic I lov'd and retain'd,
> As long as what I meant by Prelate remain'd;
> And thro' Mitres no longer will *pass* in our mart,
> I'm *episcopal* still to the core of my heart,
> No time from my name this my motto shall sever:
> 'Twill be *Non sine pulvere palma* for ever! (11.25–36)

I presume Coleridge, with the bigoted eyes of the time, sees Grenville as an "Apostate" because of his own and his cousin Pitt's courageous and stanch support of political freedom for British Catholics (Derry, 16–22). And yet what should an anti-Catholic Anglican care about "apostasy" against the Gallic Catholic Church? The satire of the English Coleridge, it must be said, is very mild compared to that of the French, where the body is made the determinative signifier.

The French satirical cartoons—exploited by Lacour-Gayet's negative biography of Talleyrand—show him with a sign indicating a crippled foot; although the actual affected foot was the right, the limp was so slight that the satirists sometimes attached an appliance to the left foot (or, where Talleyrand is portrayed in animal form, the right rear paw) and at other times to the truly afflicted foot. The representations, moreover, inevitably include the bishop's crosier. Contemporaneous

French writers were to continue this reading of Talleyrand through his body and related signs. Talleyrand discourse depends to a surprising degree upon reading the physiognomy, which has so often been attached to Others categorized by class and race, as well as to upposed criminal types and the insane—I am thinking of Lavater, Gall, Géricault, Tressaert, and, later, Lombroso.[5] This reading-the-body discourse had an astounding currency in Romantic culture and in that immediately following.

Interestingly, Paléologue culminates his early twentieth-century biography of Talleyrand with quotations from Victor Hugo's attack shortly after the statesperson's death, May 19, 1839 (Paléologue, 60–63); the biographer almost certainly does this because of the brilliant violence with which Hugo reads and writes everything through the body. This oddly enough, is the same writer who seven years before, in *Notre-Dame de Paris*, rhetorically guided his readers to a sort of sympathy for what lay beneath the limping deformity of his hunchback. Hugo overtly stresses the lame foot: Talleyrand is "lame like the devil." Hugo reads the outward infirmity as a correspondence for an inner deformity: "It might be said that everything within him limped as he did himself." Physiognomy becomes for Hugo the portal of the soul. The weight of Romantic associations comes thick and heavy to cluster around this foot—an image of parental neglect. Foremost, there is the limp of Goethe's Mephistopheles, of whom a drunk in the Auerbach-Cellar scene says, "Why does the fellow limp with one foot?" (I. 2184: *Werke* 5:208). Goethe's limping devil ma have already added satanic coloring to the halting Byron—adding yet another association for Talleyrand. Hugo establishes on the multifaceted satanic metaphor the correspondence of outward shape and inner ethos, and then he reads the diplomat through it. To describe this aspect of Talleyrand, Hugo alludes to literary archetypes recently revalidated by Romantic criticism: the already expansive Talleyrand discourse is extended even more by means of a whole arsenal of words and archetypes common in the literature from or about the Middle Ages and Renaissance. The paradox of Dante's Satan—who is fixed in the depths of Hell at the center of the earth, yet able to emanate effective and powerful evil from this position—is used to describe Talleyrand's control of the world: "For thirty years, from the depths of his palace, he practically controlled Europe." The still-radical Shakespeare seems to offer Hugo the type of the cynical and politic psychologist, Richard III, also with a limp, to elaborate this "Talleyrand": "He had approached, known, observed, plumbed, toyed with, turned inside out, examined, mocked all the men of this time, all the thought of his century." Even the hyperbole of this passage freights significance: Talleyrand surely must have been incarnate Satan to have accomplished all that Hugo attributes to him. Sir Walter Scott's own variation on the Richard III archetype—Louis XI, the spider king of Quentin Durward—must surely be the prototype here: "Into the palace [the Hôtel de Talleyrand], as a spider into its web, he enticed and captured one by one heroes, thinkers, conquerors, kings, princes, emperors, all the gilded and glittering flies that buzz through the history of these last forty years" (Paléologue, 63). Limping devil, omnipotent and omniscient Satan, entrapping spider—Talleyrand is anything but a human for **Hugo**.⁶

The adulterous lover of Hugo's wife, Sainte-Beuve, writes his own little moral sermon on the body of Talleyrand in a wordplay revolving around "wound," "gnawing ulcer," "his vices," and that word for public corruption that hints at a departure from its actual etymology into the realm of private acts—"venality." It is, above all, the body that dominates the passage:

> Venality, as it were, is Talleyrand's wound, a hideous wound, a gnawing ulcer that invades below the skin. A public person, like everyone, has his faults, his passions, or even his vices; but it is not necessarily the case, as it is with Talleyrand, where the vices take over everything else and occupy the entire ground of his being. (Saint-Beuve, 129)

According to Crane Brinton, "[i]t is this essay which fixed Talleyrand's evil reputation in the minds of cultivated people" (306). In short, from this discursive fantasia on the body sprang much of the Talleyrand legend.

George Sand, like Hugo and Sainte-Beuve, writes her text upon the body of Talleyrand, even though one might have thought that this deeply aware woman could have seen the danger of such body-centered discourse. Her attack, entitled "Le Prince," was first published in 1834, three weeks after she had imposed on, and accepted, the hospitality of Talleyrand's Chateau Valençay (Paléologue, 59; Bernard, 590; Cate, 330–31). In 1837, the author incorporated this attack into her *Letters of a Traveler*. It is in this guise that the attack is so well known to students not only of the author but also of the diplomat. Sand's whole appeal to physiognomy as a sign for the soul, in her body-reading, is clearly part of the tradition leading from Lavater to Lombroso; moreover, there is an analogy to the animal that is often found in colonialists dealing with the presumed racial Other:

> ... that lip, convex and pursed, like a cat's, broad and sagging like that of a satyr, mixes dissimulation with lasciviousness; ... that disdainful fold in the pronounced brow; that arrogant nose, together with that reptile glance—such contrasts in a human face all reveal a man born for great vices and for small actions. Never has that heart felt the warmth of generous emotion, never has a thought of loyalty passed through that thick head. The man is a freak of nature, a monstrosity.... (Sand, 2:865)

To do Sand credit, in the 1850s she came to regret the rhetoric of this attack

(2:219–20). After all, the words "freak" and "monstrosity" would have us believe that the body is the totality of the human being and that the body is her/his destiny: in this case, the destiny of the outcast Other.

## II

Controlling spider, treasonous monster of ingratitude, limping opportunist—metaphors of Romantic poets seem to control the historical valuations of the diplomat. It seems to me that the real Romantic essence of Talleyrand diplomacy can be revealed, first, by disproving the Richard III/Louis XI image and, second, by revealing an organic vision for the newly emerging nationalism of Europe: the histories written with a particular agenda, especially of the Bonapartists, offer the clearest point of departure for both. Rightly or more probably wrongly, the duke d'Enghien was presumed to have been a political plotter and assassin—in today's political parlance, a "terrorist," a label that often seems to put individuals beyond the usual rules of law. The duke's guilt is not beyond possibility; that he seemed a real threat at the time is even less possible. Lacour-Gayet, in his massive multi-volume compilation of "facts" surrounding Talleyrand, quotes Count Molé: "The Duke d'Enghien perished because of the intrigue of Talleyrand and of Fouché, who wanted to entrap Napoleon and put him under their power by a crime which would make him complicit with them, and after that he would be unable to reproach them for their revolutionary life" (Lacour-Gayet, 2:127; cf. Molé, *Sa Vie*, 4:348–49). And Lacour-Gayet—not content with Molé's having exonerated Napoleon—exonerates Fouché (2:127). For Lacour-Gayet, as in the passage from Molé that he quotes, the controlling metaphors here are the same as Hugo's: Talleyrand is the weaving and entrapping spider, and only a Richard III type would be monster enough to direct the crime. In short, Lacour-Gayet turns the whole chapter into a trial brief in defense of his adored Napoleon and against Talleyrand (2: 123–42). Although Emile Dard is less obvious than Lacour-Gayet, he does let slip, in the course of his discussion of the Duke d'Enghien affair, an astounding phrase about Napoleon: he "was the least cruel of men" (76). Obviously, "cruel" is, for Dard, a signifier not meant to encompass the graves at Jena, Austerlitz, or Borodino.

One of the other great points of attack on Talleyrand is the diplomat's behavior at Erfurt. By this time, he viewed Napoleon as lost—even though to all appearances the emperor was winning on all sides. Although Talleyrand remained a courtier, he had resigned as foreign minister. However, Napoleon still commanded his presence at Erfurt. The French emperor was trying to get Tsar Alexander to agree to the dismantling of the Hapsburg domain. Talleyrand, who had long argued for a strong Austria to set against Russia and Prussia, worked secretly against Napoleon's designs. Paléologue, who made such strategic use of Hugo's attack, terms Talleyrand's behavior as "treachery" and "infamy."—To whom? To Napoleon, of course (20). Lacour-Gayet makes it clear that he sides with Napoleon against Talleyrand, whose deeds at Erfurt "not only bear the characteristics of disobedience: a much more serious word might be uttered—that of treason" (2:247). If Talleyrand had been still the foreign minister and his disagreement with Napoleon on this point and others unclear to the emperor, then the accusation might be debatable. In fact, Talleyrand followed his own consistent international policy and had a deep feeling of duty for France and for Europe.

First of all, Talleyrand's vision was seldom one of pure *Realpolitik*. The diplomat's last public address is about this feeling of duty. The speech is in honor of another diplomat, M. Reinhard, and comes from a key part of the Talleyrand discourse—his own words. He says that Reinhard derived his qualities as a states person "from an honest and deep feeling that governed all his actions: in the feeling for duty. People are not sufficiently aware of the power generated by this feeling" (French text in Lytton Bulwer, 230–52; quoted 242). The insistent recurrence of the word "feeling" makes up in sincerity of sentiment what it loses in style. This awareness of the power of emotions, perhaps, hints at Romanticism.

Secondly, Talleyrand had a consistent policy of offering his dissenting views to Napoleon. As the secret, official correspondence preserved in the archives of the Affaires Etrangères demonstrates, repeatedly, Talleyrand was polite but candid with Napoleon. His letter of October 13, 1806 argues that, if Austria is made to suffer too much, then Europe as a whole would suffer (*Lettres inédites*, 161). Later in the same letter, Talleyrand makes the point from the interest of France: "Austria, natural enemy of Russia, will have in France a natural ally" (163). If all this seems like Baroque balance-of-power politics, it has a new twist: Talleyrand wants an alliance with Austria, while Napoleon wants to culminate the goals of Louis XIV—the annihilation of Hapsburg power. As early as the Directory, in a foreign policy report of July 10, 1798, Talleyrand is calling for a hard line against Russia (*Correspondance Diplomatique*, 244–49) and a moderate one toward Austria (272–75). Talleyrand shows a consistency in his diplomacy—in that respect, he is certainly no early nineteenth-century version of the Vicar of Bray.

Thirdly, Madame de Remusat recounts a conversation with Talleyrand in which—after stating that Napoleon is, in the short run, necessary for France—he outlines the master plan behind his working with the emperor and all his diplomacy; however, since it was a plan that emphasized national autonomy at the expense of imperial glory, it gained only fragmentary compliance from Napoleon:

> The Emperor has refused to see that he had been called by his destiny to be

everywhere and always the man of international vision [*l'homme des nations*]—the founder of useful and realizable innovations. To restore religion, ethics, and order in France; to applaud the civilization of England while restraining her political ambitions; to fortify his frontiers with the Confederation of the Rhine; to make Italy a kingdom independent of Austria and of Napoleon himself; to keep the tsar shut up in Russia by creating this obvious barrier offered by Poland—all these should have been the eternal designs of the Emperor, and it was toward these ends that every one of my treaties sought to direct him." (Rémusat, 3:269; italics are hers.)

The hope of achieving these principles had guided Talleyrand's support of Napoleon; however, when he spoke these words in 1807, the diplomat was on the verge of giving up as hopeless the increasingly erratic emperor. These principles indicate an organic—thus Romantic—unity to the diplomatic vision behind the treaties in which Talleyrand had a part. A love of order was always a guiding principle, and it guided him, along with millions of French people, to Napoleon. A dislike of disorder made him become an exile in 1793; the same dislike may have been the source of his complicity in the Duke d'Enghien affair. The point on religion is key, too. He never wanted to be priest or bishop, but there is no conclusive evidence that he had abandoned, in any internal sense, his religion.

Talleyrand's concern for the integrity of a Germany not under Austria or Prussia, and of an Italy not under France guided the goals outlined to Rémusat—goals which might have saved an ocean of blood in the last two centuries. Napoleon's desire to entice Tsar Alexander into a treaty to dismantle Austria had been the reason for Talleyrand's working against Napoleon at Erfurt and his ceasing to be a Bonapartist. The mention of Poland is the most telling: laying aside Talleyrand's own testimony about how important Polish independence was to the balance of power in Europe (letter dated December 21, 1830, in *Mémoires*, 3:427), a witness says that even as a young *abbé*, he joined in a discussion with the former foreign minister, Choiseul—all decrying the first partition of that country (Lacour-Gayet, 1:66). In the final analysis, *Talleyrand* was the "man of international vision"—not Napoleon. I see, too, that same Romantic awareness of growing nationalism, rather like that found in the work of Germaine de Staël (see Isbel). This Romantic concept of national sovereignty underpinned Talleyrand's banner words "legitimacy" and "non-interference," which gave organic unity to his diplomacy from the Congress of Vienna through the July Revolution.

## III

Talleyrand's own writings reveal Romantic organicism, binding word and deed together. Perhaps the real key to Tallyrand's Romanticism is found in his writings on his journey to and through the United States of America. The passages describing America in his *Mémoires* are extraordinary—extraordinary because they show his poetic side. The following passage, especially the opening, suggests that Talleyrand is not the cold-blooded rationalist suggested by writers from Sand to Brinton:

> I was struck with astonishment; less than fifty leagues from the capital [then, Philadelphia], I no longer saw any traces of human handwork; I found nature entirely raw and untamed: forests as ancient as the world; the debris of plants and trees dead from old age littering the ground that has produced them without cultivation; others that, in their turn, grow and die; the vines which often opposed our passage; the margins of rivers carpeted with a flourishing and vigorous verdure; several great expanses of natural meadows; in other spots, some flowers new to me; next the traces of past tornadoes that have pushed over all that was standing in their path. Extensive battered remains of trees, which had been laid out in the same direction, attest to the astounding power of these terrible phenomena. (Mémoires, 1:233–34).

This American apperception seems quite as Romantic as those of Chateaubriand.[7] Talleyrand gives clear expression to a sort of sublime shudder at the great expanse of the New World:

> Upon reaching a slightly elevated spot, one's eyes are able to wander over the most varied and agreeable prospect as far as they can see. The tops of the trees and the undulations of the terrain are the only things that break the regularity of the immense space, and the result is able to produce an uncanny effect. (*Mémoires*, 1:234)

The Baron de Vitrolles records the diplomatist's strategic outbreak of emotions concerning American landscapes:

> It is such a beautiful country! you don't know this country, do you, M. de Vitrolles? myself, I know it; I have traversed it; I have lived there; it is a superb country. There are rivers with which we Europeans are not familiar—the Potomac, for example—nothing is more beautiful than the Potomac! And then the magnificent forests.... (Vitrolles, 3:200)

The style suggests that this is more than just a cover for a political maneuver.

Talleyrand's reaction to America had utilitarian aspects, too. In his extensive correspondence from America with Germaine de Staël, he speaks almost entirely of finances, particularly investments in real estate: "There is no better place for recouping ones fortune than here" (letter, Boston, April 4, 1791; Talleyrand,

"Lettres," 213). Around this time he had been reading, in manuscript it seems, Staël's *On Literature as Regards its Interrelation with Social Institutions* (February 18, 1797; Talleyrand, "Lettres"); this is interesting because in his notes on America, he—like Staël—examines how landscape and climate affect human character.[8] It does not make his vision any less Romantic when his imagination transforms the Turneresque sublime into the Constablean beautiful and useful:

> Our imagination was then stimulated by this vast expanse; there, we envisioned cities, villages, hamlets; the forests remained untouched on the mountaintops, the hillocks were covered with crops, and already, the flocks came to graze in the pastures of the valley we envisioned before us. Viewing such landscapes through the future lends them an inexpressible charm. (*Mémoires*, 1:234)

The future provides a sort of looking-glass through which to imagine a landscape transformed by human progress. Talleyrand, here as so often elsewhere in his words and deeds, displays an ability to view things under the aspect of a Romantic *becoming*.

This ability of casting the present in terms of the future is an aspect of modernity—a concept that the Romantics were so instrumental in creating. Cambon writes of Talleyrand's reaction to the New World, "It was a new world, and he did not have fear of new ideas" (50). Elsewhere, this writer on history relates that Talleyrand "had the gift of foresight" and that "he had his eyes fixed on what would happen the next day, and it was the next day that determined his conduct" (49). This was how Talleyrand described his mode of viewing of the American landscape: through the future. Modernity had arrived, but it is surprising how few realized it: Napoleon, Louis XVIII, and Charles X thought like Augustus, Charlemagne, or Louis XIV.

The fearlessness with which Talleyrand faced the future—the dangers of which he had no doubt—is clearest when he faces the ocean during the voyage to America. This is the Atlantic Ocean that was so fearsome to Hugo, Crèvecoeur, and even Melville (see Farnsworth).[9] Talleyrand utterly and fearlessly exulted very much like Byron did, through the titular persona of *Childe Harold* (Canto 3, ll.5–18; *Poetical Works*, 2: 77): "I depart ..." Byron proclaims, "the hour's gone by,/When Albion's lessening shores could grieve or glad mine eye." "Once more upon the waters! yet once more!" he shouts, " ... Welcome, to their roar!" Then, He concludes with his characteristic fearlessness in confronting change: "I am a weed,/Flung from the rock, on Ocean's foam, to sail/Where'er the surge may sweep, or tempest's breath prevail." The English poet expresses in ringing phrases what the Frenchman conveys in a dramatic placement of human figures:

> We sailed out from Falmouth. The wind was good; every one of the passengers—up on deck, eyes turned toward the shore—was saying with an expression of pleasure: "I still can see land." I alone felt relieved when we could see it no longer. At this moment, the sea possessed a special charm for me; the sensations I derived from it were peculiarly suited to my disposition. (*Mémoires*, 1:231–32)

Whether this is a memory of a real event or a bit of Byronic posing apart from the crowd, years after the fact and after Byron, does not matter. It is Romantic either way. Only a Romantic could identify his disposition so fully with the ocean and face a voyage on the open sea so fearlessly, or just as valid, later imagine that he had done so. Memories of the ocean continue to haunt Talleyrand amid the American landscape (233).

## IV

The United States and the Atlantic Ocean—two great symbols of change—Talleyrand faced in the same spirit with which he, upon his return, faced the metamorphoses of France in an organically holistic way. It was the same conservative but not reactionary, radical but not rash, spirit with which many of the great European Romantics confronted their unprecedented age of change: a mediation between the opposite types of chaos resulting from too much change and not enough change (see Farnsworth). In terms of practical politics, this spirit seeks the *via media* and finds a great proponent in Talleyrand.

Talleyrand's greatest political moment in 1814 when Paris was awaiting the arrival of the Bourbons backed up by the allies. Aimée de Coigny presents Talleyrand laying out the course that France was to take after Napoleon and during the Restoration:

> It is necessary: that the Senate assemble.... That the Senate, then, constitute a National Assembly; that it send out to all the deputies the order to assemble and deliberate.... That it declare France to be a constitutional monarchy by means of three or four laws carefully written, indicating clearly the liberties of the people and call it either *charter* or *constitution*, as it chooses. Then, that it call the brother of Louis XVI to the throne. (249–50).

Even the hostile writers on history cannot deny that this is the basic course taken by events or that Talleyrand, with an unusually overt dispatch and zeal, was in clear charge of those events. In 1789 the appearance of the term "*assemblée nationale*" is not accidental: it can be taken as a sign of continuity in Talleyrand's political thoughts and actions. Central to his thinking was always the often forgotten fact that, in 1789, France gained and never lost constitutional and representative government, however battered or ignored at times. Now, in 1814, Talleyrand seemed to believe that in this one not-inconsiderable way the French Revolution had been a success. A clear view of this continuity can be found in the 1867 biography by Sir Henry Lytton Bulwer, Lord Dalling (1801–1872), the brother of the more famous novelist. He lived his four decades during the height of English and French Romanticism, so we may suppose that Talleyrand found one sympathetic, if late, in him, Romantic biographer. Lord Dalling finds a deep organic wholeness to the Frenchman's political vision: "M. de Talleyrand aided in reviving that nation, and giving it the framework of a constitutional system, under a legitimate monarchy;—almost, in fact, that very system which thirty-five years before he had wished to see established" (248). In this way, Talleyrand participated in a crucial form of Romantic mediation between the excesses of order and chaos.

When viewed in historical context, Talleyrand comes off rather well. In his relatively consistent support of limited monarchy, representative government, and freedom of the press—the essential goals of the 1789 Revolutionaries, sustained by him in 1814—he seems progressive even when viewed as a Frenchman of his time; however, when compared to the larger continental scene—Tsar Alexander or Metternich, with their love of Divine Right and hatred of constitutional government—Talleyrand seems radical. We see Talleyrand taking a *via media*: between the chaos emerging from Bourbon stasis and that resulting from the excessive changes of the popular sovereignty of the First Republic; between the chaos potentially arising from the stagnation at the end of the Directory or that from Napoleon's extreme reaches into plebiscite tyranny and empire; between the Ultras and those seeking another republic. His negotiation between extremes allowed him to support whatever seemingly effective form the limited representation and constitutional monarchy (or the Directory's pentarchy) might take after the summer of 1789. He turned from them when they set a course toward chaos. In 1814 and 1830, he played an active part in the creation of this middle path in statecraft and diplomacy, but when compared with the generality, royal or common, around him, he seems radical. On that fateful eve of the Restoration in 1814, he worked with uncharacteristic zeal to preserve French representative government.

To be fair to Talleyrand, therefore, one might apply the acid test of that great political thinker, Frederick Douglass; although he is American, his ideas cross national boundaries and can be applied to the French scenario. In speaking of Lincoln as an abolitionist, Douglass wrote: "Viewed from the genuine abolition ground, Mr. Lincoln seemed tardy, cold, dull, and indifferent: but measuring him by the sentiment of his country, a sentiment he was bound as a statesman to consult, he was swift, zealous, radical, and determined" (4:436). By this measure,

Talleyrand is certainly progressive. His consistent, progressive strategy for political *becoming* permeates his own writings—not only in his letters, papers, speeches and conversations, but above all in reaction to the American landscape, the people, and the ocean. These American texts embalm a certain attitude of mind that demonstrates the best capacity to negotiate drastic changes in the practical sphere. Talleyrand's own discourse is the surest guide to understanding his diplomacy and statecraft, and it is perhaps as Romantic as that concerning his body, cane, and crosier.

## Notes

1   For help in physiognomy and criminology, my thanks to Barry Hancock, dean of SPEA, Indiana-Purdue University Fort Wayne; for the immense numbers of multi-volume collections of letters, political documents, and memoirs that I had to consult and only in a few cases cite, my thanks to librarian Cheryl Truesdell and her document delivery staff, Helmke Library, IPFW: Christine A Smith; Mark Watrous, and Francis Smith; my thanks are also owed to librarian Sue Skekloff, Shirley Champion, Professor Lidan Lin, and Professor Jeanette Clausen, Associate Dean of Academic Affairs.
   I have used the term "writers on history" rather than "historians," because although there are historians in the strictest sense among them, there are also those who wrote significant *belles-lettres* essays in history, including biographies. On this point, I bow to the great theorist on history, R. G. Collingwood, who wrote: "a biography ... however much history it contains, is constructed on principles that are not only non-historical but anti-historical. Its limits are biological events, the birth and death of a human organism: its framework is thus a framework not of thought but of natural process" (304).
2   Throughout the chapter all translations of French and German sources are mine.
3   During the *ancienrégime*, proudly displaying articulating limbs was a sign of royal potency—indeed, of both political and sexual power. This is why kings—especially Louis XIV –were pictured by artists with a leg thrust aggressively forward (Zanger, 43–48). Talleyrand's poorly articulated leg combined with his boudoir prowess was an unforgiveable contradiction of the normative iconography.
4   An otherwise neglected work, this satire is treated by Schulz (24 and 198–99).
5   On the various applications of physiognomy to the Other among Talleyrand's near contemporaries see: Johnson (148–51); Gilman (151–55); Hagan (127–31); Flaherty (284–85).
6   I am not forgetting the earlier—perhaps "pre-Romantic"—line of descent for the limping-devil archetype: Vélez de Guevara's *El Diablo cojuelo* and the French work it inspired, Alain René Lesage's *Le Diable boiteux*.
7   The comparative scholar Baldensperger finds this same passage of Talleyrand's "less lyrical" than Chateaubriand's, but the "impressions" of the former "are not less sincere" than the latter (373). I fail to see the Talleyrand prose I

have cited as falling short of his great political opponent in lyricism. These American passages of the *Mémoires*, it is true, may find a more apt comparison in the controlled lyricism of Alphonse de Lamartine, of whose poetry, Talleyrand was among "the earliest and most devoted admirers" (Bernard 601).

8   See Huth and Pugh 74–75 and 80–81; this collection only published Talleyrand's writings in an English translation; I have yet to find a published version of the French originals; hence, I have had to give them passing treatment.

9   I did not treat Talleyrand in my *Mediating Order and Chaos*, however, I see in him a exemplar of the view of Romanticism I argued for in that study. I have also used some of the findings of that study for comparative context.

**Works Cited**

Baldenberger, Fernand. "Le Sejour de Talleyrand aux Etats-Unis." *Le Revue de Paris* 15 November 1924:364–87.
Bernard, J.F. *Talleyrand: A Biography*. New York: Capricorn-Putnam, 1974.
Brinton, Crane. *The Lives of Talleyrand*. 1936. New York: Norton, 1963.
Byron, Lord. *The Complete Poetical Works*. Ed. Jerome I. McGann. 7 vols. Oxford: Clarendon, 1980.
Cambon, Jules. *Le Diplomate*. Paris: Hachette, 1926.
Cate, Curtis. *George Sand*. Boston: Houghton, 1975.
Coigny, duchesse de Fleury, Anne Française Aimée de. *Mémoires de Aimée de Coigny*. Paris: Calmann, 1906.
Coleridge, Samuel Taylor. *Poems*. Ed. Ernest Hartley Coleridge. London: Oxford UP, 1912.
Collingwood, R. G. *The Idea of History*. 1946. New York: Oxford UP, 1956.
Cooper, Duff. *Talleyrand*. 1932. The Bedford Historical Series edn. London: Jonathan Cape, 1938.
Dard, Emile. *Napoléon et Talleyrand*. Paris: Pion, 1935.
Derry, John W. *Reaction and Reform: England in the Early Nineteenth Century*. New York: Humanities, 1963.
Douglass, Frederick. *The Frederick Douglass Papers. Series One*. Eds. John W. Blassingame and John R. McKivigan. 4 vols. New Haven, CT: Yale UP, 1991.
Farnsworth, Rodney. *Mediating Order and Chaos: The Water-Cycle in the Complex Adaptive Systems of Romantic Culture*. Internationale Forschungen zur Allegemeinen und Vergleichenden Literaturwissenschaft, 56. Amsterdam: Rodopi, 2001.
Flaherty, Gloria. "The Non-Normal Sciences: Survivals of Renaissance Thought in the Eighteenth Century." *Inventing Human Science: Eighteenth-Century Domains*. Eds. Christopher Fox, Roy Porter, and Robert Wokler. Berkeley: University of California Press, 1995. 271–91.
Gilman, Sander L. "The Jewish Nose: Are Jews White? Or, The History of the Nose Job." *Encountering the Other(s): Studies in Literature, History, and Culture*. Ed. Gisela Brinker-Gabler. Albany: State University of New York Press, 1995. 149–82.

Goethe, Johann Wolfgang von. *Gedenkausgabe der Werke, Briefe und Gespräche.* Ed. Ernst Beutler et al. 24 vols. Zurich: Artemis, 1949.

Hagan, Frank E. *Introduction to Criminology: Theories, Methods, and Criminal Behavior.* Belmont: Wadsworth, 2002.

Huth, Hans, and Wilma J. Pugh. *Talleyrand in America as a Financial Promoter, 1794–96: Unpublished Letters and Memoirs.* The Annual Report of the American Historical Association. Washington: US Government Printing Office, 1942.

Isbel, John Claiborne. *The Birth of European Romanticism: Truth and Propaganda in Staël's "De L'Allemagne," 1810–1813.* Cambridge: Cambridge UP, 1994.

Johnson, Dorothy. *Jacques-Louis David: Art in Metamorphosis.* Princeton, NJ: Princeton UP, 1993.

Lacour-Gayet, Georges. *Talleyrand, 1754–1838.* 3 vols. Paris: Payot, 1930–31.

Lytton Bulwer, Sir Henry, Lord Dalling. *Historical Characters: Machintosh, Talleyrand, Canning, Cobbett, and Peel.* 5th edn. 1867. London: [Bentley], 1876.

McCabe, Joseph. *Talleyrand: A Biographical Study.* London: Hutchinson, 1906.

Molé, Le Comte. *Le Comte Molé, 1781–1855: Sa Vie—ses mémoires.* Ed. Marquis de Noailles. 4th edn. 6 vols. Paris: Champion, 1925.

Paléologue, Maurice. *Romantisme et diplomatie: Talleyrand, Metternich, Chateaubriand.* Paris: Hachette, 1924.

Rémusat, Madame de. *Mémoires.* Ed. Paul de Rémusat. Paris: Lévy, 1880.

Sainte-Beuve, C. A. *Monsieur de Talleyrand.* Ed. Leon Noël. Monaco: Roche, 1958.

Sand, George. *Œuvres autobiographiques.* Ed. Georges Lubin. 2 vols. Bibliothèque de la Pleiade. Paris: Gallimard, 1970–71.

Schulz, Max F. *The Poetic Voices of Coleridge: A Study of His Desire for Spontaneity and Passions for Order.* Detroit: Wayne State UP, 1963.

Talleyrand-Périgord, Charles Maurice de, prince de Bénévent. *Correspondance diplomatique de Talleyrand: Le Ministère de Talleyrand sous le Directoire.* Ed. G. Pallain. Paris: [Pion], 1891.

———. "Lettres de M. de Talleyrand à Madame de Staël." *Revue d'histoire diplomatique* 4 (1890): 79 and 210–21.

———. *Lettres inédites de Talleyrand à Napoléon, 1800–1809.* Ed. Pierre Bertrand. 2nd edn. Paris: [Perrin], 1889.

———. *Mémoires du Prince de Talleyrand.* Ed. Le Duc de Broglie. 5 vols. Paris: [Lévy], 1891.

Veblen, Thorstein. *The Theory of the Leisure Class: An Economic Study of Institution.* New York: Mentor-NAL, 1953.

Vitrolles, Eugène François Auguste d' Arnaud, Baron de, *Mémoires et relations politiques.* 3 vols. Ed. Eugène Forgues. Paris: [Charpentier], 1884.

Zanger, Abby. "Lim(b)inal Images: 'Betwixt and Between' Louis XIV's Martial and Marital Bodies." *From the Royal to the Republican Body: Incorporating the Political in Seventeenth-and Eighteenth-Century France.* Eds. Sara E. Melzer and Kathryn Norberg. Berkeley: University of California Press, 1998. 32–63.

## Chapter Thirteen

# Byron and *Manfred*:
# Epistolary Journal into Dramatic Poem

### D.L. Macdonald

Between September 17 and 29, 1816, Byron toured the Swiss Alps with his friend John Cam Hobhouse. During this trip, he kept a journal, which he sent to his sister, Augusta Leigh. Later, in response to the suggestion that his first dramatic poem, *Manfred*, was an imitation of Goethe's *Faust*, he repeatedly insisted that its real inspiration was the scenery he had seen on that trip and described in that journal (*Letters*, 5:268, 7:113). He even claimed to have written the poem "*for the sake of* introducing the Alpine scenery in description" (5:188; emphasis added). In the past, I (and many others) have written about *Manfred* as a Faustian tragedy; taking Byron at his word and concentrating on the scenery should help us to put the poem in a new perspective.

Echoes of Byron's Alpine journal—often startlingly precise in their recall of its wording—occur throughout the first half of the poem (the second half is set indoors and has little scope for scenery).[1] Almost all of them are given to Manfred—in case anybody doubted Byron's identification with his hero. The "torrent ... like the *tail* of a white horse streaming in the wind" that Byron saw on September 22 (*Letters*, 5:101) turns up, along with the biblical reference it suggested to him (Rev. 6:8)—but without the snug curate's cottage he noticed opposite to it—just before Manfred's encounter with the Witch of the Alps (2.2.1–8). The comparison of a glacier to "a *frozen hurricane*" (5:102) recurs—without any mention of the dinner Byron ate before going to see it—in the opening speech of the First Destiny (2.3.4–8). Most of these echoes, however, occur in Manfred's soliloquy on the Jungfrau, just before his suicide attempt is frustrated by the Chamois Hunter, a fact which, together with Byron's claims about the importance of the scenery, suggests that this scene has as much right to be considered the center of the poem as Manfred's Faustian incantations (1.1), his confrontation with the spirit of Astarte (2.4), or his final defiance of the devils (3.4), and a fact which might tend to confirm Jerome McGann's contention that insofar as the poem is autobiographical, it expresses Byron's guilt, not so much for incest as for having "'filed [his] mind' (*Childe Harold's Pilgrimage*, III. st. 113) by trafficking with contemptible people during his 'Years of Fame'" (Byron, *CPW*, 4:467).

This essay will explore the transformation of Byron's Alpine journal into Manfred's soliloquy—of the private discourse of the epistolary journal into the public (if closeted) discourse of the dramatic poem, examining the significance of what Byron retains, what he omits, and what he adds in the process. In each case, the transformation is from what Anne K. Mellor calls Romantic irony into what McGann calls the Romantic ideology.

The first six and a half lines are essentially a summary of the preceding scene. Then Manfred makes the "turn to Nature" that McGann considers characteristic of the Romantic ideology (*RI*, 67–68):

> *My* mother Earth!
> And thou fresh breaking Day, and you, ye Mountains,
> Why are ye beautiful? *I* cannot love ye.
> And thou, the bright eye of the universe,
> That openest over all, and unto all
> Art a delight—thou shin'st not on *my* heart.
> And you, ye crags, upon whose extreme edge
> *I* stand, and on the torrent's brink beneath
> Behold the tall pines dwindled as to shrubs
> In dizziness of distance; when a leap,
> A stir, a motion, even a breath, would bring
> *My* breast upon its rocky bosom's bed
> To rest for ever—wherefore do *I* pause?
> *I* feel the impulse—yet *I* do not plunge;
> *I* see the peril—yet do not recede;
> And *my* brain reels—and yet *my* foot is firm:
> There is a power upon *me* which withholds
> And makes it *my* fatality to live;
> If it be life to wear within *myself*
> This barrenness of spirit, and to be
> *My own* soul's sepulchre, for I have ceased
> To justify *my* deeds unto *myself*—
> The last infirmity of evil. (1.2.7–29; emphasis added)

This passage recalls the peroration of the Alpine journal (September 28):

> In the weather for this tour (of 13 days) *I* have been very fortunate—fortunate in a companion (Mr. H[obhous]e) fortunate in *our* prospects—and exempt even from the little petty accidents & delays which often render journeys in a less wild country—disappointing—*I* was disposed to be pleased—I am a lover of Nature—and an Admirer of Beauty—*I* can bear fatigue—& welcome privation—and have seen some of the noblest views in the world.—But in all this—the recollections of bitterness—& more especially of recent & more

home desolation—which must accompany *me* through life—have preyed upon *me* here—and neither the music of the Shepherd—the crashing of the Avalanche—nor the torrent—the mountain—the Glacier-the Forest—nor the Cloud—have for one moment—lightened the weight upon *my* heart—nor enabled *me* to lose *my own* wretched identity in the majesty & the power and the Glory—around—above—& beneath *me*.—*I* am past reproaches—and there is a time for all things—*I* am past the wish of vengeance—and *I* know of none like for what *I* have suffered—but the hour will come—when what *I* feel must be felt—& the——but enough.——(*BLJ*, 5:104–05; emphasis added)

What the poem retains from its prose source is, above all, what McGann calls the "implacable nihilism" that is Byron's special contribution to the Romantic ideology (*RI*, 76; cf. Mellor 26).[2]

This nihilism is accompanied by an equally implacable narcissism—"since after all," as Freud points out, "one's libido must go somewhere" (18:65; cf. Richardson, 48). The poem intensifies both. Just as Byron seems to assume that the only point of the shepherd, the avalanche, the torrent, the mountain, the glacier, the forest, and the cloud would be to lighten the weight on his heart, so Manfred seems to assume that there is no point in the earth, the day, and the mountains being beautiful if he cannot love them. In the journal passage, which is 210 words long, there are sixteen self-references, or usages of the first-person pronoun—7.6 percent of the total, already a pretty high proportion. In the passage from the poem, which is only 175 words long, there are eighteen self-references, or 10.3 percent. Accompanying this enhanced narcissism is an enhanced sense of subjecthood: in the journal passage, Byron, or one of his parts or attributes, is a subject nine times, or in 56.2 percent of the self-references ("*I* have been very fortunate ... *I* was disposed to be pleased—*I* am a lover of Nature") and an object seven times, or in 43.8 percent. In the soliloquy, Manfred is the subject eleven times, or in 61.1 percent of the self-references, and the object only seven, or in 38.9 percent. Manfred is thus somewhat more of an agent, less of a passive sufferer, than his creator. The change in the sense of the integrity of the subject is more emphatic: in the journal, Byron refers to himself as a whole thirteen times, or in 81.3 percent of the self references, and to parts or attributes of himself ("*my* heart ... *my* own wretched identity") only three times, or in 18.7 percent; in the soliloquy, Manfred refers to himself as a whole only ten times, or in 55.6 percent of the self-references, and to parts or attributes of himself fully eight times, or in 44.4 percent—an incidence more than three times as high as in the journal. Manfred's self-division, which is so important on the thematic level of the poem, is also evident on the stylistic level.

The rhetorical form of the passage—an apostrophe—also enhances its narcissism: Byron addresses his Alpine journal to his sister; Manfred addresses only the earth, the day, the mountains, and the sun—inanimate objects that have only the consciousness he grants them. The poem intensifies both the nihilism and the narcissism of the journal by replacing Byron's obscure, but outwardly directed, threat of vengeance with Manfred's threat of suicide—an introverted form of death, just as Manfred and Astarte's incest was an introverted form of love. (This, at any rate, seems to be how Byron conceives of incest and suicide—which, in "The Prisoner of Chillon," he calls "a selfish death" [230]). Astarte's death also seems to have been a suicide (2.4.82).

It is odd that a poem so replete with biblical allusions should omit the journal's allusion to the Lord's Prayer (Matthew 6:13); at this point, Manfred is unwilling to attribute "the power and the Glory" to anyone—even to God. (His attitude will change by 2.4.46–49, when he will invite Arimanes to kneel to God with him.) But the poem's most striking omission—the omission that most strikingly confirms its turn towards narcissism—is the companionship of someone like "Mr. H[obhous]e," a companionship so intimate that Byron uses the first person plural—"*our* prospects"—to refer to the two of them. Manfred has no companions, and he uses the first person plural almost exclusively to refer to himself and the dead Astarte.

The poem's most striking addition to the journal—the allusion to "Lycidas"—also confirms its turn towards the narcissistic: for Milton, the desire for fame is the "last infirmity of noble mind" (71; cf. McGann, *BR*, 29, 69, 148–49); for Manfred, to cease "To justify [his] deeds unto [him]self" is "The last infirmity of evil" (1.2.29). What is striking is not just the degradation of nobility to evil (like Faustus [5.2.14–15], Manfred is proud to be worse than anybody else) but the replacement of a desire for fame—approbation by others—with a narcissistic desire for self-approbation.

Following this passage is another apostrophe (not based on the Alpine journal) to an eagle—not as an element of the Alpine ecosystem, but as a transcendent, "winged and cloud-cleaving minister" possibly sent to inflict a Promethean punishment on Manfred himself (1.2.30)—and a meditation on human duality, "Half dust, half deity" (1.2.40), which is also reminiscent of "Prometheus" (47–48). Then Manfred turns back to the scenery:

> Hark! the note,
> [*The Shepherd's pipe in the distance is heard*]
> The natural music of the mountain reed—
> For here the patriarchal days are not
> A pastoral fable—pipes in the liberal air,
> Mix'd with the sweet bells of the sauntering herd;

My soul would drink those echoes.—Oh, that I were
The viewless spirit of a lovely sound,
A living voice, a breathing harmony,
A bodiless enjoyment—born and dying
With the blest tone which made me! (1.2.48–56)

This passage recalls the Alpine journal's entry for September 19:

> The music of the Cows' bells (for their wealth like the Patriarchs is cattle) in the pastures (which reach to a height far above any mountains in Britain—) and the Shepherds' shouting to us from crag to crag & playing on their reeds where the steeps appeared almost inaccessible, with the surrounding scenery—realized all that I have ever heard or imagined of a pastoral existence—much more so than Greece or Asia Minor—for there we are a little too much of the sabre & musquet order—and if there is a Crook in one hand, you are sure to see a gun in the other—but this was pure and unmixed—solitary—savage and patriarchal—the effect I cannot describe—as we went they played the "Ranz des Vaches" and other airs by way of farewell.—I have recently repeopled my mind with Nature. (*BLJ*, 5:99)

In this case, the poem retains the imagery of the journal—in even greater detail than in the first pair of parallel passages—together with the biblical and pastoral allusions it suggests. It adds Manfred's desire to become the "viewless spirit of a lovely sound" (1.2.54), a proto-Paterian aspiration to the condition of music—or a typically Romantic aspiration to "'Unity of Being'" (McGann, *RI*, 40, quoting Geoffrey Hartman), thus enhancing the sense of the "pure and unmixed" which is already present, though not in pure and unmixed form, in the journal.[3] "[V]iewless" is Shakespearean/Miltonic: in *Measure for Measure* (3.1.124), it describes the winds in which Claudio fears to be imprisoned after death; in *Comus* (92), the form assumed by the Attendant Spirit as Comus enters; in *Paradise Lost* (3.518), the retracted stairway to Heaven. These allusions emphasize the spiritual nature of Manfred's aspiration.

The poem omits all the political, economic, and social contexts (the Swiss national air, "Ranz des Vaches," the function of cattle as wealth in biblical Palestine and modern Switzerland, the prevalence of violent robbery in Greece)—a context of which Byron is aware of himself as a part ("*we* are a little too much of the sabre & musquet order"). As Marjean D. Purinton points out, the entries in the Alpine journal "do not reflect a writer dazzled and mesmerized by an idealized or romanticized landscape" (68).[4] The poem, by contrast, reflects just such a writer. As McGann argues, "One of the basic illusions of Romantic Ideology is that only a poet and his works can transcend a corrupting appropriation by 'the world' of politics and money" (*RI*, 13). Perhaps most importantly, the poem omits Byron's concluding claim to have "repeopled [his] mind with Nature," which flatly contradicts the implacable nihilism both of the journal's peroration, and of the poem. The Byron of the Alpine journal is often willing to be pleased. As Mellor puts it,

> He [the Romantic ironist] must acknowledge the inevitable limitations of his own finite consciousness and of all man-made structures or myths. But even as he denies the absolute validity of his own perceptions and structuring conceptions of the universe, even as he consciously deconstructs his mystifications of the self and the world, he must affirm and celebrate the process of life by creating new images and ideas. Thus the romantic ironist sustains his participation in a creative process that extends beyond the limits of his own mind. (5)

Manfred, by contrast, is only a Romantic ideologist. As Mellor explains, "rather than accepting [his] ironic awareness of human finitude as a mode of possibility and part of the process of self-transcendence ... Manfred bitterly rebels against the limitations of his own humanity. He thus locks himself into a tragic view of life" (35). From such a viewpoint, the back-and-forth movement of Romantic irony looks like self-division:

> ... *we*, who name ourselves [the world's] sovereigns, *we*,
> Half dust, half deity, alike unfit
> To sink or soar, with *our* mix'd essence make
> A conflict of its elements, and breathe
> The breath of degradation and of pride,
> Contending with low wants and lofty will
> Till *our* mortality predominates,
> And men are—what they name not to themselves,
> And trust not to each other. (1.2.39–47; emphasis added)

Significantly, this ideological passage has no parallel in the ironic Alpine journal. The rare use of the first person plural marks the only kind of solidarity with the rest of living humanity that Manfred is prepared, at this point, to grant: their common subjection to the tragically divided human condition. Over the course of the passage, the agency of humanity, either pretentious and futile ("*we* ... name ourselves [the world's] sovereigns") or self-dividing ("*we* ... make/A conflict of [the] elements" of "*our* mix'd essence") to start with, yields, in a stylistic self-disintegration, to the agency of one of its attributes, half of its "mix'd essence" ("*our* mortality predominates")—thus erasing even the ideological view of Romantic irony as self-division—and finally to the self-alienation of the third person: it is no longer "we" but "men" who "are—what they name not to themselves, / And trust not to each other."

After the Chamois Hunter's first speech, which (in another indication of his narcissism [Richardson 47–48]) he does not hear, Manfred continues:

> To be thus—
> Grey-hair'd with anguish, like these blasted pines,
> Wrecks of a single winter, barkless, branchless,
> A blighted trunk upon a cursed root,
> Which but supplies a feeling to decay—
> And to be thus, eternally but thus,
> Having been otherwise! (1.2.65–71)

This recalls the Alpine journal's entry for September 23:

> Starlight—beautiful—but a devil of a path—never mind—got safe in—a little lightning—but the whole of the day as fine in point of weather—as the day on which Paradise was made.—Passed *whole woods of withered pines—all withered*—trunks stripped and barkless—branches lifeless—done by a single winter—their appearance reminded me of me & my family.—(*BLJ*, 5:102)

It would be hard to find a more perfect example of the back-and-forth movement of Romantic irony than that first sentence: "Starlight—beautiful—*but a devil of a path*—never mind—got safe in—*a little lightning*—but the whole of the day as fine in point of weather—as the day on which Paradise was made." The poem omits all this. It retains Byron's narcissistic identification with the pines, intensifying the narcissism by omitting any suggestion that anyone but Manfred suffers from this blight: Byron refers to his family, but Manfred doesn't even mention Astarte. It adds the ambiguous opening formula, "To be thus," an expression both of Manfred's desire for and his dread of death—which, at this point in the soliloquy, Manfred images in purely material terms, rather than the spiritual terms of the "viewless spirit of a lovely sound" passage. Above all, the poem extends the blight both backwards and forwards in time. Despite the later contention of Manfred's retainer, Manuel, that Manfred's father was a happy man (3.3.25), and despite Manfred's own contention, in this very speech, that the pines are the "Wrecks of a single winter," Manfred still insists that the source of his problem is hereditary, "a cursed root" extending indefinitely down into the past. That Manfred should contradict not only Manuel—who has no reason to lie—but also himself suggests that we should be critical of this insistence. We should presumably be equally critical of his prediction that his problem will never end—that he will be "thus, eternally but thus." After all, he will die, apparently at peace, at the end of the poem. Again, of the two poles of Romantic irony, Manfred insists on the pole of despair—of the Romantic ideology.

Finally, just before his suicide attempt and the Chamois Hunter's rescue, Manfred indulges in yet another apostrophe:

> Ye toppling crags of ice!
> Ye avalanches, whom a breath draws down
> In mountainous o'erwhelming, come and crush me—
> I hear ye momently above, beneath,
> Crash with a frequent conflict; but ye pass,
> And only fall on things which still would live;
> On the young flourishing forest, or the hut
> And hamlet of the harmless villager....
> The mists boil up around the glaciers; clouds
> Rise curling fast beneath me, white and sulphury,
> Like foam from the roused ocean of deep Hell,
> Whose every wave breaks on a living shore,
> Heaped with the damn'd like pebbles.—I am giddy. (1.2.74–89)

This recalls another passage from the September 23 entry in the Alpine journal—one referring explicitly to the Jungfrau, the site of Manfred's soliloquy:

> The height of the Yung frau is 13000 feet above the sea—and 11000 above the valley—she is the highest of this range,—heard the Avalanches falling every five minutes nearly—as if God was pelting the Devil down from Heaven with snow balls—from where we stood on the *Wengren* [sic] Alp—we had all these in view on one side—on the other the clouds rose from the opposite valley curling up perpendicular precipices—like the foam of the Ocean of Hell during a Springtide—it was white & sulphery—and immeasurably deep in appearance— ... I made a snowball & pelted H. with it—got down to our horses again—eat something-remounted—heard the Avalanches still—(*BLJ*, 5:101–02)

The poem omits the absurd blasphemy of God's pelting the devil with snowballs—and the further absurdity of Byron's pelting the notoriously non-Satanic Hobhouse in imitation. It omits, as usual, all the chaotic details of companionship, horses, and food. It adds an apocalyptic image of disaster reminiscent of "Darkness"—the destruction of the forest, hut, and hamlet—and also the surrealistic image of the shore of hell, "Heaped with the damn'd like pebbles," which vastly extends the suffering in space, as well as extending it indefinitely in time, as in the passage about the blasted pines. At the end of the poem, he, Abbot, will dread to think where Manfred has gone (3.4.153), but since he will have beaten back the baffled fiends (3.4.140), it presumably will not be to hell.

In turning his Alpine journal into Manfred's soliloquy, Byron has, at every point, reduced Romantic irony into a "pure and unmixed" expression of the Romantic ideology. In a sense, the story of the rest of the poem is Manfred's discovery—or recovery—of irony: his journey from this narcissistic and ideological soliloquy to his other-directed and ironic exit line, "Old man! 'tis not so difficult to die" (3.4.151).[5]

**Notes**

1  Byron's use of his journal resembles William Wordsworth's use of Dorothy Wordsworth's journals in his poems, except that in this case, the journalist and the poet are the same person.
2  There is, of course, some resemblance between Byronic nihilism and Coleridgean dejection.
3  In metafictional terms, Manfred actually is "The viewless spirit of a lovely sound": he exists only in the medium of Byron's beautiful verse. But that verse is directed outward, towards the reading public; within the diegesis, Manfred's soliloquy is directed only at himself.
4  Purinton is surely right to contend that Mangred also deals with political issues, in a displaced way (68). But it is precisely this displacement that makes him ideological.
5  An earlier version of this essay was presented at the International Conference on Romanticism, Marquette University, 15 November 2003. I am grateful to Craig Franson, Emily Bernhard Jackson, Jerome McGann, Richard Nanian, Jeff Schragel, Matt Squires, and Paul Westover for their comments.

**Works Cited**

Byron, George Gordon Noel. *Byron's Letters and Journals*. Ed. Leslie A. Marchand. 12 vols. London: John Murray, 1973–82.
———. *The Complete Poetical Works*. Ed. Jerome J. McGann. 7 vols. Oxford: Clarendon Press, 1980–91.
Freud, Sigmund. *The Standard Edition of the Complete Psychological Works of Sigmund Freud*. Ed. and trans. James Strachey et al. 24 vols. London: Hogarth Press, 1953–74.
Macdonald, D.L. "Incest, Narcissism and Demonality in Byron's *Manfred*." *Mosaic* 25.2 (1992): 25–38.
Marlowe, Christopher. *Doctor Faustus: A 1604-Version Edition*. Ed. Michael Keefer. Peterborough: Broadview Press, 1991.
McGann, Jerome J. *Byron and Romanticism*. Ed. James Soderholm. Cambridge: Cambridge UP, 2002.
———. *The Romantic Ideology: A Critical Investigation*. Chicago: University of Chicago Press, 1983.
Mellor, Anne K. *English Romantic Irony*. Cambridge MA: Harvard UP, 1980.

Milton, John. *The Complete Poetry of John Milton*. Ed. John T. Shawcross. Rev. edn. Garden City, NY: Anchor, 1971.

Purinton, Marjean D. *Romantic Ideology Unmasked: The Mentally Constructed Tyrannies in Dramas of William Wordsworth, Lord Byron, Percy Shelley, and Joanna Baillie*. Newark: University of Delaware Press, 1994.

Richardson, Alan. *A Mental Theater: Poetic Drama and Consciousness in the Romantic Age*. University Park: Pennsylvania State UP, 1988.

Chapter Fourteen

# The Romantic Artist on the Couch: A Freudian Approach to Wackenroder's Musician, Berglinger

Sonja E. Klocke

Many scholars have analyzed the so-called typical Romantic artist, and have characterized him as overly sensitive and suffering from his surroundings. Furthermore, his misery often ends in death.[1] Nevertheless, explanations for this particular typification are generally absent, which may be due to the difficulties inherent in the quest for a person's underlying and possibly psychologically motivated makeup. This complexity becomes even more intricate when one is dealing with a fictional character created by a writer. I definitely do not want to draw conclusions from the text and transfer them onto the author Wackenroder, as has been done before.[2] The relatively recent critical edition (1991) of Wackenroder's works exemplifies the different strata research has followed over the years (359–363) and also stresses the closeness of Berglinger and Wackenroder (363). Although biographical influences cannot necessarily be denied, I am not concerned with the author Wackenroder, but exclusively with his artistic product, Joseph Berglinger. Consequently, the claims I am making about his musician should not be transferred onto the author.

Since Romantic authors were increasingly interested in the unconscious and its influence on the human mind and soul, there is some justification for applying psychoanalysis and Freud's theory to Romantic art. The famous Viennese analyzed Hoffmann's Nathanael as he is presented in *The Sandman* in "The Uncanny." This 1919 essay offers readers an increased insight into the psychological make-up of Hoffmann's artist because the psychoanalyst manages to uncover character traits that otherwise would have remained hidden. It is precisely for this reason that I will investigate the make-up of the musician Berglinger in Wackenroder's "The Strange Musical Life of the Musical Artist Joseph Berglinger" from *Confessions from the Heart of an Art-loving Friar*,[3] and look at the influence of childhood and family on his development. Returning to Freud for this purpose will permits an interpretation that can reconstruct the latent text underlying Wackenroder's novella. This analysis shall by no means reduce the story to a manifest text, whose underlying problematic sexual complex could then be considered the focal point; rather, it is intended to overcome limits inherent in common interpretations by offering an additional aspect that should be taken into consideration when analyzing Berglinger's life story. I will argue that Berglinger, a representative of the "typical" Romantic artist, is determined by an unsolved oedipal conflict, which in turn can even allow us to question the quality of his artistic production.

According to Wackenroder, God presents himself in two languages: nature and art (SCH, 118–120; WA, 97–100). Nature as God's immediate creation corresponds with art, which is regarded as a human artifact. God grants the artist the ability to produce art, exemplifying "the highest human perfection" (SCH, 120).[4] Therefore art mirrors God's ability to create and cannot be dissociated from religion. The artist, on the other hand, is no more than "a weak instrument" (SCH, 157):[5] characterized as weak and nothing but a tool, the good artist's mission is not self-expression but the illustration of the divine will. Hence, God can be detected in every work of art because He participates in its production. Yet not only the creation, but also the reception, of art attains the significance of religion. We find this notion of an "art-religion," or *Kunstreligion*, explicitly expressed in Wackenroder's statement: "I compare the enjoyment of the more noble works of art to prayer" (SCH, 126).[6] Although Wackenroder compares the two, he does not suggest substituting art by religion;[7] he merely links the bond established between believer and God in prayer with the kind of *unio mystica* the observer of a work of art arrives at when contemplating the object of his gaze, which contains God. Consequently, the enjoyment of art equals "prayer" for him (SCH, 126; WA, 106), museums may be considered "temples" (SCH, 126; WA, 106), and the artist Raphael has to be considered "divine" (SCH, 85; WA, 58).

Wackenroder's proclaimed paradise on earth can best be found in music, which he (in contrast to the early Romantics in Jena who believed poetry to be the most advanced art) deems superior to all other forms of art. Wackenroder explicitly states his ideas in "The Marvels of the Musical Art" (SCH, 178–181),[8] and in "Concerning the Various Genres in Every Art and Especially Concerning Various Types of Church Music" (SCH, 182–185).[9] Due to what Adorno signifies as the "theological conception" (Adorno/Ashton) of music,[10] we are dealing with "the language of angels" (SCH, 180) according to both Wackenroder and Adorno.[11] Their concept of music as "a language, but a language without concepts" (Adorno/Ashton, 44)[12] is also adopted by Brantner. According to her, music succeeds over language, an arbitrary system of signs, precisely because of its linguistic distance, its ability to elude a rational definition.[13] The word, by definition, cannot be immediate; thus it ironically lengthens the distance that it tries to overcome. By contrast, music bridges this gap because of its ability to express feelings directly. As Wackenroder puts it, one must "consider music to be the most marvelous of these inventions, because it portrays human feelings in a superhuman way" (SCH, 180).[14]

These ideas concerning art and the ideal artist are accentuated in the novella narrating Joseph Berglinger's life story. Berglinger lacks the abilities that would enable him to qualify as God's tool. He repeatedly asks God to bestow upon him artistic abilities: "he fell upon his knees because of the ardent drive of his heart and begged God that He might guide him, so that he might one day become a truly magnificent artist in the eyes of heaven and earth" (SCH, 152).[15] Although Berglinger perceives the divine origins of art, he still wants to misuse art to serve his own egoistic interests—to express his own feelings and to be acclaimed by his audience. His request to be granted creative competence is not based on a desire to serve God in an exhibition of the divine glory, but on a yearning to celebrate himself. Therefore, he fails to serve as God's instrument on earth.

Berglinger is thus established as what Karoli signifies as the "romantic artist par excellence":[16] the torn individual trapped in a tension evolving from his idealistic enthusiasm, his subjectivism, his dangerous passivity, and his wish to dissolve his life in musical sounds. He proves inept at accepting the superiority of art over the subject of the artist, and turns out to be incapable of mediating between art and reality. Thus, he is unable to fulfill the Romantic artist's mission of poeticizing the world in Novalis's sense and is doomed to fail.

In addition, Joseph finds himself in a conflict with a family and a society that lacks an appreciation for the artist and is inimical towards art.[17] He constantly suffers from the antagonism between his enthusiasm for art and prosaic reality. According to Brantner, this renders him a typical representative not only of the artist, but more specifically of the musician in Romantic literature. As a matter of principle, he lives in poor financial circumstances; his father tries to suppress the child's musicality, and social need constrains.[18] Escape, therefore, appears to be Joseph's sole remaining alternative. First, he flees his father's house; when he realizes that he is incompetent at producing art and feels unappreciated by the court, he longs to leave everything behind again: "I would like to leave all this culture in the lurch and take refuge with the simple Swiss shepherd in the mountains and play his Alpine songs with him, according to which he becomes homesick everywhere" (SCH, 157).[19] He suffers from the clash between his expectations of composing godly music and a reality that demands the display of social skills. And since the "Swiss shepherds" constitute an illusory perception, Berglinger eventually retreats into isolation. Nevertheless, he still has to deal with the audience he loathes and, due to the self-reference of his artistic products, cannot communicate with.

While many scholars follow the idea that Joseph cannot succeed because of society's constraints,[20] Frey suggests that the explanation for his failure is inherent in the configuration of his personality. She stresses that in Wackenroder's *Confessions from the Heart* only those artists equipped with special sensitivity, fail to qualify as true artists.[21] And since Berglinger is never satisfied with his own artistic production, his qualification as an artist needs to be questioned. Therefore I consider it vital to investigate the circumstances in which the "Romantic artist" Berglinger lives, and examine their influence on his psyche and his inability to produce art.

In his 1919 essay "The Uncanny" Freud analyzes Hoffmann's *The Sandman* exclusively from a psychoanalytic perspective. He establishes the father image, which is divided into a "good father" and a "bad father". The latter threatens to remove Nathanael's eyes when he is a little boy, thus establishing castration anxiety as reason for little Nathanael wishing to see this "bad father" dead. When on the contrary the "good father" is killed by the hand of the "bad father," Coppelius/Sandman, it is the latter who fulfills Nathanael's suppressed desire.

The *Berglinger-Novella* establishes a similar situation. At the beginning Wackenroder, through the persona of the friar, explicitly points to the positive aspect of the father-image: "This father was originally a gentle and very good-hearted man who liked to do nothing better than to help, counsel, and give alms, as much as his means allowed" (SCH, 147).[22] Consequently, Joseph loves this soft, good-hearted father with "sincere love" (SCH, 147).[23] However, the word "originally" (in German, *ursprünglich*), already insinuates the father's dark side. The text accentuates this aspect, and moreover implies that the study of medicine and his vocation as a doctor have evoked a negative father who lusts after illnesses: "This industrious studying had become for him a secret, nerve-deadening poison, which penetrated all his veins and ate away at many resonant strings of the human heart within him" (SCH, 147).[24] Studying illnesses has turned out to be toxic. Furthermore, this poison is "secret," (*heimlich*), which, according to Freud, is just another version of "uncanny," or *unheimlich*:[25] it acts secretly, cannot be explained in any rational way, and provokes an eerie feeling in the reader who does not want to imagine a doctor engaged in mysterious and supernatural arts. The "nerve-deadening poison," which has conquered the entire body through the bloodstream, deadens the man's nerves and suggests a mysterious union with an evil spirit.

The science which Berglinger's father engages in is medicine. Wackenroder uses the older version of the word, *Arzneygelehrsamkeit*, (WA, 130) which stresses the studying of pharmaceutical herbs, and alludes to the use of poisonous plants or even witchcraft. The text further emphasizes the mysterious aspect involved in the father's profession when referring to specific interests that also cause him delight: "He ... had taken pleasure in nothing but in the knowledge of strange things which lie hidden within the human body" (SCH, 147).[26] Thus Berglinger senior, like Nathanael's fathers, seeks knowledge about creation, procreation, and especially about the mysterious, or even occult, aspects of what constitutes life. And like Nathanael, Joseph has to learn that the quest for this knowledge is punished. Even though his father lives, he is increasingly penalized: first through his wife's death, then by growing unhappiness and poverty. Those conditions reflect back on the boy's childhood and adolescence, and cause his feelings of sadness and despair: "How miserable and dejected he felt to be again in a family whose entire living and activity revolved solely around the meager satisfaction of the most necessary physical needs" (SCH, 150).[27] Joseph repeatedly rejects his father's preaching that it is his duty to take care of his fellow human beings, and to "bind up loathsome wounds and heal odious illnesses!" (SCH, 151).[28] He is convinced that he is "born for a loftier, more noble end," (SCH, 151)[29] and thus, unsurprisingly, he blames his father for the calamity he feels trapped in.

I have already noted the family's neediness and the father's attempt to suppress the child's musicality as representing conditions typically suffered by the Romantic artist. Furthermore, the absence of a mother left Joseph without anybody to turn his affection to and be loved by, thus rendering it impossible for him to overcome his oedipal conflict. He is left with his fantasies and dreams, forced to flee into "a realm of beautiful fantasy and divine dreams ... and ... inner fantasies" (SCH, 147/148).[30] According to Freud in "Creative Writers and Day-Dreaming,"[31] only the unsatisfied fantasize: "We may lay it down that a happy person never phantasies, only an unsatisfied one. The motive forces of phantasies are unsatisfied wishes, and every single phantasy is the fulfillment of a wish, a correction of unsatisfying reality" (Freud, *Complete Psychological Works*, IX: 146).[32] Joseph doubtlessly qualifies as an unhappy child. Furthermore, the lack of a loving female renders him unsatisfied. His fantasies have to serve as the correction of his gruesome reality, but the reader remains in the dark about the content of his dreams.

This sensitive child deprived of his mother and unable to connect with the world around him causes his father to "consider him also slightly perverse and of weak mind" (SCH, 148).[33] Should the reader therefore deem little Joseph a rather difficult child, or instead mistrust the father's account? If we keep Freud's observations from "Creative Writers and Day-Dreaming" in mind, we see that Berglinger senior cannot be considered to be entirely mistaken: "If phantasies become over-luxuriant and over-powerful, the conditions are laid for an onset of neurosis or psychosis. Phantasies, moreover, are the immediate mental precursors of the distressing symptoms complained of by our patients" (Freud, *Complete Psychological Works*, IX: 148).[34] If Freud is right, the father's rather hostile attitude toward his son will cause the latter to fantasize excessively and therefore amplify the deficiency caused by the mother's absence. Joseph is thus perfectly preconditioned for generating a neurosis. Furthermore, his family's lack of sympathy increasingly forces the little boy to retreat into narcissistic self-love: "he valued his own inner soul above all else and kept it concealed and hidden from others. One keeps a little treasure chest hidden in this way, whose key one entrusts to no other person's hands" (SCH, 148).[35] The "concealed" here is *heimlich* and can also be read as "secret." An awareness of the close relationship between *heimlich* and *unheimlich* established by Freud and referred to earlier, as well as the secrecy implied by the "hidden" (*verborgen*) and Joseph's refusal to grant anyone access to his personality, leaves the reader with an uncanny feeling. The suggestion of suppressed feelings, which is, according to Freud, a prerequisite for artistic production, links Berglinger to the psychoanalyst's ideas concerning aesthetics as established in "The Uncanny," while at the same time alluding to a medical-psychological condition. Wackenroder's choice of word, *verborgen*, further stresses this aspect: it is the same word that the poet employed to describe Joseph's father's interest in gaining "knowledge of strange things which lie hidden within the human body" (SCH, 147). For Joseph's father, his son's "inner soul" must be as great a secret and simultaneously as troublesome a disease as the ugly illnesses he constantly attempts to cure.

At the same time, the doctor enforces his son's medical-psychological condition through his lack of understanding for the child's early love for music, resulting in repeated attempts to turn him away from this passion. The friar recalls the father's attitude and behavior:

> From the beginning he had regarded with displeasure the fact that his Joseph had become so very fond of music; and now, since this love was growing greater and greater in the boy, he was making a persistent and serious attempt to convert him from this ruinous inclination toward an art, the practice of which was not much better than indolence and which merely satisfied the senses, to medicine. (SCH, 150)[36]

This evokes a similar conflict to that which the father and son would have engaged in over the mother's love, had she survived Joseph's birth. Because the boy has decided to direct his love to music, his father feels obliged to turn him away from this love. The way in which music replaces for the mother figure is obvious it is a longing (*Lust*). Berglinger senior envies the younger one's pleasure in this longing, just like a father who is jealous of his son's love for the mother. On the grounds of the observable absence of women in Berglinger's life, Yee has already shown that Joseph turns to music instead of the female sex. However, he failed to provide a possible reason behind this observation. Freud offers an explanation in his analysis of Hoffmann's Nathanael: "The psychological truth of the situation in which the young man, fixated upon his father by his castration-complex, is incapable of loving a woman, is amply proved by numerous analyses of patients" (Freud, *Studies in Parapsychology*, 39).[37] Berglinger has proved incapable of engaging in relationships with women. Adult women are entirely absent from the bandmaster's life, and merely setting eyes on his sisters, the only females to appear in the novella, causes him despair (SCH, 158; WA, 143). Thus the father's reaction to Joseph's love for music makes the similarity to an oedipal situation very palpable: the doctor is jealous of his son's affection for music which results in his total withdrawal from the parent and ends the already weak father–son bond.

Berglinger senior considers Joseph's love for music "ruinous" precisely because it satisfies his son's longing, his "desire of the senses." We are reminded of Joseph's fantasies signifying his repressed wishes; apparently he has finally found an outlet for those desires in music. At the same time one recalls Joseph's father's perverted lust resulting from his dealings with sickness. Freud established the connection between art, sickness, and the oedipal conflict in "Totem and Taboo":[38]

> At the conclusion, then, of this exceedingly condensed inquiry, I should like to insist that its outcome shows that the beginnings of religion, morals, society and art converge in the Oedipus complex. This is in complete agreement with the psychoanalytic finding that the same complex constitutes the nucleus of all neuroses. (Freud, *Complete Psychological Works*, XIII:56–157)[39]

Freud explicitly names the oedipal complex as the basic nucleus of all the phenomena observable in the *Berglinger-Novella* which cause the artist both enthusiastic pleasure and abysmal pain, namely all culture, religion, art, morality, and society.

Mahlendorf, referring to Hoffmann's *The Sandman*, specifically links the Romantic artist's "oedipal phase of development ... to his creativity" (218). She also considers the influence of a rather difficult relationship between family and artist significant if one wants to gain insights into possible causes for the success or failure of the creative work. Concerns regarding an artist's achievement or failure are also significant for Berglinger. He is generally considered to be a problematic musician, mainly because of his problems with society. Yee, however, is skeptical about Berglinger's artistic gift: "In fact, Berglinger's ability is questionable ... The Friar states that Berglinger's last composition 'ewig ein Meisterstück bleiben wird' (144), ["will eternally be a masterpiece" (SCH, 159)]. She then goes on to imply that Berglinger should never have attempted to be a composer: "Soll ich sagen, daß er vielleicht mehr dazu geschaffen war, Kunst zu *genießen* statt *auszuüben*?" (144) ["Shall I say that he was perhaps created more to *enjoy* art than to *practice* it?" (144; SCH, 159)]. On the basis of those lines one cannot discard a link between Berglinger's apparent difficulties which, as we have seen, are predicated on an oedipal situation. and his debatable abilities. In accordance with Wackenroder's standards for "good art"—that is, an art that does not express the artist's emotions but celebrates God—Joseph has to fail. This means that exclusively blaming society and a family hostile to art for Joseph's dilemma is hardly justifiable. He might just as well be not very talented as a musician.

Hence Berglinger, like Hoffmann's Nathanael, is not only conditioned by an oedipal conflict, but his artistic abilities also have to be seriously doubted. Even though he has been depicted as the Romantic artist *par excellence* by a variety of scholars, his inability to focus on the production of "good art" corresponding with Wackenroder's ideals must also be considered. Resting upon Freud's statements with reference to the relationship between art and the oedipal conflict, I consider Berglinger unsuccessful precisely because of his unsolved oedipal situation.

For future research, it would be fascinating to follow this idea and examine other artistic characters in literature, not only from the Romantic period. Scholars like Müller-Seidel have already pointed to the relationship between modernism and the Romantic period. Hasselbach gives a detailed comparative analysis of Wackenroder's *Berlinger-Novella* and Thomas Mann's *Doktor Faustus*, and other critics such as Thewalt, Ellis, Hilzinger, Bollacher, Frey, and Brantner have pointed to the chain of artists that starts out with Joseph Berglinger and continues with Hoffmann's Johannes Kreisler, Thomas Mann's Tonio Kröger and his Adrian Leverkühn, to name a few. If we focus on those as well as other artists and their family backgrounds and upbringing as described in the literature, we might find that they and their lives can also be understood and interpreted by the discourse of the unresolved, unsolved oedipal complex.

## Notes

1 For an analysis of this specific kind of artist see especially Brantner; Ellis; Frey; Hasselbach; Karoli; and Thewalt.
2 See Hertrich; Neumann. For an evaluation of this approach see Yee.
3 The novella is called "Das merkwürdige musikalische Leben des Tonkünstlers Joseph Berglinger." It is the last piece from a collection called *Herzensergießungen eines kunstliebenden Klosterbruders*. I shall quote in English, marked as SCH, and refer to the translation by Schubert as given in the "Works Cited." The original text, cited as WA and referring to the critical edition given in the "Works Cited," can be found in the notes below.
4 "Die Kunst stellt uns die höchste menschliche Vollendung dar" (WA, 99).
5 "Wahrhaftig, die Kunst ist es, was man verehren muß , nicht den Künstler; - der ist nichts meh, als ein schwaches Werkzeug" (WA, 141).
6 "Ich vergleiche den Genuß der edle,en Kunstwerke dem Gebet" (WA, 106).
7 See Hertrich (136).
8 "Die Wunde, der Tonkunst" (WA, 205–08).
9 "Von den verschiedenen Gattungen injede, Kunst und insbesondere von verschiedenen Arten der Kirchenmusik" (WA, 209–13).
10 Adorno calls it "die theologische Konzeption der Musik" (55).
11 Wackenroder and Adorno both call it the "Sprache der Engel," (WA, 207; Adorno, 55) which Ashton translates into "the angels' tongue" (44).

12  Adorno's phrasing of "eine Sprache, aber eine ohne Begriffe" (54) seems to be more accessible, since the German *Begriff* includes the notion of a specific terminology in addition to the idea of a concept.
13  "Fähigkeit, sich einer rationalen Definition zu entziehen" (Brantner, 167).
14  "Die Musik aber halte ich für, die wunderbarste dieser Erfindungen, weil sie menschliche Gefühle auf eine übermenschliche Art schildert" (WA, 207).
15  "Viele werden es für, ... Erdichtung halten, allein es ist reine Wahrheit, ... daß er oftmals ... auf die Knie fiel und Gott bat, er möchte ihn doch also führen, daß er einst ein echt herrlicher Künstler vor dem Himmel und vor der Erde werden möchte" (WA, 136).
16  Karoli terms and describes him as the "romantischer Künstler par excellence" (191).
17  Cf. Frey (53); Ellis determines the following three main reasons for the conflict: "his overly imaginative and introspective nature," "the misfortune of being born into a family which has so little understanding for his musical inclinations," and society itself, in which "the musical experience has been stripped completely of its spiritual significance" (78).
18  As Brantner phrases it: "Grundsätzlich lebt er in armen Verhältnissen, der Vater versucht die kindliche Musikalität zu unterdrücken, [und] soziale Not schränkt ein" (37).
19  "Ich möchte all diese Kultur im Stiche lassen und mich zu den simplen Schweizerhirten ins Gebirge hinflüchten und seine Alpenlieder, wonach er überall das Heimweh bekömmt, mit ihm spielen" (WA, 142).
20  See Bollacher (381); Dahnke (196); Ellis (9, 76); Hertrich (31, 50, 56); Neumann (185, 189); Strack (374); Zipes (252, 253).
21  Frey talks about those, "die nicht echte Künstler sind" (54–55).
22  "Dieser Vater war ursprünglich ein weicher und sehr gutherziger Mann, der nichts lieber thun mochte, als helfen, rathen und Almosen geben, so viel er nur vermögend war" (WA, 130).
23  "Man muß ... Von tiefer Wehmut und herzlicher Liebe ergriffen werden ..." (WA, 130).
24  "Dieses eifrige Studium nun war ihm ... ein heimliches, nervenbetäubendes Gift geworden, das all seine Adem durchdrang, und viele klingende Saiten des menschlichen Busens bey ihm zernagte" (WA, 131).
25  For an impressive philological analysis of the German word *unheimlich*, as well as of its implications for psychoanalysis, see Freud's essay "Das Unheimliche."
26  "Er [hatte] an nichts als an der Kenntniß der seltsamen Dinge, die im menschlichen Körper verborgen liegen ... seine Lust gehabt" (WA, 131).
27  "Wie kläglich und niedergedrückt fühlte er sich wieder in einer Familie, deren ganzes Leben und Weben sich nur um die kümmerliche Befriedigung der nothwendigsten physischen Bedürfnisse drehte" (WA, 134).
28  "Und ... mein Vater predigt es immer, daß es die Pflicht und Bestimmung des Menschen sey, ... ekelhafte Wunden zu verbinden, und häßliche Krankheiten zu heilen" (WA, 135–136).
29  "Und doch ruft mir wieder eine innere Stimme ganz laut zu: Nein! nein! du bist zu einem höheren, edleren Ziel gebohren" (WA, 136).
30  "In diese Familie konnte niemand weniger passen, als Joseph, der immer in

schöner Einbildung und himmlischen Träumen ... und ... seinen inneren Phantaseyen [lebte]" (WA, 131).
31  The title is "Der Dichter und das Phantasieren."
32  "Man darf sagen, der Glückliche phantasiert nie, nur der Unbefriedigte. Unbefriedigte Wünsche sind die Triebkräfte der Phantasie, und jede einzelne Phantasie ist eine Wunscherfüllung, eine Korrektur der unbefriedigten Wirklichkeit" (Freud, *Studienausgabe*, X: 173–74).
33  "... drum hielt der Vater auch ihn ein wenig verkehrt und blöden Geistes" (WA, 131).
34  "Das Überwuchern und Übermächtigwerden der Phantasien stellt die Bedingungen für den Verfall in Neurose oder Psychose her; die Phantasien sind auch die nächsten seelischen Vorstufen der Leidenssymptome, über welche unsere Kranken klagen" (Freud, *Studienausgabe*, X: 175).
35  "Sein Inneres schätzte er über alles, und hielt es vor andern heimlich und verborgen. So hält man ein Schatzkästlein verborgen, zu welchem man den Schlüssel niemanden in die Hände gibt" (WA, 131).
36  "Schon von jeher hatte er es mit Mißvergnügen gesehen, daß sein Joseph sich so sehr an die Musik gehängt hatte; und nun, da diese Liebe in dem Knaben immer höher wuchs, machte er einen anhaltenden und ernstlichen Versuch, ihn von dem verderblichen Hange zu einer Kunst, deren Ausübung nicht viel besser als Müssiggang sey, und die bloße Lüsternheit der Sinne befriedige, zur Medicin ... zu bekehren" (WA, 134).
37  "Wie psychologisch richtig es aber ist, daß der durch den Kastrationskomplex an den Vater fixierte Jüngling der Liebe zum Weibe unfähig wird, zeigen zahlreiche Krankenanalysen." (Freud, *Studienausgabe*, IV: 256)
38  The title is "Totem und Tabu."
39  "So möchte ich denn zum Schlusse dieser ... Untersuchung das Ergebnis aussprechen, daß im Ödipuskomplex die Anfänge von Religion, Sittlichkeit, Gesellschaft und Kunst zusammentreffen, in voller Übereinstimmung mit der Feststellung der Psychoanalyse, daß dieser Komplex den Kern aller Neurosen bildet" (Freud, *Studienausgabe*, IX: 439).

**Works Cited**

Adorno, Theodor W. *Einleitung in die Musiksoziologie. Zwölf theoretische Vorlesungen.* Frankfurt am Main: Suhrkamp, 1962.
———. *Introduction to the Sociology of Music.* Trans. E. B. Ashton. New York: The Seabury Press, 1976.
Bollacher, Martin. "Wackenroders Kunst-Religion. Überlegungen zur Genesis de frühromantischen Kunstanschauung." *Germanisch-Romanische Monatsschrift* 30 (1980): 377–394.
———. *Wackenroder und die Kunstauffassung der frühen Romantik.* Erträge der Forschung. Vol. 202. Darmstadt: Wissenschaftliche Buchgesellschaft, 1983.
Brantner, Christina E. "Fritz Dalbergs 'Blicke eines Tonkünstiers in die Musik der Geister und Wilhelm Heinrich Wackenroders Äußerungen zur Musik."

*Aurora. Jahrbuch der Eichendorffgesellschaft.* Vol. 49. Ed. Franz Heiduk et al. Sigmaringen: J. Thorbecke, 1989. 203–10.

———. *Robert Schumann und das Tonkünstler-Bild der Romantiker.* Studies in Modern German Literature. Vol. 32. New York: Peter Lang, 1991.

Dahnke, Hans-Dietrich. "Wilhelm Heinrich Wackenroder." *Romantik. Erläuterungen zur deutschen Literatur.* Ed. Kollektiv für Literaturgeschichte im Volkseigenen Verlag Volk und Wissen. Berlin: VEB Volk und Wissen, 1967. 191–97.

Ellis, John. *Joseph Berglinger in Perspective. A Contribution to the Understanding of the Problematic Modern Artist in Wackenroder/Tieck's "Herzensergießungen eines Kunstliebenden Klosterbruders."* Europäische Hochschulschriften. Reihe 1. Deutsche Sprache und Literatur. Vol. 851. Bern, Frankfurt am Main, New York: Peter Lang, 1985.

Freud, Sigmund. "Der Dichter und das Phantasieren." (1908 [1907]) *Bildende Kunst und Literatur.* Studienausgabe Vol. X. Eds Alexander Mitscherlich, Angela Richards, and James Strachey. Frankfurt: Fischer, 1969. 169–179.

———. "Creative Writers and Day-Dreaming." (1908 [1907]) *The Standard Edition of the Complete Psychological Works of Sigmund Freud.* Vol. IX. Ed. and trans. James Strachey, Anna Freud, Alix Strachey, Alan Tyson. London: Hogarth, 1959. 141–153.

———. "Das Unheimliche." (1919) *Psychologische Schriften.* Studienausgabe Vol. IV. Ed. Alexander Mitscherlich, Angela Richards, James Strachey. Frankfurt: Fischer, 1970. 241–74.

———. "The Uncanny." (1919) *Studies in Parapsychology.* Ed. Philip Rieff. New York: Collier, 1963. 19–60.

———. "Totem und Tabu." (1912–1913) *Fragen der Gesellschaft und Ursprünge der Religion.* Studienausgabe Vol. IX. Ed Alexander Mitscherlich, Angela Richards, James Strachey. Frankfurt: Fischer, 1974. 287–444.

———. "Totem and Taboo." (1912 [1912–1913]) *The Standard Edition of the Complete Psychological Works of Sigmund Freud.* Vol. IX. Eds and trans. James Strachey, Anna Freud, Alix Strachey, Alan Tyson. London: Hogarth, 1955. 1–162.

Frey, Marianne. *Der Künstler und sein Werk bei WH. Wackenroder und E.T.A. Hoffmann.* Europäische Hochschulschriften. Reihe 1. Deutsche Sprache und Literatur. Vol. 29. Bern: Peter Lang, 1970.

Hasselbach, Ingrid. "Paradigmatische Musik: Wackenroders 'Joseph Berglinger' als Vorläufer von Thomas Manns 'Doktor Faustus'." *The Romantic Tradition. German Literature and Music in the Nineteenth Century.* Eds Gerard Chapple et al. Lanham: UP of America, 1992. 95–112.

Hertrich, Elmar. *Joseph Berglinger. Eine Studie zu Wackenroders Musiker-Dichtung.*Quellen und Forschungen zur Sprachund Kulturgeschichte der germanischenVölker. Eds Hermann Kunisch et al. Berlin: De Gruyter, 1969.

———. "Wer war Wackenroder? Gedanken zur Forschungslage." *Aurora* 48 (1988): 131–48.

Hilzinger, Klaus Harro. "Die Leiden der Kapellmeister. Der Beginn einer litearischen Reihe im 18. Jahrhundert." *Euphorion* 78 (1984): 95–110.
Karoli, Christa. *Ideal und Krise enthusiastischen Künstlertums in der deutschen Romantik*. Bonn: H. Bouvier, 1968.
Mahlendorf, Ursula. "E.T.A. Hoffmann's *The Sandman*: The Fictional Psycho Biography of a Romantic Poet." *American Imago* 32 (1975): 217–39.
Müller-Seidel, Walter. "Epochenverwandtschaft. Zum Verhältnis von Moderne und Romantik im deutschen Sprachgebiet." *Geschichtlichkeit und Aktualität. Studien zur deutschen Literatur seit der Romantik. Festschrift für Hans-Joachim Mähl zum 65. Geburtstag*. Eds Klaus-Detlef Müller et al. Tübingen: Niemeyer, 1988. 370–92.
Neumann, Michael. *Unterwegs zu den Inseln des Scheins. Kunstbegriff und literarische Form in der Romantik van Navalis bis Nietzsche*. Frankfurt am Main: Klostermann, 1991.
Schubert, Mary Hurst. *Wilhelm Heinrich Wackenroder's Confessions and Fantasies. Translated and Annotated with a Critical Introduction by M.H. Schubert*. University Park and London: Pennsylvania State UP, 1971.
Strack, Friedrich. "Die 'göttliche' Kunst und ihre Sprache. Zum Kunst- und Religionsbegriff bei Wackenroder, Tieck und Novalis." *Deutsche Vierteljahreszeitschrift für Literaturwissenschaft und Geistesgeschichte* 52 (1978); Sonderband: *Romantik in Deutschland. Ein interdisziplinäres. Symposium*. Ed. Richard Brinkmann. Stuttgart, 1978. 369–91.
Thewalt, Patrick. *Die Leiden der Kapellmeister. Zur Umwertung van Musik und Künstlertum bei W.H. Wackenroder und E.T.A. Hoffmann*. Bochumer Schriften zur deutschen Literatur. Vol. 20. Frankfurt: Peter Lang, 1990.
Wackenroder, Wilhelm Heinrich. *Sämtliche Werke und Briefe*. Historisch-kritische Ausgabe. Eds. Silvio Vietta and Richard Littlejohns. Vol. 1. Ed. Silvio Vietta. Heidelberg: Carl Winter, 1991.
Yee, Kevin F. "Identification, Patriarch, and Aesthetic Homosociality in Wackenroder's and Tieck's Works." Doctoral dissertation. University of California, Irvine, 1997.
———. *Aesthetic Homosociality in Wackenroder and Tieck*. New York: Peter Lang, 2000.
Zipes, Jack D. "W.H. Wackenroder: In Defense of His Romanticism." *The German Review* 44 (1969): 247–58.

# Index

Abrams, Meyer 2, 65–6
adjectives relating to different senses 48
Adorno, Theodor W. 192
*Affktenlehre* doctrine 14
*Agnes Grey* 5, 143–50
Aiken, M. 101
Alexander, Tsar 170, 172, 176
Althusser, Louis 2
America, images of 93, 173–4, 177
"anarchistic" works (White) 12–13
Anderson, Benedict 29, 133
anti-clericalism 20
*The Antiquary* 5, 156–62
Aristotle 39, 73
artifacts, literary works seen as 35–6, 49–50
*Aucassin et Nicolette* 26
Austen, Jane 117–18, 121, 143
Avison, Charles 14

Bachelard, Gaston 4, 87–95
Backsheider, Paula 12
Baillie, Joanna 14, 75, 77, 81–2
Bakhtin, Mikhail 59
Balfe, Michael William 17
Balthazar, Scott 28
Bannatyne Club 5, 155–6, 159, 162
Bartolomeo, Joseph 87
Beattie, James 14
Beattie, John M. 74
Beaumarchais, Pierre Augustin Caron de 19, 21, 24
Beethoven, Ludwig van 15, 18, 27
*Belinda* 5, 121–9
Bentham, Jeremy 73–7
Bernard, J.F. 166
Berton, H.-M. 23
*Bildung* 5, 143–8
Bilger, Audrey 119–20

*Biographia Literaria* 43, 55, 57, 63, 66
Blackstone, Sir William 74
Blair, Hugh 107
Blood, Fanny 108
Bloom, Harold 2, 5, 43, 117–18
*Blue Beard* 17
Boaden, James 11, 76, 78–80
body-centred discourse 6, 165, 168–9
Bollacher, Martin 198
Bonstetten, Karl Victor von 131–2
Bouilly, Jean-Nicolas 23, 27–8
bourgeois society 13, 74
Brantner, Christina E. 192–3, 198
Brinton, Crane 166, 169, 173
Brontë, Anne 5, 143–6
Brooks, Peter 12, 25
Browning, Elizabeth Barrett 131–2, 139–40
Brun, Friederike 5, 131–5, 138–40
Buckley, Jerome 144–5
Bulwer, Sir Henry Lytton 176
Bunn, Alfred 17
Burke, Edmund 101–12
Burney, Frances (Fanny) 76–9, 103
Butler, Marilyn 101–2
Byron, George Gordon 6, 168, 175, 181–9

*Caleb Williams* 75, 80
Cambon, Jules 166, 174
*Camilla, ossia Il sotterano* 23–4
Cammaille-Saint-Aubin, M.-C. 17
Canova, Antonio 131
Caroline of Brunswick 77
*The Castle of Otranto* 16
Catholic Church 19, 167
Chadwick, Edwin 75
Charles X 174

Charlton, David 14–15, 20
*Le Château des Appenins
    ou le fantôme vivant* 17
*Le Château du diable* 18, 20
Cherubini, Luigi 23
*Childe Harold* 174
Chitham, Edward 150
Choiseul, Duc de 172
"Christabel" 45–7
Christensen, Jerome 2
Cisneros, Sandra 95
class divisions 12–13
*Coelina ou l'enfant du mystère*
    19, 24
Coigny, Aimée de 175
Coleridge, Samuel Taylor 1, 4, 43–7,
    55–66, 107–8, 131, 135, 167
Colman, George 17, 80–81
Colquhoun, Patrick 74–7, 81–2
*Le Comte D'Albert* 16, 28
*Comus* 185
*Conciones ad Populum* 58–9
Condorcet, Marquis de 113
Cox, Jeffrey 12
Crawford, Robert 156
criminal justice 4, 73–81
critical discourse 3

Dacre, Charlotte 11
Dalayrac, Nicolas 17, 23–4, 28
Dante 168
Dard, Emile 165, 170
De Quincey, Thomas 73, 75, 81, 132
Dean, Winton 15
Deffand, Madame de 27
*Le déserteur* 28
*Les deux journées* 23
dialect 162
dialectic, Romantic 65
Dickens, Charles 144–5
Diderot, Denis 21, 24–5
discourse and instability 1–5
Dodsley, Robert 25
Donne, John 42
Douglas, Frederick 176

Duncan, Ian 156

East India Company 102–3, 111
Edgeworth, Maria 5, 117–24, 128
Edgeworth, Richard Lovell 117–18
*Edinburgh Review* 161
*Edwy and Elgiva* 76–9
Elfenbein, Andrew 107
Ellis, John 198
d'Enghien, Duke 170, 172
Enlightenment, the 166
epistemology 4
Esterhammer, Angela 132, 135
*Euphrosine* 23
"The Eve of St Agnes" 47–9
everythingness, poetic value of 3, 37

fantasies 195, 197
fathers, literal and literary 117–18
*Faust*, 6, 181
"Fears in Solitude" 4, 55–66
Ferris, Ina 159–60
*Fidelio* 15, 18, 27–8
Fletcher, Loraine 87, 93
*La forêt périlleuse des
    brigands de la Calabre*
    20–21
*The Fortunes of Nigel* 160–61
Foucault, Michel 1–2, 13
Fouché, Joseph 170
Fox, Charles James 108
Francis, Sir Philip 108
French Revolution 12–13,
    18–22, 27–30, 58–9,
    62–3, 80, 87, 102, 166, 176
Freud, Sigmund 183, 191, 194–8
Frey, Marianne 193–4, 198
Fryer, Judith 95
*I Fuoruscii de Firenze* 24
Fuseli, Henry 102, 124

Gall, Franz 168
Galland, Antoine 102
gaming houses 81–2

Garrick, David 21, 27
Gaveaux, Pierre 27
gender relations and distinctions 12, 29, 76, 87, 106–8
genius, concept of 107
Géricault, Théodore 168
Gerin, Winifred 143, 150
Gilbert, S.M. 5, 117–20
Godwin, William 75, 80
Goethe, Johann Wolfgang 6, 131, 135, 168
Gossman, Lionnel 26
gothic drama 11–13
gothic novels 3, 11–12, 15–18, 21–4, 30
Grétry, André E.-M. 17
Greuze, Jean-Baptiste 23
Gubar, Susan 5, 117–20

Handel, G.F. 14, 29
Hapsburg rule 170–71
Hasselbach, Ingrid 198
Hastings, Warren 102–4, 108–12
Hazlitt, William 155
Hegel, G.W.F. 3, 144
Heine, Heinrich 1, 6–7
Hemans, Felicia 131–5
Hervey, James 18
*Herzensergiessungen eines kunstliebenden Klosterbruders* 6
Hilzinger, Klaus Harro 198
historical novels 5–6, 156, 159–62
Hobhouse, John Cam 181, 184, 188
Hoffman, François B. 17
Hoffmann, E.T.A. 191, 194–8 *passim*
home, images of 93
Hugo, Victor 168–71, 174
Humboldt, Caroline von 131
Humboldt, Wilhelm von 131
Hume, David 161
Hussey, Dyneley 15

"Ich denke Dein" 5, 131–4
ideology 2, 11; *see also* Romantic ideology
imagination 61, 63, 66; *see also* secondary imagination
imagined communities 29, 133
Imlay, Gilbert 109
Inchbald, Elizabeth 102
India 103–4, 109–11
*The Iron Chest* 80–81
Islam 99, 109; *see also* Mahometanism

Jephson, Robert 76–9
Jewsbury, Maria Jane 137
Johnson, Samuel 11, 104, 109
Jones, Sir William 102
Jost, François 147

Kant, Immanuel 66
Karoli, Christa 193
Kauffman, Angelica 131
Keats, John 47–9
Keith-Smith, Brian 134
Kelly, Michael 17
Kemble, John Philip 17
King, Kathryn R. 87
King, Peter 74
Kirkpatrick, Kathryn 124
Klob, Karl M. 15
Kowaleski-Wallace, Elizabeth 118–19
"Kubla Khan" 43, 62

Lacour-Gayet, Georges 165, 167, 170–71
Landau, Norma 74
Landon, Letitia 131–2, 135–9
*The Law of Lombardy* 76–9
Ledbury, Mark 21, 23, 25–6
Leigh, Augusta 181, 184
*Léon, ou Le Château de Montenero* 17

Lessing, G.E. 24
Lewis, Matthew 11, 17
Lincoln, Abraham 176–7
literary criticism 35–6
Loaisel-Tréogate, Joseph 18, 20–21
*Lodoiska* 17
Lombroso, Cesare 168–9
Longinus 37
Louis XI 168–9
Louis XVI 19, 175
Louis XVIII 174
Löwy, Michael 3
"loyalty gothic" 13, 23

Macaulay, Thomas Babington 103, 110–12
McCabe, Joseph 166
McGann, Jerome 2, 181–6
Machiavelli, Niccolò 165
Macpherson, James 161–2
Magnuson, Paul 59, 64
Mahlendorf, Ursula 197
Mahometanism 4, 99–104, 109, 112–13
*The Maid of Artois* 17–18
*Maillard ou Paris sauvé* 26–7
Mallarmé, Stéphane 37
*Manfred* 6, 181–9
Mann, Thomas 146–7, 198
Manzoni, Alessandro 1
*Maria, or the Wrongs of Woman* 107
*Le Mariage de Figaro* 19
marriage laws 76–7
*Mary, a Fiction* 107
*A Masque* (Milton) 126, 128–9
mass culture 12
Matthisson, Friedrich 132
*Measure for Measure* 185
medievalism 26
Méhul, Etienne 23
Mellor, Anne K. 182, 186
melodramas 12, 15–25 *passim*
Melville, Herman 174
Mercier, Louis-Sébastien 24

metaphors 35–6
  of the body 165
Metternich, Klemens 176
Miles, David 146
Miles, Robert 13
Mileur, Jean-Pierre 61
Miller, J. Hillis 2
Milton, John 5, 99, 117–28, 184–5
misogyny 117–18
*Le Moine* 17
Molé, Count 170
monarchy 12–13, 16, 20, 176
*The Monk* 17
Moon, Penderel 103–4
Moore, George 143
More, Hannah 118
Müller-Seidel, Walter 198
music 192–3, 197
*The Mysteries of Udolpho* 17
myth of origins 13

Napoleon 19, 27, 165–6, 170–76 *passim*
narcissism 183–4, 187, 189, 195
Nash, Julie and Barbara A. 143
nationalism 3, 29–30, 170, 172
"negative capability" (Keats) 47
Nelson, Henry 132
Newman, Gerald 29
nihilism 183–4
Nodier, Charles 19, 21
nothingness, poetic value of 3, 37
Novalis 193
Noverre, Jean-George 21–2, 27

oedipal conflict 6, 195–8
*The Old English Baron* 16
*The Old Manor House* 4, 87–96
Olivares, Julian 95
*opera semiseria* 15, 23–4, 28
*opera seria* 15
orientalism 101
Osborne, Marianne 143, 146

Paër, Ferdinando 23–4, 28

Paine, Tom 102
Paléologue, Maurice 165–6, 168, 171
*Paradise Lost* 5, 118–24, 127–8, 185
passions 14
past participles used as adjectives 47–8
patriarchy 16, 20, 99, 101, 109, 111, 117–20
Pearson, Jacqueline 118–19
Pitt, William (the younger) 58
Pixérécourt, René-Charles Guilbert 15, 17–19, 24
plerosis 37–44, 47–9
power structures 3
Price, Richard 101–2
"The Prisoner of Chillon" 184
prostitution 76, 110
Pruitt, Kristin 119
psychoanalysis 191, 194
Purinton, Marjean D. 185

*Quentin Durward* 168–9

Radcliffe, Ann 11, 21, 23
Rahill, Frank 18
*Raoul, Sire de Créqui* 23, 28
Raphael 192
*Die Raüber* 14
readerly activism 160–61
reading experiene, the 36
*Redgauntlet* 160–61
Reeve, Clara 16
"Reflections on Having Left a Place of Retirement" 60–61
Reinhard, M. 171
Remusat, Madame de 171–2
"rescue" operas 3, 12–17, 22–3, 26, 29–30
revolution, fear of 11–12, 29
Ribié, César 17

*Richard couer-de-lion* 15–17, 19
*Les rigueurs du cloître* 23
Rimbaud, Arthur 37
"The Rime of the Ancient Mariner" 44, 63
Robertson, William 110
Robespierre, Maximilien de 20, 58, 62–3
Roe, Nicholas 62–3
*Le Roi et le fermier* 16, 25–6
Romantic artists 6, 191–5, 198
Romantic criticism 168
Romantic ideology 2, 182–9
Romantic irony 182, 186–9
Romantic love 133
Romanticism
  and aesthetics 37–9, 43, 49, 61–2, 65–6, 143–4
  and drama 4, 12, 75, 77
  and genre 1, 24–7, 30, 166
  and history 5–6, 155–6, 159–62
  and human development 144, 146, 175–6, 185
  and language 37–8, 49, 65, 165, 168
  and psychology 61, 66, 125, 183, 191, 194–8
  and religion 100, 106, 113, 146, 149
  and sociology 73–5, 82, 101, 104, 111–12
  and typology 3, 131, 144
Rosenblum, R. 23
Rousseau, Jean-Jacques 19, 21, 105, 125

Sade, Marquis de 23
Sainte-Beuve, C.A. 169
Saintsbury, George 143
Sand, George 169–70, 173
*The Sandman* 191
Sayre, Robert 3

Schiller, Friedrich 14
Schlegel, Friedrich 1, 143
Schmidgall, Gary 14
Schwab, Raymond 101–2
Scott, Jonathan 104
Scott, P.J.M. 143, 145
Scott, Walter 5, 155–7, 160–63, 168
secondary imagination 4, 55, 57, 66
*The Secret Tribunal* 78–80
secularism 3, 29
Sedaine, Michel-Jean 15–28
sentimental novels 4, 96
Sewell, Elizabeth 36–9, 44
Shaftesbury, Earl of 14
Shakespeare, William 22, 26–7, 29–30, 168, 185
Shawcross, John 119
Shelley, P.B. 112
Sheridan, Richard B. 108–9
*A Sicilian Romance* 21, 23–4
Siddons, Henry 11, 109
Siddons, Sarah 78
signification 36, 38
Siskin, Clifford 61–2
Sismondi, J.C.L. Simonde de 131
slavery and the slave trade 62–3, 135–7
Smith, Charlotte 4, 87–90, 93, 96
Sontag, Susan 36
soul, the, theories of 4, 99, 104–8, 112–13
space as depicted in fiction 4, 87–95
Staël, Germaine de 1, 131–4, 172–4
Stanford, Derek 150
Stewart, Susan 162–3
Storace, Stephen 17
"The strange musical Life of the Musical Artist Joseph Berglinger" 6, 191–9
*The Stripling* 81–2
Sutherland, Kathryn 156
Swales, Martin 144
Swift, Jonathan 11

synaesthesia 48
Talleyrand-Perigord, Charles Maurice de 6, 110, 165–77
Thackeray, William Makepeace 144–5
Thewalt, Patrick 198
Thorwaldsen, Bertel 131
"Tintern Abbey" 39–43, 136
tragedy, types of 24
Troyes, Chrétien de 26
Trumpener, Katie 162

Veblen, Thorstein 165
Virgil 125
Vitrolles, Baron de 173

Wackenroder, Wilhelm Heinrich 6, 191–4, 197–8
Walpole, Horace 11, 16, 27
Warren, Robert Penn 63
*The Watchman* (journal) 62
Watelet, Claude-Henri 25
Watt, James 13
*Waverley* 160
White, Hayden 12, 156
Whitman, Walt 49
Winnifrith, Tom 143
Wittreich, Joseph 119
Wolfson, Susan 106
Wollstonecraft, Mary 4, 99–113
women poets 132
women's rights and status 99–113
Woolf, Virginia 108
Wordsworth, Dorothy 41–2, 136
Wordsworth, William 1, 38–43, 47, 56, 62, 119, 131, 135–8

Yee, Kevin F. 196–7
Young, Brian 109
Young, Edward 18

For Product Safety Concerns and Information please contact our EU
representative  GPSR@taylorandfrancis.com
Taylor & Francis Verlag GmbH, Kaufingerstraße 24, 80331 München, Germany

www.ingramcontent.com/pod-product-compliance
Lightning Source LLC
Chambersburg PA
CBHW070257230426
43664CB00014B/2563